Women & Men in Management

Women & Men in *Management*

GARY N. POWELL

 SAGE PUBLICATIONS
The Publishers of Professional Social Science
Newbury Park   Beverly Hills   London   New Delhi

For information address:

SAGE Publications, Inc.
2111 West Hillcrest Drive
Newbury Park, California 91320

SAGE Publications Inc.
275 South Beverly Drive
Beverly Hills
California 90212

SAGE Publications Ltd.
28 Banner Street
London EC1Y 8QE
England

SAGE PUBLICATIONS India Pvt. Ltd.
M-32 Market
Greater Kailash I
New Delhi 110 048 India

Printed in the United States of America

Library of Congress Cataloging-in-Publication Data

Powell, Gary N.
    Women and men in management / by Gary N.
Powell.
        p.   cm.
Bibliography: p.
Includes index.
ISBN 0-8039-2796-7 : ISBN 0-8039-2797-5 (pbk.)
    1. Women executives.   2. Executives.   3. Sex role in the work
environment.   I. Title.
HD6054.3.P69   1988
658.4'095—dc19

87-28803
CIP

FIRST PRINTING 1988

Contents

Dedicated to
Laura Graves
for her love and support
and
to the memory of my grandmother
Edna Powell
for all the quarters and much more

Preface

With this book, a circle has been successfully turned and closed. Not in the sense of people closed out, because Professor Powell's book is inclusive, rather than exclusive. The circle I refer to is the circle that "women in management" thinking and research has defined over the past two decades.

When I wrote *Women in Management* in the mid-1970s with Marion Wood, I did it defensively. I needed a book for a new course I had been persuaded to teach; the course carried the same name as the book. One by one, I had called in the sales representatives of the leading publishing houses and had asked them for a book that might be used in the course. There was none available. A clever representative of one of the largest firms volunteered that I should write it . . . but that her firm would not publish it because the women thing would certainly prove to be a passing fad.

The "fad" has, of course, never passed. Women in management seem here to stay; women are now half of the enrollment at some major schools of business, and women are moving into some key positions after graduation. The move is slow and often difficult—many good individuals still find their careers stunted and some give up the effort to succeed. Others are succeeding, and by their success inevitably and irretrievably alter our image of what management is all about. It has been an exciting change to watch.

Change has occurred as well in how we construe the topic. At the start, a good deal of time was devoted to consciousness-raising for women students and to cheering them on to realize their ambitions. Men who stumbled into such a course were generally either naive or masochistic. Clearly, women in management was a class for them only by omission. That seemed appropriate, because every other course spoke to men in a male voice.

But, as I say, change has occurred. The success of the women's movement has raised consciousness all around. The number of women moving into positions teaching management is now increasing dramatically. Most of them are aware of their rights and aware of their women students. They don't rely on case examples with male bosses and women secretaries; they don't use sexist language either in the class or in their own writing. They don't allow their male colleagues to do so either.

As important, most (but still not all) of their male colleagues agree with the women management faculty. We haven't entered an era in which pushy women suddenly dominate acquiescent men; rather, we've come to the point in which both sexes are increasingly sensitive to the needs of their colleagues as individuals, and in which they are aware of their responsibilities as educators to help prepare their students irrespective of the sex of the students.

What that means is neatly capsulized in Professor Powell's book. The students in these special courses are *both* women and men, for equality and just plain human respect demand that we welcome both. Both sexes have something to learn and something to gain. They will need to work together, and they will be planning their lives together. It is critical that both sexes be sensitized to the situation—needs, interests, life cycle, opportunities—that they face at work and outside of it. It is similarly critical that they recognize that their own situation is not necessarily identical to that of the opposite sex. Finally, it is important that the students recognize that there is no one model that is best or preferable, that people of either sex are individuals.

This set of recognitions enriches the lives of those understanding them, of course. Perhaps less understood, the recognitions enrich the lives of others in organizations—both men and women—when they are no longer forced into ill-fitting stereotypic categories and when their opportunities are no longer circumscribed without reference to their abilities. I consider it of equal importance that the final result *should* help to make organizations (and their societies) more competitively successful. Moving women into management and other career positions doubles the number of capable people available to our businesses and our society. The counterpart, understanding that men are not automatons who must either succeed or admit failure and opening the full panoply of career and stylistic choices to men, should help eliminate a good deal of the stress experienced by career-oriented men and should allow those who prefer to spend more time with richer experiences with families and alternative types of employment.

I'd like to see a society in which all of these changes have occurred already. But change takes time and effort. This book is a singularly important part of that effort, because it marks a watershed in thinking . . . now about women *and* men. I look forward to using it in my courses.

—Laurie Larwood
Dean, School of Business
State University of New York
Albany

Acknowledgments

While I did all the writing, there are many people who have contributed to the preparation of this book. I wish to express my deep gratitude to

(1) colleagues who read all or a portion of the manuscript and offered helpful comments: Len Chusmir, Carolyn Dexter, Ellen Fagenson, Laura Graves, Laurie Larwood, Lisa Mainiero, Lynda Moore, Barry Posner, Susan Taylor, and Jack Veiga;

(2) Cheryl Lison for her capable job of copy-editing;

(3) Rise Daniels for her assistance with the research for this book;

(4) Ann West at Sage Publications for being as supportive an editor as an author could want;

(5) Tony Butterfield for being my mentor and valued colleague;

(6) The School of Business Administration of the University of Connecticut, for giving me the opportunity to teach the course on Women and Men in Management, which won the American Assembly of Collegiate Schools of Business (AACSB) Committee on Equal Opportunity for Women Innovation Award and led to the writing of this book;

(7) my many colleagues in the Women in Management Division of the Academy of Management, for providing both a forum for the sharing of research findings and a stimulus for creative thinking on this topic;

(8) Louis Cohn-Haft for his counsel and friendship;

(9) my parents, Norm and Zina Powell, for encouraging me to display both my masculine side and my feminine side; and

(10) most of all, Laura Graves, my wife, collaborator, and favorite colleague, for standing by (not behind) me and encouraging me all the way.

Introduction

This book will chronicle and examine the transition that is taking place in female/male work relationships in American organizations. Significant changes have occurred in the status of and interactions between women and men at work in recent years. In fact, some believe that all the changes that needed to take place have already happened and that a person's sex no longer has any effect on what happens to him or her at work. According to many people now entering the work force, or anticipating entry, the days when women had trouble getting into jobs compared to men are long past. Gender issues have not entirely disappeared from the workplace, however.

For example, consider the statistics regarding the proportions of women and men in management. The proportion of women who hold management, executive, or administrative positions in organizations has been rising consistently since 1970 and is currently 38%. The proportion of women who hold *top* management positions, however, continues to be very small, no more than 2% according to most surveys. What has changed is that more women are in management. What hasn't changed is that women are concentrated in the lower levels of management and hold positions with less authority overall than men. Is it just a matter of time before the proportions of women in upper, middle, and lower management positions become approximately the same? As we shall see, maybe and maybe not.

When I first told colleagues that I was planning to write a book on women and men in management, I heard a variety of reactions:

(1) A male colleague smugly said, "Well, that seems to include everyone unless they are excluded by child labor laws." I could not quarrel with the accuracy of his observation, but clearly he was poking fun at the writing project.

(2) Some nodded sagely and said, "Sounds great!" although it was obvious by the puzzled expressions on their faces that they had no idea what the book would be about.

(3) A female colleague who is a prominent researcher in the field of women in management concluded that I must be trying to shift the focus of the field from women's issues to interactions between the sexes. She felt unsure about why "women" comes first in the title, however. She thought that this may reflect my uncertainty about whether I wish to reach a large audience with the book. As an afterthought, she wondered whether I am making a point about men usually coming first in such a title.

(4) Another male colleague simply asked, "Why 'women and men' in that order, rather than 'men and women' like everyone is used to saying?" Before I could reply, someone within earshot answered, "If you need to ask a question like that, you need to read the book!"

Let's consider the issues that these reactions raise, in order.

The *first reaction* reflects the fact that my colleague did not take the project seriously. This attitude is not surprising. Until recently, men and women were assumed to be very different from one another in psychological as well as physiological attributes. The differences didn't need to be discussed, and any book or article that pertained to one sex was assumed to be irrelevant to the other. Many people still have beliefs about what women and men are "really like," how they should interact in the workplace, and the contributions that members of each sex can best make. The following statements are examples: Men should clean up their language when women are present. Women should be expected to act as representatives of their sex and be able to speak for "what women think" on an issue. Female subordinates should be managed differently than male subordinates. He is careful about details—she is picky. He loses his temper because he is so involved in his job—she is bitchy. Flirting, sexual innuendoes, and teasing are acceptable in the workplace as long they don't have an adverse effect on productivity. Men are better at some jobs than women and vice versa, but men make the better managers.

The purposes of this book are (a) to bring to light such beliefs, (b) to examine critically their relevance to the world of work today, and (c) to recommend ways for individuals and organizations to respond to them successfully. In so doing, it will increase our understanding of the interactions between women and men in work settings. These interactions are having ever greater impact as the proportion of women in the workplace, especially in management positions, steadily increases. Many employees are bringing new attitudes about male-female roles to their jobs. Considerable resistance to the shifting of economic roles between the sexes remains, however. Hence problems that arise in male-female work relationships, the sources of these problems—individual, organizational, and societal—and possible solutions to them deserve our close attention.

The *second reaction*, as well as the first to some extent, reflects the fact that the term *women and men in management* is unfamiliar to many people. Other books on this general topic in the recent past have been devoted primarily to issues related to women in management and secondarily to issues related to male/female interactions and men in management. These books were a healthy antidote to the prevailing trend in the management literature until the early 1970s, which was to write as if all managers were men. Reflecting the fact that women were entering the management profession in greater numbers than ever before, the books were designed both to advocate that women could be effective managers and to highlight the special problems that women faced in entering the management profession. The message of these books has been heard. The proportion of women in managerial positions continues to rise, and writers on the topic of management no longer question their presence in management but instead talk about managers in terms that include both sexes.

This is not to say, however, that women have been totally assimilated into the management profession and are indistinguishable from men. A successful middle manager in a Hartford, Connecticut, insurance company has the mock nameplate, "Boss Lady," on her desk and says that she is still called that by most of her peers (affectionately or derisively so, she does not say!). The psychologist Sandra Bem asked an audience whether they had ever known anyone personally and had not thought to notice whether the person was male or female. Even with the popularity of unisex dress and grooming styles in the recent past, few could answer the question yes. A person's sex remains an important characteristic to most of us in forming an impression of the person, and people often react to others at least in part according to their sex.

Now that women are in managerial ranks to stay, it is appropriate to focus attention on how women and men interact in the workplace rather than on whether women belong in management positions and how to get them there. Moreover, it also makes sense to recognize that men should not be regarded as having their acts all together while women are the ones with the problems. Men have problems related to male/female interactions too. For example, they have to cope with the fact that some men get ahead in organizations while most do not. As women have to adjust to holding positions with high status, men have to adjust to working with women who hold such positions, sometimes as their managers, often as peers, and ever more frequently as their subordinates. In discussing the issues that arise between women and men in organizations today, it is helpful to consider both female and male perspectives. In simple terms, if men have been part of the problem, they can also be part of the solution. To provide the complete background necessary for understanding these issues, we need to examine the work and prework experiences of both men and women.

The *third and fourth reactions* to the book's title reflect the fact that *women and men* is an unusual order for these two terms in writing and in speech. I am not uncertain about the audience I am trying to reach with this book, however. Its potential audience includes *all* men and women (or women and men) who presently work in organizations, expect to work in them, or are interested in how work is conducted within them. Moreover, the colleague who wondered why the terms appear in the order they do will probably gain from reading this book, as will many others.

I have chosen "women and men" in the title simply to call attention to the typical and unconscious order usually used. You may have already noticed that I have been using the two orders interchangeably. If the order "women and men" makes you feel uncomfortable, try a little exercise: Repeat "women and men in management" aloud 25 times. Then repeat "men and women in management" aloud 25 times. Next, alternate phrases for 25 rounds: "women and men in management," "men and women in management," "women and men in management," and so on. Which phrase sounds more natural now? If it's still "men and women in management," go through the whole exercise again (and again, if necessary, and again . . .). After a while, you will find that it really doesn't matter which phrase you use. That's the *real* point to be made.

ORGANIZATION OF THE BOOK

The book begins its analysis of the transition in female/male work relationships by looking back in time. Chapter 1 provides a historical perspective on the economic roles of women and men. Most individuals have been exposed to "traditional" stereotypes about the traits that females and males possess and are supposed to display. To understand these "gender stereotypes" fully, as they shall be called, we need to understand the traditions on which they are based. The chapter traces the historical influences that have shaped these traditions and affected the distribution of work roles between women and men over the course of American history. By comparing the public norms with the economic realities at various points in time, we can better understand the present allocation of work roles.

Chapter 2 examines individual differences that affect the behavior of women and men at work and the origins of these differences. It compares gender stereotypes with the facts that have emerged from research studies about actual sex differences. It introduces the concept of androgyny as a new ideal proposed by some people for how both males and females should behave. The chapter investigates the influence of socialization experiences provided by parents, schools, and the mass media on the development of young girls and boys. It also explores the consequences of these experiences on the health of adult women and men.

Chapter 3 investigates how individuals and organizations make decisions about whether to establish an employment relationship with each other. For individuals, these decisions entail whether, when, and where to work. For organizations, these decisions entail which job applicants to hire. The chapter describes how both types of decisions are influenced by the sex segregation of occupations, which itself is the result of past employment decisions by individuals and organizations and has decreased only slightly in recent years. Individuals' decisions are also influenced by their own personal characteristics and life situations, which may differ for males and females. Organizations' decisions to hire female or male applicants may be affected by the conscious or unconscious biases of their recruiters and by the steps they take to prevent these biases from determining hiring decisions.

Chapter 4 examines the effects of gender stereotypes on the work relationships between male and female peers. It explores whether actual differences exist between female and male peers that could serve as the basis for stereotypes. It then details the factors that tend to promote or prevent gender stereotyping of peers, particularly the sex ratios of work groups. The chapter also examines issues pertaining to the expression of sexuality in the workplace. This expression may consist of unwelcome sexual attention directed toward others, or sexual harassment. It also may consist of welcome sexual attention directed by coworkers toward each other, or organizational romances. Both types of attention, even the welcome type, may have negative consequences for the individuals and their work group and call for management action.

Chapter 5 extends the analysis of the effects of gender stereotypes to the work relationships between managers and their subordinates. It compares these stereotypes with stereotypes of managers and then with the actual characteristics of women and men managers. The chapter reports that sex differences in managerial behavior, motivation, commitment, stress, and responses elicited from subordinates are rare and do not support the traditional belief that men make better managers. It also concludes that the belief that better managers are masculine is not supported and that androgynous managers are likely to be more effective.

Chapter 6 examines the career paths typically followed by men and women. Sex differences in these paths have been diminishing but still remain. The chapter documents the lack of an accepted theory of career development, which applies to both women's and men's careers. It identifies the various factors that should be included in such a theory, including societal factors, organizational practices, personal factors, and family factors. It then discusses how both individuals and organizations can act in their own self-interest while reducing the sex difference in career patterns even further.

Chapter 7 investigates issues related to the promoting of equal opportunity for women and men in organizations. It presents the relevant laws and guidelines that have been enacted to restrict sex discrimination by organizations. It examines why inequalities according to sex exist in organizations and why many employees, including the intended beneficiaries of affirmative action programs, resist attempts to end sex discrimination. It then makes recommendations for how organizations may best promote equal opportunity within their boundaries.

Chapter 8 completes the book's analysis by looking ahead in time.

It poses questions about the factors that seem most likely to shape the future of female/male work relationships. While it does not predict the answers to these questions, it considers how different answers may affect the status of and interactions between women and men in different ways. The chapter ends with the presentation of two possible scenarios for the future.

In summary, *Women and Men in Management* covers a wide range of topics. It addresses preorganizational and organizational entry issues for women and men as well as issues that arise in the workplace. It examines issues pertaining to individuals at different developmental stages, in work groups, organizations, and society as a whole. It considers what it is like for men and women to work with others as peers, to manage others, and to be managed. It observes female/male relations in past eras, examines their present nature, and speculates about what they may be like in the future.

In so doing, this book offers managers two types of useful information. First, it gives them further insight into themselves— how they relate to the managerial role, how they conduct themselves as managers, and how they respond to managerial actions by others. Second, it provides further insight into how other individuals in organizations relate to and conduct themselves in their own work roles, whether managerial or nonmanagerial. You do not need to be a manager, however, to benefit from reading this book.

1

Looking Back

A Silent Revolution

As a boy I lived for some time in the family of a pioneer uncle from Iowa. His log cabin was a perfect fairyland for a child because of the fascinating industries carried on in it. . . . Nearly all that was eaten and worn in the family had been manufactured by the hands of its womenfolk. In those days nothing was heard as to the "economic dependence" of the wife, of her being "supported." My aunt, busy in and about the house, was as strong a prop of the family's prosperity as my uncle afield with his team. Uncle knew it, and, what is more, *she knew* he knew it.

Gradually, however, a silent revolution has taken place in the lot of the home-staying woman. The machine in the factory has been slipping invisible tentacles into the home and picking out, unobserved by us, this, that, and the other industrial process. . . . So, one by one, the operations shift from home to factory until the only parts of the housewife's work which remain unaffected are cooking, washing, cleaning, and the care of children. . . .

With the industrial decay of the home, it is more and more often the case that the husband "supports" the wife. In the well-to-do homes— and it is chiefly here that the status of women is determined—the wife has lost her economic footing. Apart from motherhood, her role is chiefly ornamental. He is the one who counts, whose strength must be conserved, who cannot afford to be sick. . . . She is tempted to pay for support with subservience, to mold her manner and her personality to his liking, to make up to him by her grace and charm for her exemption from work. This "being agreeable" means often that she must subordinate her individuality, hide her divergent wishes and opinions, or adopt his.

—Edward A. Ross, 1922[1]

21

Traditional sex roles, as the term is commonly used, emphasize the differences rather than similarities between women and men. These differences are typically assumed to be innate. Traditional sex roles also suggest that women should behave in a "feminine" manner, in accordance with their presumed feminine attributes, and that men should behave in a "masculine" manner, in accordance with their presumed masculine attributes. To deviate from these prescriptions, according to traditional thinking, is to engage in abnormal behavior. These sex roles have had a profound impact on relations between women and men in our society in all spheres of life—in the family, educational system, and workplace, and in both management and nonmanagement ranks within the workplace.

This perspective on sex roles, although true as far as it goes, raises more questions than it answers. Does the adjective *traditional* mean that sex roles have been handed down unchanged, from generation to generation, since the beginning of civilization, or have sex roles differed over time or among cultures? If sex roles have not been constant, isn't the label of "traditional" misleading? To which traditions are we then referring? Why are we choosing these traditions over others to be called "traditional"? How were these traditions developed? How well have they reflected the actual distribution of economic roles between the sexes?

In this chapter, we will address such questions. First, we will examine the development of the traditions on which "traditional" sex roles are based. In so doing, we will trace the impact of diverse historical forces such as the rise of industrialization, the occurrence of major world wars, and the development and growth of the women's movement. Second, we will explore the compatibility of these traditions with the utilization of men and women in the labor force and management ranks over time. Finally, we will examine the implications of the difference between expressed traditions and economic realities on the work relationships that exist between men and women today.

A MATTER OF EVOLUTION?[2]

Before we begin our historical analysis, we need to examine the view that sex roles are *not* shaped by particular historical events, but instead are simply the result of evolutionary tendencies. Evolutionary theory suggests that organisms and societies that are best able to adapt to their environment have the best chance of survival. People have used this theory to justify the notion that inborn psychological differences between the sexes complement obvious physical differences. For example, the average man is larger in stature and physically dominant over the average woman. Consequently, it has been argued as "natural" that the man assume the dominant position of manager in work organizations and that the woman assume the submissive position of subordinate. The chain of reasoning is as follows: (1) Differences exist in the division of labor between women and men, with most management positions held by men. (2) The differences evolved as our species developed. (3) The differences must have some function in ensuring our survival as a species. (4) Therefore, the differences are natural and must not be altered.

This kind of argument could be used to justify almost every difference between the behavior and status of men and women that exists today. It has its limitations, however. Sex differences that may have been necessary in the past may be unnecessary at this time, and they could be undesirable in the future. As a solution to a survival problem, sex differences could remain in a society after the problem has disappeared. Moreover, some patterns of behavior may neither help nor hinder the society's survival.

Evolutionary theory has also been used as the basis for claims that sex differences that exist today were originally established in hunting and gathering societies. The activities of hunters of food (i.e., men) have frequently been portrayed as more important than the activities of food gatherers (i.e., women). Some researchers who studied societies that were organized around hunting assumed that all hunting and gathering societies were similarly organized. Hence, we have such conclusions as "Hunting is the master behavior pattern of the human species," and, "Our intellect, interests, emotions and basic social life—all are evolutionary products of the success of the hunting adaptation."[3] Lionel Tiger and Robin Fox went further to conclude that, in accordance with their hunting activities, men have always been natural killers.[4] From this argument, it is a small leap forward to the argument that, as men learned how to be successful at dominating other species during the hunt, they also learned how to be successful at dominating (managing) other people in today's work organizations. Such arguments, however, ignore the often greater importance of gathering activities to the survival of cultures. They also diminish the intellectual and other capabilities that were required to gather food.

The famed anthropologist Margaret Mead pointed out the fallacy of assuming that sex differences in a particular society are natural and the result of evolution. Based on her observations of several Pacific cultures, she concluded:

> In every known society, mankind has elaborated the biological division of labor into forms often very remotely related to the original biological differences that provided the original clues. Upon the contrast in bodily form and function, men have built analogies between sun and moon, night and day, goodness and evil, strength and tenderness, steadfastness and fickleness, endurance and vulnerability. Sometimes one quality has been assigned to one sex, sometimes to the other. Now it is boys who are thought of as infinitely vulnerable and in need of special cherishing care, now it is girls. In some societies it is girls for whom parents must collect a dowry or make husband-catching magic, in others the parental worry is over the difficulty of marrying off the boys. Some peoples think of women as too weak to work out of doors, others regard women as the appropriate bearers of heavy burdens, "because their heads are stronger than men's." The periodicities of female reproductive functions have appealed to some peoples as making women the natural sources of magical or religious power, to others as directly antithetical to those powers; some religions, including our European traditional religions, have assigned women an inferior role in the religious hierarchy, others have built their whole symbolic relationship with the supernatural world upon male imitations of the natural functions of women. In some cultures women are regarded as sieves through which the best-guarded secrets will sift; in others it is the men who are the gossips. Whether we deal with small matters or with large, with the frivolities of ornament and cosmetics or the sanctities of man's place in the universe, we find this great variety of ways, often flatly contradictory one to the other, in which the roles of the two sexes have been patterned.[5]

A comprehensive study of cross-cultural occupational differences reached a similar conclusion. This study compiled data on the division of labor by sex in 224 different, mostly subsistence-level, cultures. Only three activities—preparing and planting the soil, crafting leather goods, and making ornaments—were equally likely to be given to men or women. Other occupations were labeled masculine or feminine according to which sex was more likely to perform them. As some proponents of evolutionary theory would expect, masculine roles included hunting and trapping, while cooking and gathering herbs were feminine roles. Nonetheless, only a few occupations—metal working, weapon making, pursuit of sea mammals, and hunting—were nearly always relegated to males, and no occupation was nearly always relegated to females. While a particular society could be quite rigid in sex roles, there was considerable variability in sex roles across societies.[6]

In conclusion, the evidence accumulated by anthropologists suggests that no one pattern of sex roles prevails across all societies. If sex roles are dictated by the lessons of evolution, different lessons have been learned by different societies. Therefore, it is unlikely that our "traditional" conceptions of sex roles are the result of principles of evolution at work. To understand the relationship between the sexes in our own society, we need to look elsewhere.

AMERICAN SOCIETY
PRIOR TO 1900

Although societies around the world have differed in their conceptions of sex roles, Western societies have shared some similar notions. Throughout the recorded history of Western civilizations, a patriarchal social system in which the male has authority over the female has almost always prevailed, or at least has been the public norm.

Early American society was no exception. Puritan New Englanders, who were prominent in the founding of the American colonies, believed in a hierarchy within the family, with the man as head and the women and children as subordinates. Man's role in the home was seen as similar to God's role in the universe, that is, in charge. The Puritans weren't the only group to endorse the concept of patriarchy, however. Members of other religious groups who were early American settlers shared the same values regarding male supremacy.

These attitudes were in force as the colonists wrested control over their affairs from Great Britain in the Revolutionary War and formed their own government. The decision to rebel against Great Britain was made by men. The Preamble of the Constitution referred only to men. In the conferences that led to formation of the new nation, it was never considered that anyone other than men should have the same rights and privileges that men had bestowed upon themselves. The right to vote was not given to women until 1920, long after it was theoretically given to men who were former slaves, and only then after a half-century of resistance. As far as the conduct of public affairs was concerned, women played little direct role in the early shaping of the American republic.[7]

Although disenfranchised, women played a considerable role in the economic system of early American society. Prior to the 1800s, the society was predominantly agrarian, with most work taking place in or around the home. Women and men were engaged in different activities—for example, men being responsible for activities that called for lifting heavy burdens and women for those related to clothing and food preparation—but the activities of both sexes were equally essential to the family economy. All household members, children included, worked at productive tasks.

Women became managers of shops, businesses, plantations, or farms only through the early deaths of their husbands. According to English Common Law, which governed the colonies until the Revolutionary War, a woman could not appear in court, enter into a contract, or inherit from heirs without the approval of a male relative or guardian. Nonetheless, economic needs took precedence over legalities. Women were too skilled a resource not to be fully utilized in preindustrial America.[8]

The slow rise of a market economy and the later industrial revolution altered the relationship between the sexes markedly. Better production and distribution methods began to allow the sale in the marketplace of farm produce and crafted goods that were not needed by the family. Because of the types of activities that men and women had performed, the products that men made were more likely to enter the marketplace than those produced by women. For example, milk, wheat, and wool, produced by men or both women and men, could be sold to townspeople who did not have farms. Butter, bread, and cloth, produced by women, could then be readily manufactured within most of those families. As a result, men, more often than women, received and thereby controlled the money coming into the family. Their control was legitimized by the religious and social doctrines that had been paid lip service but had been effectively dormant for some time.

During the same period, the American legal system was refined and tightened, and previously unwritten laws were codified. The cultural doctrines supporting male supremacy had been unofficial since the English Common Law had become no longer applicable. They were now formalized in a manner compatible with the new market economy in which men dominated economic life. Wives became legally obligated to serve the wishes of their husbands, and husbands were legally elevated to the position of almost total dominance and responsibility.

The labor of wives was still valuable after the advent of the market economy, but it could not be sold as easily. Its value depended on the use the family could make of it. When piecework manufacturing methods were later developed, women who worked in their homes could also earn wages outside the home. By this time, however, the laws formalizing women's subordinate position to men were already in place. Had the laws been codified earlier, they might have recognized the de facto equality between the sexes then in existence. Had they been codified later, they also might have accorded men and women equal status. The legal system was well established by the time the industrial revolution was under way.

Despite its apparent rigidity after the advent of the market economy, the economic system in America ordinarily would have been expected to continue changing to allow for the most efficient division of labor. The industrial revolution temporarily suspended the need for further changes, however, by allowing economic superiority to be achieved through the superior organization of production. With surplus production, it became possible for more affluent husbands to keep their wives at home rather than allow them outside work. Thus the stay-at-home wife became a status symbol for men in American society. This division of labor outwardly copied the earlier fashion of life among European nobility, allowed the conspicuous demonstration of affluence, and reaffirmed the legally defined superior/subordinate relationship between the husband and the wife. Growing general affluence allowed the practice to spread gradually until it became institutionalized as an ideal, the standard against which other allocations of roles between the sexes were judged. This ideal, however, was largely based on the experiences of white middle-class families, which differed greatly from the experiences of minority and lower-class families. The impact of similar historical forces produced comparable results in other Western cultures.[9]

Unmarried women were subject to a different set of economic forces but the same social norms.They were relied upon as workers in the early days of the industrial revolution. To avoid the miserable working conditions and abuse of female and child labor that had taken place in British factories, Francis Cabot Lowell introduced the "Waltham system" of large-scale manufacturing to the New England textile industry in the 1810s. Factory communities built by Lowell and his associates in mill towns throughout New England were designed with adult females in mind as the workers. The female workers, primarily single and from farming families, were required to reside in boardinghouses under direction of a matron employed by the company. The matron enforced regulations regarding proper behavior, including a ten o'clock curfew, and mandatory church attendance. These arrangements were intended to assure Yankee farmers that their daughters would not be working in places of sin and corruption, and the community that the invasion of a large number of young women would not drastically alter its social fabric.

The women mainly tended the roving and spinning frames and minded the looms in the mills. Men were employed primarily as overseers, machinists, and in other heavy occupations, or in those requiring a definite skill such as printing. Men's wages were typically set at the prevailing New England wage rate for the appropriate skill or trade. Women's wages were set at a level high enough to induce them to leave the farms and stay away from other forms of employment such as domestic service, but low enough to offer an advantage for employing females rather than males and to compete with the wages of unskilled workers in British textile factories.

Female factory workers, whose ranks gradually came to include widows and wives from poorer families as well as single women, did not conform to the female role being developed in affluent middle-class families. Of course, they had no choice. Their wages often made them the primary earners in their families, which became all the more important when New England's farming economy began a long period of decline in the 1830s. As a life-style of genteel leisure became the ideal for all women, those in the growing female work force were looked down upon for having to work. Thus the spread of industrial-ization was affecting women throughout society. For some, it meant long hours in the factory. For others, it meant isolation in the home. [10]

The industrial revolution also greatly affected the lives of men. Toward the end of the nineteenth century, men were required to work in factories in increasing numbers due to the rise of heavy industry, for which women were regarded as too frail. The shift from an agricultural to an industrial society changed the ways in which men made use of their abilities and assessed their self-worth. In much earlier days, men proved their worth by demonstrating their physical prowess at killing animals for food. More recently, men had been admired as craftsmen for their skills at making things. Now, the role of strong provider and skilled artisan was being replaced by the role of keeper of the machines. Even though the industrial revolution provided mass-produced goods and a less strenuous way of life for most, it also robbed many men of their opportunity for creativity and accomplishment, and of their sense of purpose.[11]

By 1922, when he wrote the passage from *The Social Trend* that begins this chapter, Edward Ross could describe the dramatic contrast between the economically equal household of the log cabin in Iowa and the economically unequal households of his contemporary society. Ross's aunt and uncle knew that they were both important contributors to the family economy. They didn't perform the same roles, but they performed equally necessary ones. There was no distinction in the wages their roles earned. With the rise of the market economy and then the industrial revolution, both women and men realized that the man was providing the major economic support for the family. Their attitudes changed to conform to their new economic relationship. The passage describes changes in wives' attitudes to make themselves more subordinate to their husbands' desires. We can expect that husbands' attitudes changed in the direction of feeling more superior to their wives than they did before, even though they weren't as fulfilled by their factory work. Social doctrine had been declaring for some time that men were already superior to women. It had been expressing the official and unofficial norms of American society, however, rather than the economic reality. Now, at least for the more affluent, reality had caught up with the norms.

Recognition of this new reality provides us some answers to the questions that were raised at the onset. Sex roles have *not* been handed down unchanged, from generation to generation, since the beginning of civilization. Cultures have differed widely in their expectations for behavior from the sexes. Western societies, however, have tended to endorse a male-dominated social system. Early American society did not adhere to this norm, because of the demands of the primarily agricultural, home-based economy. The industrial revolution placed different demands on families. One member of the family, most often the man, was required to earn wages away from home while the woman continued to work at home on an unpaid basis.

Thus we have identified the source of what have come to be known as "traditional" sex roles in our society. These sex roles, developed within white middle-class families that could afford to have the woman not earn wages, provided an ideal that was supposed to apply to all families. The label of "traditional," however, is somewhat misleading. It implies a constancy in the actual economic roles of women and men that simply has not been present in American society, although public norms about economic roles have varied less. Why did this particular set of traditions become cast as ideal, rather than traditions based on the greater sexual equality in economic roles that had prevailed before? Probably because they most agreed with the doctrine of a patriarchal social system, which had been brought to America by its original settlers. Certainly not because they were adhered to by all social classes, and not because they reflected the distribution of economic roles that was to emerge in the years to come.

AMERICAN SOCIETY SINCE 1900

By the beginning of the twentieth century, the labor force was clearly differentiated according to sex. Census statistics showed that 19% of all women and 80% of all men were in the labor force in 1900 (Table 1.1). In other words, four out of every five women *were not* engaged in paid employment, whereas four out of every five men *were* engaged in paid employment. Only 4% of nonfarm executives, administrators, and managers (called simply "managers" from now on) were women. Men were firmly established as the dominant sex in the workplace, both in numbers and in positions of authority.

In the decades between 1900 and 1940, labor force participation rates for men and women remained essentially the same, despite the occurrence of several major events. World War I, waged from 1914 to 1918, created new job opportunities for women at higher wages than they were used to earning, as large numbers of men went off to war. No sustained change in the employment of women resulted, however. In fact, the employment rate of women in 1920 (21%) was slightly lower than it had been in 1910 (23%). Labor unions, government, and

TABLE 1.1
Labor Force Participation Rates

Year	Percentage Employed	
	Women	Men
1870	13	75
1880	15	79
1890	17	79
1900	19	80
1910	23	81
1920	21	78
1930	22	76
1940	25	79
1950	31	80
1960	35	79
1970	42	78
1980	52	77
1987	56	78

SOURCE: 1870-1970: U.S. Department of Commerce, Bureau of the Census, *Historical Statistics of the United States: Colonial Times to 1970,* series D14 (Washington, DC: Government Printing Office, 1975), pp. 127-28; 1980: U.S. Department of Labor, Bureau of Labor Statistics, *Handbook of Labor Statistics* (Washington, DC: Government Printing Office, 1983), pp. 16-19, table 4; 1987: U.S. Department of Labor, Bureau of Labor Statistics, *Employment and Earnings* 34, no. 6 (June 1987), p. 55, table A33.
NOTE: 1870-1930: data for persons 10 years old and over; 1940-1960: data for persons 14 years old and over; 1970-1980: data for persons 16 years old and over; 1987: data for persons 20 years old and over.

American society in general were not ready for more than a temporary change in the economic role of women. When men returned from the war, they received priority in hiring, and many women were forced out of the labor force, to their resentment.

The passage of the Nineteenth Amendment to the Constitution in 1920, which gave women the right to vote, could have influenced economic roles in America. Backers of the amendment hoped that, by ending sex discrimination in the right to vote, it would stimulate the dismantling of sex discrimination in other areas of life. Women's suffrage, however, brought about little change in their economic status. By 1940, the employment rate of women was only 4% higher, at 25%, than it had been in 1920.

The Depression of the 1930s threw millions of American workers out of work. The unemployment rate was above 14% in each year of the decade, peaking at 25% during 1933. These conditions contributed to an identity crisis for unemployed men. In the book *Puzzled America*, published in 1935, Sherwood Anderson concluded, "The breaking down of the moral fiber of the American man through being out of a job, losing that sense of being some part of the moving world of activity, so essential to an American man's sense of his manhood—the loss of this essential something in the jobless can never be measured in dollars."[12] The Depression caused great strains in family relations, as unemployed men suffered a loss of status in their families. Those who relied upon holding an authoritative role in the family and society felt humbled and disgraced. In addition, the Depression triggered resentment toward working women. With all the attention being lavished on the problems of men, the general attitude intensified that a woman who held a job was taking it away from a male breadwinner. Labor force participation rates were basically unchanged during the Depression, though, because unemployed workers who were looking for a job were still counted in the labor force.[13]

World War II, which closely followed the Depression, marked a turning point in the distribution of economic roles between women and men in the twentieth century, although it did not necessarily cause the massive changes that were to follow. Similar to World War I, it created what was expected to be a temporarily high demand for female labor. Women were attracted to war-related industries by an advertising campaign appealing to their patriotism as well as self-interest, and they were given access to the more skilled, higher paying jobs that were usually held by men. After the war was won in 1945, however, the labor force did not quickly "return to normal" as it did after World War I. Instead, it has never been the same.

Changes in the relative economic roles played by the sexes after World War II took several forms. The labor force participation rate of women, already at a century-high figure of 31% in 1950, rose steadily in the years to come (Table 1.1). By 1980, over half of American women were in the labor force. In contrast, the labor force participation rate of men held fairly constant throughout the century. The employment rate of men still exceeded that of women, but the gap was narrowing.

The increased employment of women coincided with a rise in the proportion of "white-collar" jobs—or those that did not require manual labor—in the economy. In 1940, about one-third of all jobs were white collar, and about one-third of these jobs were held by

TABLE 1.2

Participation in White-Collar Occupations

Year	White-Collar Total	Nonfarm Executives, Administrators, and Managers	Professional and Technical	Clerical Workers	Sales Workers
Percentage of Total Labor Force					
1900	18	6	4	3	5
1910	21	6	5	5	5
1920	25	7	5	8	5
1930	29	7	7	9	6
1940	31	7	7	10	7
1950	36	9	8	12	7
1960	40	8	11	14	7
1970	47	8	14	18	7
1980	52	11	16	19	6
1987	56	12	16	–	–
Percentage of Female Workers in Occupation					
1900	19	4	35	24	17
1910	24	6	41	35	22
1920	32	7	44	48	26
1930	33	8	45	52	24
1940	35	11	41	54	27
1950	40	14	40	62	34
1960	43	15	38	68	36
1970	49	16	40	74	40
1980	53	26	44	80	45
1987	56	38	49	–	–

SOURCE: 1900-1970: U.S. Department of Commerce, Bureau of the Census, *Historical Statistics of the United States: Colonial Times to 1970*, series D182-232 (Washington, DC: Government Printing Office, 1975), pp. 139-40; 1980: U.S. Department of Labor, Bureau of Labor Statistics, *Handbook of Labor Statistics* (Washington, DC: Government Printing Office, 1983), pp. 44-48, table 16; 1987: U.S. Department of Labor, Bureau of Labor Statistics, *Employment and Earnings* 34, no. 6 (June 1987), p. 46, table A22.

NOTE: – indicates that 1987 data were not compatible with earlier data.

women (Table 1.2). By 1980, over half of all jobs were white collar, and over half of these jobs were held by women. Women held an increasing proportion of clerical and sales jobs. Professional and technical jobs (i.e., engineers, lawyers, teachers, health technicians, and so on), about 40% of which had consistently been held by women, were growing in proportion in the economy. Most important

TABLE 1.3

Marital Status of the Labor Force: Women

Year	Percentage Distribution of Female Labor Force			Female Labor Force as Percentage of Female Population		
	Single	Married, Spouse Present	Widowed/ Separated/ Divorced	Single	Married, Spouse Present	Widowed/ Separated/ Divorced
1890	68	14	18	41	5	30
1900	66	16	18	44	6	33
1910	60	25	15	51	11	34
1920	77	23	–	46	9	–
1930	54	29	17	51	12	34
1940	49	36	15	46	16	30
1950	32	48	20	51	24	38
1960	24	54	22	44	31	40
1970	22	59	19	53	41	39
1980	25	55	20	62	50	44
1984	26	54	20	63	53	45

SOURCE: 1890-1940: U.S. Department of Commerce, Bureau of the Census, *Historical Statistics of the United States: Colonial Times to 1970*, series D49-62 (Washington, DC: Government Printing Office, 1975), p. 133; 1950-1984: U.S. Department of Labor, Bureau of Labor Statistics, *Handbook of Labor Statistics* (Washington, DC: Government Printing Office, 1985), pp. 115-17, table 50.

NOTE: 1890-1940: Married, spouse present data include separated women. 1920: Single data include widowed or divorced women.

for the balance of power held by women and men in the economy, the proportion of women managers was increasing. In 1900, this proportion was only 4%, or 1 in every 25. By 1940, it was 11%, or about 1 in every 10. In 1970, it was 16%, or 1 in every 6. In 1980, it was 26%, or 1 in every 4. By 1987, it had increased to 38%, or greater than 1 in every 3. Women were rapidly gaining in numbers and influence in managerial ranks, with the greatest changes taking place most recently.

The marital status of the labor force was also changing, especially for women. In 1900, single women constituted two-thirds of the female labor force (Table 1.3). The proportion of married women who worked, which had been 6% in 1900, was still only 16% in 1940. This proportion dramatically increased after World War II, so that half of all married women were employed in 1980. By 1960, over half of the female labor force was married, reversing the trend in place at the start of the century. This shift did not result from a decline in

TABLE 1.4
Marital Status of the Labor Force: Men

Year	Percentage Distribution of Male Labor Force			Male Labor Force as Percentage of Male Population		
	Single	Married, Spouse Present	Widowed/ Separated/ Divorced	Single	Married, Spouse Present	Widowed/ Separated/ Divorced
1950	20	74	6	63	92	63
1960	18	76	6	56	89	59
1970	18	76	6	61	87	54
1980	26	66	8	71	81	67
1984	27	63	10	71	79	68

SOURCE: U.S. Department of Labor, Bureau of Labor Statistics, *Handbook of Labor Statistics* (Washington, DC: Government Printing Office, 1985), pp. 115-17, table 50.

working single women. The employment rate for single women increased by 17% between 1940 and 1984, but it more than tripled for married women during the same period. The marital status of male workers changed to a lesser extent (Table 1.4). Between 1950 and 1984, there was a 13% decline in the proportion of married men who worked and an 8% increase in this proportion for single men. Married men, however, still constituted about two-thirds of the male labor force in 1984.

The working mother has moved from the periphery of the American labor force into its mainstream during the twentieth century.[14] Postwar changes in the female labor force demonstrated increasing disregard for the public norm that the woman's proper place is in the home. At the beginning of the century, single women were the women most accepted into the workplace, and their rate of participation in the labor force is still the highest. Employment of single women required the least adjustment to the public norm; the notion that the *mother's* proper place was in the home could still be held as a standard while single women worked. The next women to enter the labor force in large numbers were older married women. Between 1940 and 1960, the proportion of 45- to 64-year-old women who worked went from 20% to 42%. These women were past their peak child-raising years. Their increasing presence in the workplace could be begrudgingly accepted by defenders of the public norm as long as *young* mothers still stayed home. The final group of women to increase its labor force participation consisted of younger married women with preschool- or school-age children. By 1984, almost two-thirds of women with children between 6 and 18 years old and over half of those with children under the age of 6 were in the labor force. Their employment effectively ended adherence to the public norm concerning women's place in any age group.[15]

The women who entered the labor force after World War II came increasingly from the middle class. The war legitimized employment for all women regardless of their class, as female employment became a patriotic gesture rather than questionable behavior. The growth in white-collar occupations also created jobs that were not incompatible with middle-class status. Aspirations for a higher standard of living, consumerism, the desire to send children to college, and inflation made it necessary for middle-class women to work to achieve and maintain a middle-class standard of living.

Traditional attitudes concerning women's proper place in society persisted, however. During the 1950s, the mass media promoted an image of family togetherness that defined the mother's role as central to all domestic activity. Betty Friedan called this attitude "the feminine mystique." It is succinctly described in the following passage:

The suburban housewife—she was the dream image of the young American women and the envy, it was said, of women all over the world. The American housewife—freed by science and labor-saving appliances from the drudgery, the dangers of childbirth and the illnesses of her grandmother. She was healthy, beautiful, educated, concerned only about her husband, her children, her home. She had found true feminine fulfillment. As a housewife and mother, she was respected as a full and equal partner to man in his world. She was free to choose automobiles, clothes, appliances, supermarkets; she had everything that women ever dreamed of.

In the fifteen years after World War II, this mystique of feminine fulfillment became the cherished and self-perpetuating core of contemporary American culture. Millions of women lived their lives in the image of those pretty pictures of the American suburban housewife, kissing their husbands goodbye in front of the picture window, depositing their stationwagonsful of children at school, and smiling as they ran the new electric waxer over the spotless kitchen floor. They baked their own bread, sewed their own and their children's clothes, kept their new washing machines and dryers running all day. They changed the sheets on the beds twice a week instead of once, took the rug-hooking class in adult education, and pitied their poor frustrated mothers, who had dreamed of having a career. Their only ambition was to be perfect wives and mothers; their highest ambition to have five children and a beautiful house, their only fight to get and keep their husbands. They had no thought for the unfeminine problems of the world outside the home; they wanted the men to make the major decisions. They gloried in their role as women, and wrote proudly on the census blank: "Occupation: housewife."[16]

Women were supposed to revel in this role and happily surrender control of and participation in economic and public life to men. According to opinion polls, both women and men accepted such an allocation of sex roles. Yet, the statistics that have been presented show that something else was actually happening in the workplace. As one observer put it, "A visitor from another planet who read the magazines and newspapers of the 1950s would never have guessed that the women portrayed as being engaged exclusively in homemaking activities were also joining the job market in unprecedented numbers."[17]

During this period, women workers were not perceived as crusading to achieve economic equality with men. Instead, their increased economic activity could be interpreted as consistent with their primary role as helpmates to their spouses. Most women who worked were citing "economic need" as the reason for their employment, even when the family income was solidly in the middle-class range. If women had not been portrayed, or portrayed themselves, as working temporarily to help meet immediate needs, they may not have been allowed to enter the workplace as easily.

Nonetheless, the contradiction between traditional attitudes and actual behavior could not last without something giving, especially when the contradiction became greater each year. What eventually "gave" was the unvarying public acceptance of traditional sex roles. In the late 1960s and early 1970s, a women's movement emerged that had a major impact on the attitudes of women, and indirectly men, about the roles they played. It was spurred both by the experiences of younger women in the civil rights movement of the 1960s and by the increasing resentment of middle-class business and professional women toward the barriers that held back their further progress. Their discontent found an early voice in Friedan's *The Feminine Mystique*, but recognition of the limits on their achievements placed by society's attitudes was not enough. This recognition now led to a

full-fledged push for legislative and economic action that would
bring closer the goal of equality, or at least equal opportunity, for
American men and women.

Women's groups, operating in a decentralized fashion with
organizations like the National Organization of Women (NOW),
which played the most visible role, were successful in promoting
change in a multitude of areas. Through law suits or the threat of
them, groups pressured large corporations into initiating affirmative
action programs to increase their hiring and promotion of women.
Women pressured the federal government into investigating sex
discrimination in federally funded contracts and federally sponsored
programs and then devising programs to end it. Women's studies
courses were added to the curriculum at many colleges and universities. Other actions reduced the emphasis on sex role stereotypes
in children's books and stimulated the opening of day-care centers.
Pressure from the women's movement contributed to the elimination
of sexist language in professional journals and of separate advertising
for "women's jobs" and "men's jobs" in the classified sections of
newspapers. The women's movement had impact in many ways,
large and small, and a whole generation of women became aware of
the possibilities that could be open to them if their lives were not lived
according to traditional norms.[18]

The women's movement elicited mixed reactions in men. The men
most threatened by it were those most committed to traditional roles
in the family, the economy, and public affairs. They were alarmed as
much because it challenged their power as because it violated their
principles. Other men were concerned about the impact on their job
security and future advancement as more women entered the workplace. These men were inclined to see affirmative action programs as
promoting "reverse discrimination," considered as bad as the original
discrimination and not a proper substitute for it.

A small number of men had the opposite reaction and promoted
"men's liberation." Using consciousness-raising techniques borrowed
from the women's movement, their goal was the liberation of men
from the constraints imposed by the masculine sex role stereotype.
"Men's studies" courses focusing on the male experience were offered
on nearly 200 college campuses by 1984. These courses rankled many
people with an interest in women's studies, who tended to believe that
men's studies courses weren't legitimate and were marginally useful
at best. The director of the National Women's Studies Association

argued that *every* college course could be called a men's studies course.[19]

Most men, however, after first reacting to the women's movement with amusement, came to view it with ambivalence and anxiety. They now took it seriously, but they still didn't know what to make of it or how to respond to it. In a nationwide survey of men over 16 in 1986, one-third said that the new relationship between women and men had left them confused over what was expected of them. Younger men (between ages 16 and 34) and older men (age 50 and over) were the most confused. Given the breakdown of traditional roles, it was no longer clear what being a man, or a woman, meant in American society.[20]

IMPLICATIONS FOR MANAGEMENT

For manager-subordinate relationships to work best, each party needs to understand the other's needs, attitudes, skills, and goals. Without such understanding, communication is distorted, arriving at consensus solutions is difficult, and establishing the sense of teamwork and shared vision that characterizes excellent organizations is nearly impossible. One of the purposes of this book is to help men and women in both managerial and nonmanagerial roles to achieve such an understanding. As we have seen, it has seldom been present in American society, as public norms and economic realities have rarely converged.

According to the historical evidence, there has been no consistent distribution of economic roles between the sexes in the United States. In early American society, cultural norms regarding male supremacy were embraced in public speech but ignored in private actions. The introduction of the market economy and the industrial revolution resulted in the least difference between these norms and economic activities. The allocation of roles between the sexes in the more affluent families of that time came to be regarded as "traditional" sex roles by our time. These roles were generally adhered to in economic life until World War II, but have been increasingly ignored since. Traditional sex roles have less to do with present-day economic realities than at any time in American history.

The changes experienced by women in the labor force in this

century have been striking. The changes experienced by men during this period have been less apparent. Men in different age groups and with different marital status have been employed at approximately the same rates for at least 80 years. Men have been increasingly required to adapt, however, to the presence of women as their peers, superiors, and subordinates. In turn, women entering male-dominated organizations have gone from being the only member of their sex holding a particular job, to being a member of a small group of women in the midst of a larger group of men in the job, to sometimes being a member of the majority group and often being in charge. Adjustment has been necessary for members of both sexes at every level—personal, interpersonal, and organizational.

Yet, some important differences between the economic roles played by women and men remain. Men still hold almost two-thirds of all management positions in organizations. Even when organizations consist of predominantly female employees, the leaders are typically male. Women have had virtually no success in gaining access to the highest management positions in American corporations. In 1986, only two of the 500 largest industrial and 500 largest service companies had a woman chief executive. One, Katherine Graham of the Washington Post Company, said that she got the job because her family owns a controlling share of the corporation. The other, Marion O. Sandler of the Golden West Financial Corporation, shared the job with her husband.[21]

The gap between male and female wages also persists. Working women have held the same relative earnings position compared to men for some time, averaging no more than 70 cents for every dollar earned by a man. Even with the same job in the same occupation, women's average earnings are typically lower than those of men. The highest paid occupations are those with predominantly male workers. Pay is an important indicator of the value attached to work, and the work of women continues to be valued less than the work of men in almost all major sectors of the economy.

Thus we find ourselves in a period of flux in work relationships between the sexes. Even though work and its rewards are not distributed equally, enough change has occurred to make traditional sex roles no longer an appropriate guideline for workplace behavior. What *does* it mean to be a woman or a man in today's workplace? How *should* women and men take their own sex and the other's sex into account in their workplace interactions, if at all? Widely accepted answers to these questions, promoting either a unisex standard of behavior or separate standards for men and women, have not emerged. New standards of behavior have not been substituted for the old standards that have been rejected in practice.

Nonetheless, whether consciously or unconsciously, people often take their own sex and the other's sex into account in their work transactions in some way. For example, male managers in a large, male-dominated, industrial organization described their feelings about working with women as follows: "They're hard to understand." "It takes a lot of toe testing to be able to communicate." "I'm always making assumptions that turn out to be wrong." Some managers were willing to admit that this was "90 percent my problem, mostly in my head." However, they preferred to deal with people who were similar to themselves. Women as a group were seen as highly dissimilar.[22]

Due to the increase in the proportion of working women, organizations now have more interactions between people who may see themselves as dissimilar than ever before. One of the few advantages of adhering to traditional sex roles was that men and women knew how to act with each other and what to expect. That advantage is lost for now. The only way to regain it (other than by returning to the previously prescribed roles, which is unlikely) is for women and men to seek to understand each other better in their present work roles.

NOTES

1. E. A. Ross, *The Social Trend* (New York: Century, 1922), pp. 90-93.

2. This section of the chapter is primarily based on L. Larwood and M. M. Wood, Chapter 3, "A Question of Tradition," in *Women in Management* (Lexington, MA: Lexington Books, 1977).

3. W. S. Laughlin, "Hunting: An Integrated Biobehavior System and Its Evolutionary Importance," in *Man the Hunter*, ed. R. B. Lee and I. de Vore (Chicago: Aldine, 1968), p. 304; S. L. Washburn and C. S. Lancaster, "The Evolution of Hunting," in *Man the Hunter*, ed. Lee and de Vore, p. 293, quoted in B. L. Forisha, *Sex Roles and Personal Awareness* (Morristown, NJ: General Learning Press, 1978), p. 44.

4. L. Tiger and R. Fox, *The Imperial Animal* (New York: Delta, 1971).

5. M. Mead, *Male and Female* (New York: Morrow, 1949), pp. 7-8, reprinted by permission.

6. G. P. Murdock, "Comparative Data on the Division of Labor by Sex," *Social Forces* 15, no. 4 (1937): 551-53.

7. C. Ferguson, Chapter 1, "The Male Ethos," in *The Male Attitude* (Boston: Little, Brown, 1966).

8. W. H. Chafe, "Looking Backward in Order to Look Forward: Women, Work, and Social Values in America," in *Women and the American Economy: A Look to the 1980's*, ed. J. M. Kreps (Englewood Cliffs, NJ: Prentice-Hall, 1976).

9. L. A. Tilly and J. W. Scott, *Women, Work, and Family* (New York: Holt, Rinehart & Winston, 1978).

10. P. Foner, ed., "Introduction," in *The Factory Girls* (Urbana, IL: University of Illinois Press, 1977).

11. J. A. Doyle, Chapter 1, "Today's Uncertain Male," in *The Male Experience* (Dubuque, IA: Brown, 1983).

12. S. Anderson, *Puzzled America* (Mamaroneck, NY: Appel, 1935), p. 46, quoted in J. L. Dubbert, *A Man's Place: Masculinity in Tradition* (Englewood Cliffs, NJ: Prentice-Hall, 1979), p. 210.

13. M. F. Fox and S. Hesse-Biber, Chapter 2, "Women in the Work Force: Past and Present," in *Women at Work* (Palo Alto, CA: Mayfield, 1984); Dubbert, *A Man's Place*, Chapter 7, "War to Depression: Preserving Masculine Control."

14. L. Y. Weiner, *From Working Girl to Working Mother: The Female Labor Force in the United States, 1820-1980* (Chapel Hill: University of North Carolina Press, 1985).

15. U.S. Department of Commerce, Bureau of the Census, *Historical Statistics of the United States: Colonial Times to 1970*, series D29-41 (Washington, DC: Government Printing Office, 1975), pp. 131-32; U.S. Department of Labor, Bureau of Labor Statistics, *Handbook of Labor Statistics* (Washington, DC: Government Printing Office, 1985), p. 23, table 54.

16. B. Friedan, *The Feminine Mystique*, 2nd ed. (New York: Norton, 1974), p. 18, reprinted by permission.

17. Chafe, "Looking Backward in Order to Look Forward," p. 20.

18. Chafe, "Looking Backward in Order to Look Forward."

19. Doyle, *The Male Experience*, Chapter 14, "Of Clashing Values and a Questionable Future: Where to from Here?"; D. Petzke, "'Men's Studies' Catches on at Colleges, Setting Off Controversy and Infighting," *Wall Street Journal* 207, no. 29 (11 February 1986): 35.

20. B. T. Roesnner, "Men Adrift in a World of Change," *Hartford Courant* 149, no. 272, (30 September 1986): B1.

21. M. McComas, "Atop the *Fortune* 500: A Survey of the CEO's," *Fortune* 113, no. 9 (28 April 1986): 26-31.

22. R. M. Kanter, Chapter 3, "Managers," in *Men and Women of the Corporation* (New York: Basic Books, 1977), p. 58.

2

Being Good Girls and Boys

Mattel's Barbie Is No Longer
Just a Pretty Face

After 25 years of parties and dates with Ken, Mattel Inc.'s Barbie has decided to get a job. The new working-woman version of the doll made its debut this month at the American International Toy Fair in New York.

By day, the career-minded Barbie wears a pink business suit, carries a briefcase, and works at a computer terminal in her private office. At night, the sociable Barbie changes into a pink sequined evening dress in her pink and blue bedroom. "This is the first time we have positioned Barbie as a working woman," says Kathy Thorpe, a spokeswoman for Mattel, which sold $260 million worth of Barbie products last year. "Little girls see their mothers working, and their play reflects what's happening in the world."

Parents can buy the new contemporary Barbie, one of 11 models Mattel makes, for about $12, but they will have to shell out $23 more for the home and office play set. The working Barbie also comes with her own gold credit card. Unfortunately, Mattel will not let parents use it to pay for the doll.

—Business Week, 1985[1]

What sex differences, if any, exist beyond the obvious ones? What do people believe sex differences to be? What alternatives to traditional beliefs have been proposed? How are beliefs about sex differences conveyed? What effects do they have on children and adults?

These questions, introduced from a historical perspective in the last chapter, continue to be the subject of much attention and controversy. Some people believe that the only noteworthy differences that exist between women and men are physiological and hormonal, and that otherwise women and men are basically the same. According to this view, learned sex roles are mostly destructive to individuals and society because they are contrary to human nature. Others believe that women and men are and should be fundamentally different in their orientation to life, including their work-related attitudes, motivation, behaviors, and skills. Such differences may be due to heredity (i.e., they are "in the genes") or environment (i.e., they result from learned sex roles rather than innate characteristics), but, in either case, they are seen as beneficial to individuals and society.

We will address these questions by reviewing the results of relevant research. Before we proceed, it is useful to make a distinction between two terms that are frequently used in such discussions: sex and gender. *Sex* (or "biological sex") is the term suggested by biological characteristics such as the chromosomal composition and reproductive apparatus of individuals. *Gender* is a term used in a social context. It may be defined as a scheme for categorization of individuals that uses biological differences as the basis for assigning social differences. Thus the study of sex differences examines how males and females actually differ. In contrast, the study of gender differences focuses on how people think that males and females differ. An example of a gender difference would be a belief that males are higher in achievement motivation than females. This difference does not appear to be a sex difference, as we shall see, but many people think that it is.[2]

Some gender differences represent beliefs that have been stable over time and held by a large proportion of the population. In particular, men have been believed to be high in "masculine" traits such as independence, aggressiveness, and dominance, and women have been believed to be high in "feminine" traits such as gentleness, sensitivity to the feelings of others, and tactfulness. Although others have called the beliefs "sex role stereotypes" or "sex stereotypes," we will refer to them as *gender stereotypes* in accordance with the *sex/gender* distinction.[3]

As we consider the effects of sex differences on work-related behavior, we also need to consider the effects of gender differences. Sex differences influence how people actually behave in work settings. Gender differences influence how people react to others in such settings. Examining both types of differences will help us to understand male/female interactions in the workplace.

The focus of this chapter is on early influences on the behavior of females and males and the later effects of these influences. It will first separate some of the common myths about sex differences from the established facts. It will then consider the nature of gender stereotypes, or the traits that females and males traditionally have been believed to possess. The concept of androgyny, a recent development in thinking about sex roles, will be presented. The ways in which sex role expectations are conveyed to children, as well as the later effects of sex roles on adult health, will be examined. Finally, the chapter will consider the implications of sex differences, gender stereotypes, and sex role development on the practice of management. In other words, is it reasonable to believe that a working Barbie will make a difference? If so, how much and what kind of a difference?

SEX DIFFERENCES:
WHAT ARE THE FACTS?

In 1974, Eleanor Emmons Maccoby and Carol Nagy Jacklin published an exhaustive review of over 1400 published studies on the psychology of sex differences.[4] Their work was the most complete of its kind ever published. We shall examine their major findings, and update them with the major findings reached from research published since 1974.

Maccoby and Jacklin's Findings

Maccoby and Jacklin examined the validity of a wide variety of beliefs regarding the nature of sex differences. One of these beliefs was that, given that men outnumbered women in the upper ranks of most professions, men possessed a higher level of achievement motivation than women. No evidence was found to support this assertion, and, indeed, the reverse appeared to be true in school. Girls' level of academic motivation was consistently strong throughout the school years, whereas boys' motivation tended to decline during this period. Boys and girls were similar in their persistence on tasks and were influenced equally by the reactions of others such as parents and teachers to their performance.

The self-esteem of girls, which matched that of boys through childhood and adolescence, became less than that of boys in college. College women were less optimistic about their future task performance or their future grades than college men, even when they subsequently performed as well as the men. A sex difference in self-concept, however, did not extend much beyond the college years.

Tests of general intelligence did not reveal any sex differences. Tests of specific abilities related to intelligence, however, did yield some differences. There was little sex difference in verbal skills until age 10 or 11, when girls came into their own on tests of verbal proficiency. Boys' superior mathematical and visual-spatial ability demonstrated itself at about the same age and was accompanied by a greater mastery of scientific courses and interest in science. Based on these results, some researchers argued that females were superior in tasks that called for rote learning and repetitive behavior and males in tasks that called for problem solving or unique responses to situations. According to this argument, boys and girls differed in the learning process at which their sex determined they were best. Maccoby and Jacklin, however, found no support for such a difference. Both sexes shifted to higher-level problem-solving strategies from childhood to adulthood at about the same rate with equal success.

Beliefs concerning sex differences in social skills and interests were prevalent. Women were expected by many to be more dependent, more likely to ask for help, more likely to find security in the company of others, and more responsive to social approval and reinforcement than men. Such differences between the sexes in sociability would be expected to affect their job performance according to whether they worked alone or in a group. In fact, sex differences in these areas were rare. Girls did not seek more security than boys and did not show greater sensitivity to or interest in social stimuli. Girls after the age of seven did appear to establish greater intimacy in friendships by having one or two "best friends," whereas boys tended to play in larger groups of children. Such exclusiveness could imply, however, that girls were more hostile to newcomers rather than that they indulged in greater self-disclosure. Few sex differences were found in social relations skills and overall interests.

In contrast to other beliefs, the belief that males are more aggressive than females was supported by studies in a variety of settings and cultures. This sex difference was found to exist from about the age of two years. Boys exhibited a higher level of both verbal and physical aggression, as seen in exchanges of insults as well as blows. Their choice of targets was interesting: male aggression was aimed primarily at other males. This was true even though girls and boys responded similarly to aggressive behavior directed toward them. Some observers argued that the sex difference in aggression resulted from reinforcement for different types of aggression. Although girls were generally discouraged from aggression, they were allowed to show hostility in subtle ("catty") ways while boys were allowed only displays of physical aggression. This point of view suggested that, if the sanctions on girls' aggressiveness were removed, girls would be just as aggressive as boys. Maccoby and Jacklin argued against this view, citing behavior in nursery schools where boys received more reprimands for aggressive behavior and where girls were disinclined to show aggressiveness even when there were no repercussions for it.

Subsequent Findings

Several thousand studies since 1974 have attempted to verify, modify, or extend Maccoby and Jacklin's findings.[5] The sex difference in mathematical ability is now believed to exist before adolescence, the point at which Maccoby and Jacklin claimed that it began. This difference appears to occur primarily on algebraic problems, however, but not on arithmetical or geometric problems. The sex difference in visual-spatial ability also emerges prior to adolescence but is limited to specific types of skills. Moreover, training can significantly alter the mathematical and visual-spatial ability of both females and males. The sex difference in verbal ability is now considered to be weak at best.

The sex difference in aggression has been found to be characteristic only of certain types of situations. Males and females, for example, are equally likely to engage in aggression when they are provoked, but males are more likely to initiate aggression. Women are as aggressive as men in situations of marital conflict. Also, different types of situations elicit anger in men and women. Men have reported that physical aggression makes them most angry, whereas women are most angered by unfair treatment.[6]

Further sex differences have been uncovered that were not reported by Maccoby and Jacklin. For example, men tend to be more influential and women more easily influenced in most settings. This difference, however, may be attributable to the typical status difference in male/female interactions. When a difference in formal status exists, the male is more likely to hold the higher level position in the organization. Also, when someone from a male-dominated occupation (e.g., physician) interacts with someone from a female-dominated occupation (e.g., nurse), the person in the male-dominated occupation usually has the greater power and status. Thus this sex difference, when seen in work settings, may amount to the fact that more powerful people are more influential than less powerful people.[7]

Status differences between women and men may also play an important role in their nonverbal communication skills and behavior. Nonverbal communication skills include the ability to assess accurately the meaning of nonverbal cues from others, the accuracy with which one's nonverbal expressions can be judged, and the ability to recall having met or seen people. Females have higher skills than males in all three areas. This also could be because they tend to have lower status. For example, the fact that women are better able to interpret nonverbal cues could reflect their being in weaker positions and having constantly to monitor others' reactions to them.[8] These two streams of research suggest that, when sex differences exist, they can frequently be accounted for by situational factors other than sex.

An important area of male and female similarity has been established since Maccoby and Jacklin's review. Apparently, both women and men experience mood shifts according to changes in their hormones. The existence of a premenstrual syndrome for women has had widespread popular acceptance for some time, but the existence of a relationship between the hormone levels and moods of men is a relatively new discovery. Hormone cycles may differ only in that the male cycle length varies more and female cycles are accompanied by external signs. These differences may be advantages for females, because they can more easily take their cycles into account in understanding their mood swings. Both women and men, however, are generally able to cope with their hormone/mood swings in their work and personal lives.[9]

Even when sex differences exist, women and men may still follow the same behavioral processes to generate these differences. Kay Deaux demonstrated this point in her research on the causal attributions that individuals make for their performance. People can seek to explain performance by invoking unstable causes such as luck or effort, or stable causes such as ability. Deaux initially found that males' and females' explanations for their own successful performance tended to vary: what was skill for the male was luck for the female. Upon further study, she concluded that the basic process of making attributions for performance was the same for men and women. The only difference was in initial expectations for performance. When women expected to perform worse than men but actually performed as well as them, they saw their own performance as resulting more from luck and effort and less from ability compared with the men. Thus the nature of the task at hand and the expectations for performance that it generates have an important influence on whether sex differences appear.[10]

This has been a selective review of the major research findings about sex differences obtained since 1974, given that it is beyond the scope of this book to summarize the results of all of the studies on this topic. Now that we have reviewed the facts about sex differences, we shall turn to the question of what people traditionally have believed are the facts. This is because sex differences themselves play only a small role in influencing male/female interactions in the workplace. Gender differences are important as well.

GENDER DIFFERENCES: WHAT ARE THE BELIEFS?

The terms *masculinity* and *femininity* were introduced in the last chapter to describe beliefs about what males and females are really like. These terms usually are used in a historical sense. That is, they typically refer to "traditional" beliefs that have been handed down about the personal attributes of men and women. These beliefs are not necessarily held by all members of society at any given time. For the most part, the beliefs have been unguided by the facts about sex differences. Nevertheless, most members of society have been exposed to such beliefs and have been expected to live up to them at some time in their lives. Before we examine the influence of these beliefs, it is necessary to document exactly what the beliefs are.

Before we proceed, try the following exercise. In your mind, put together a mental image of the "typical woman"; then try to imagine an image of the typical woman on which most people would agree.

TABLE 2.1
Characteristics of the Masculine and Feminine Stereotypes

Feminine Stereotype	Masculine Stereotype
Incompetence:	Competence:
Not at all aggressive	Very aggressive
Not at all independent	Very independent
Very emotional	Not at all emotional
Does not hide emotions at all	Almost always hides emotions
Very subjective	Very objective
Very easily influenced	Not at all easily influenced
Very submissive	Very dominant
Dislikes math and science very much	Likes math and science very much
Very excitable in a minor crisis	Not at all excitable in a minor crisis
Very passive	Very active
Not at all competitive	Very competitive
Very illogical	Very logical
Very home-oriented	Very worldly
Not at all skilled in business	Very skilled in business
Very sneaky	Very direct
Does not know the way of the world	Knows the way of the world
Feelings easily hurt	Feelings not easily hurt
Not at all adventurous	Very adventurous
Has difficulty making decisions	Can make decisions easily
Cries very easily	Never cries
Almost never acts as a leader	Almost always acts as a leader
Not at all self-confident	Very self-confident
Very uncomfortable about being aggressive	Not at all uncomfortable about being aggressive
Not at all ambitious	Very ambitious
Unable to separate feelings from ideas	Easily able to separate feelings from ideas
Very dependent	Not at all dependent
Very conceited about appearance	Never conceited about appearance
Thinks women are always superior to men	Thinks men are always superior to women
Does not talk freely about sex with men	Talks freely about sex with men
Warmth/Expressiveness:	Distance/Inexpressiveness:
Doesn't use harsh language at all	Uses very harsh language
Very talkative	Not at all talkative
Very tactful	Very blunt
Very gentle	Very rough
Very aware of feelings of others	Not at all aware of feelings of others
Very religious	Not at all religious
Very interested in own appearance	Not at all interested in own appearance

(continued)

TABLE 2.1 Continued

Feminine Stereotype	Masculine Stereotype
Warmth/Expressiveness:	Distance/Inexpressiveness:
Very neat in habits	Very sloppy in habits
Very quiet	Very loud
Very strong need for security	Very little need for security
Enjoys art and literature	Does not enjoy art and literature
Easily expresses tender feelings	Does not express tender feelings at all

SOURCE: I. K. Broverman, S. R. Vogel, D. M. Broverman, F. E. Clarkson, and P. S. Rosenkrantz, "Sex Role Stereotypes: A Current Appraisal," *Journal of Social Issues* 28, no. 2 (1972): 59-78, reprinted by permission.

Next, provide five adjectives or phrases that complete these two sentences: (1) I think the typical woman is _____. (2) Most other people think the typical woman is _____. Now repeat the whole exercise, this time thinking about the "typical man."[11]

Let's consider your responses. You probably feel that most people would answer in a more biased manner than you, invoking gender stereotypes of what the two sexes are like. But, have you noticed the bias of the exercise itself? It is likely to have led you to focus on the differences between the sexes, when, in fact, there is considerable overlap and similarity between their characteristics.

One of the earliest and best known studies of gender stereotypes was conducted in this manner. In a study published in 1972, Inge Broverman and her colleagues asked a group of college students to list characteristics, attitudes, and behaviors in which they believed women and men differ. Examining the 122 items that appeared on the initial list, a second group rated the extent to which they agreed that the items were typical of an adult man or an adult woman. Analysis of these results yielded 41 items that were believed to differentiate between men and women (Table 2.1). The men and women who responded to the survey were in almost perfect agreement on the items. These items divided into two clusters. Men were seen as being more competent than women but as being less warm and expressive. Both competence and warmth/expressiveness were seen as desirable characteristics. Because 29 of the 41 differentiating items were favorable to the masculine rather than the feminine stereotype, the researchers concluded that masculinity is more valued than femininity in American society.[12]

Another group of researchers adapted the survey used by Broverman et al. to examine gender stereotypes but followed a different procedure. They asked a group of college students to rate the *typical* adult male and female on 138 items (the original 122 items plus 16 extras) and another group to rate the *ideal* adult male and female. A total of 55 items were identified as "stereotypic" based on differences between the ratings of the typical male and female. The 23 items that had ratings for both ideal males and ideal females on the masculine side of the scale were labeled as "male-valued." Examples of these items are "makes decisions easily," "feels superior," "acts as a leader," and "independent." The 18 items that were rated higher on the feminine side of the scale for both ideal males and ideal females, such as "emotional," "devotes self to others," "understanding," and "gentle," were labeled as "female-valued." The other 13 items (one was dropped as uninterpretable) had ratings on the masculine side for the ideal male and on the feminine side for the ideal female; these items were labeled as "sex-specific." When the male-valued and male-specific items were compared with the female-valued and female-specific items, the same groupings of competence versus warmth and expressiveness were seen.[13]

Research conducted since these studies has found little change in the gender stereotypes originally documented. Beliefs about sex differences appear to have remained essentially the same since the late 1960s, despite the increased attention given to gender stereotypes in the popular media since then.[14] Beliefs about the relationship between masculinity and femininity, however, have not remained the same. As these latter beliefs have changed, so have our notions of what females and males should be like. Let's turn now to the origin and development of the concept of androgyny.

MASCULINITY, FEMININITY, AND ANDROGYNY

Until the mid 1970s, masculinity and femininity generally were believed to be opposites. If a person was high in masculinity, he or she was regarded as low in femininity, and vice versa. Although research studies had shown that some ideal characteristics for adults in general were feminine and that others were masculine, it still was considered appropriate for an individual to conform to his or her gender stereotype. Males were supposed to be masculine, females were supposed to be feminine, and anyone who fell in the middle or at the "wrong" end of the scale was considered to be maladjusted and in need of help.

Sandra Bem challenged these assumptions and beliefs in a series of studies in the 1970s. As others had done, she identified masculine items as those that were seen as more desirable for men than women and feminine items as those seen more desirable for women than men. Instead of every item being regarded as masculine at one end of the scale and feminine at the other end, however, each masculine item was now regarded as "high in masculinity" at one end of the scale and "low in masculinity" at the other end, and each feminine item as "high in femininity" at one end and "low in femininity" at the other. This procedure resulted in masculinity and femininity being defined as separate and independent sets of characteristics, rather than opposing characteristics, in the Bem Sex-Role Inventory (BSRI). Other researchers followed suit in developing their own measures of masculinity and femininity and demonstrating the independence of these measures.[15]

The original version of the BSRI contained 20 masculine items, 20 feminine items, and 20 filler items to disguise the purpose of the instrument. Individuals were asked to rate the extent to which they thought each item was characteristic of themselves. Masculinity and femininity scores were calculated by averaging individuals' self-ratings for the respective items. Therefore, rather than measuring beliefs about others, the BSRI measured beliefs about oneself in relation to traditional concepts of masculinity and femininity. Bem called these beliefs an individual's *sex role identity*. She eventually adopted a four-quadrant classification scheme for sex role identity as follows:[16]

		Femininity Score	
		High	Low
	High	Androgynous	Masculine
Masculinity Score	Low	Feminine	Undifferentiated

Thus were born the concept of psychological androgyny and a means of measuring it. The term *androgyny* comes from the Greek words *andr* (man) and *gyne* (woman). It means both masculine and feminine. Once this term entered psychologists' vocabularies, a sense of its appropriate place in the realm of human behavior needed to be developed. This was offered by Bem and others in subsequent studies.

An androgynous sex role identity was found to be associated with higher self-esteem, a more flexible response to situations that seemed to call for either feminine or masculine behaviors, and a host of other positive factors. The individual who adheres to gender stereotypes no longer seemed the ideal of psychological health. Instead, the androgynous individual, whose self-image and behavior are less narrowly restricted along sex role lines, was seen to be more psychologically flexible and more ready to meet the complex demands of society. In short, androgyny was proposed as the new ideal.[17]

It is easy to understand why the concept of androgyny has such appeal. Androgyny is intended to represent the "best of both worlds," both highly valued masculine behaviors and highly valued feminine behaviors. And it appears to present a desirable means for individuals to move beyond the rigid constraints of sex roles. If we believe in the concept and promise of androgyny, males and females no longer need to act differently by conforming to the appropriate gender stereotype. Under the new standard, they should behave similarly and adopt characteristics of both stereotypes.

Not surprisingly, Bem's work triggered a backlash. Some criticized her for poor science because her beliefs in what is "right" for individuals were made so obvious. This is not a very good argument; *all* scientific research is value-laden, but most researchers are not as explicit in stating their values. More telling criticism was made of the items which constituted the BSRI. Here, Bem appears to have been victimized by her own methodology. The average desirability of the masculine items in the BSRI for a man was similar to the average desirability of the feminine items for a woman. The desirability of the various items, however, had not been assessed for an adult in general. Other researchers found that the masculine characteristics were more desirable than the feminine characteristics overall when rated for an adult of unspecified sex. Bem accepted this criticism, and developed a Short BSRI, which eliminated most of the items regarded as undesirable for adults.[18]

Others have argued that the masculinity and femininity components of androgyny do not equally contribute to psychological well-being, flexibility, and adjustment. According to this argument, which has been supported by the results of recent research, masculinity rather than androgyny yields positive outcomes for individuals in American society. For example, a recent review of studies of the relationship between sex role identity and self-esteem concluded that masculinity has a far greater influence on self-esteem than femininity.

Further research is needed to settle the dispute over the relative utility of being androgynous, and thereby displaying a combination of masculine and feminine characteristics, or simply being masculine.[19]

Still others have argued that masculinity and femininity could be further divided into independent concepts and that it made no sense to talk about masculinity and femininity in themselves. For example, masculinity could consist of separate characteristics pertaining to dominance or aggressiveness and to autonomy or independence. Bem counterargued that strong beliefs about sex differences suggest that the terms *masculinity* and *femininity* refer to meaningful concepts for people, even if the concepts themselves can be broken down further. She acknowledged that her early results had generated inappropriate goals and subsequently proposed the elimination of society's dependence on gender as the primary means of classifying people. Rather than everyone becoming androgynous individuals, she advocated the development of an environment where everyone is free to be themselves rather than being expected to live up to any standard of psychological health. We can *all* agree on this goal.[20]

So, here is where the controversy over masculinity, femininity, and androgyny stands. Traditional beliefs about gender differences, or what females and males *are really like*, are held by many people. Differing standards of what females and males *should be like*, however, have been proposed. One set of standards argues for conformity to feminine and masculine gender stereotypes. The other set argues that individuals should break free from gender stereotypes and pursue an androgynous ideal. The battle rages between supporters of these two sets of standards. In addition, those who reject gender stereotypes as standards do not necessarily agree with the proposition that androgynous people lead better lives. In the midst of this turmoil, children still are being brought into the world and raised by adults who have beliefs about differences between girls and boys and how they should behave.

SEX ROLE DEVELOPMENT IN CHILDREN: WHAT ARE THE INFLUENCES?

Although the concept of androgyny offers a vision of a society free of the influence of gender stereotypes, that society has not arrived yet.

Boys still grow up under the heavy influence of the masculine stereotype and girls under the influence of the feminine stereotype. To explain the effects of these influences, we need to examine how young males and females are encouraged to live up to the expectations of the appropriate sex role and be "good boys" and "good girls."

Three types of factors have been claimed by different writers to influence the early development of females and males: biological, environmental, and cognitive. No agreement has been reached as to which has the greater influence, but all three factors appear to have at least some effect. To understand these effects, we need to consider the basic assumptions of each theory.[21]

Those who focus on the effects of *biological* factors argue that the characteristics and behaviors that children display are determined mostly by their biological sex. According to this argument, boys behave the way they do simply because they are male, and girls behave as they do because they are female.

Those who focus on the effects of *environmental* factors argue that girls and boys are induced to act in accordance with sex roles by being rewarded for engaging in the "right" behaviors and punished for engaging in the "wrong" behaviors by adults and other children. According to this theory, parents play a large role in shaping their children's behavior, but other people, institutions, and the society at large can have a considerable effect as well.

Both of these theories depict the role of the individual child in his or her own development as essentially passive. In the biological view, the child's biological sex determines the nature of development. In the environmental view, the reinforcement patterns specified by others determine the nature of development. The *cognitive* theory of development assumes a more active infant or child—one who participates in, is influenced by, and in turn influences the forces that contribute to his or her development. Although these forces are similar to the reinforcing influences suggested by the environmental theory, they are more subject to modification according to the cognitive theory.

Some sex differences in characteristics and behavior emerge very early in life—according to some studies, as early as 12 weeks of age. This does not mean, however, that the differences are necessarily biological in origin, because researchers have observed differences in parental behavior toward male and female children at an equally early age. Beliefs about what activities are appropriate for girls and boys emerge at a later age. One study concluded that kindergarten children are still learning stereotypes about what the typical boy or girl chooses for activities, whereas third-graders have more firm ideas. The third-grader is more likely to agree with the proposition: "She is a girl, so she will behave as a girl." Children are not born with knowledge about gender stereotypes but learn about them as they grow older.[22]

The "heredity versus environment" question is far from settled, and it is beyond the scope of this book to settle it here. Instead, while recognizing that heredity has at least some influence on the behavioral development of children, we shall focus on the interactions with external forces suggested by both the environmental and the cognitive theories. Although these two theories differ considerably in their basic assumptions, they agree on the predominant influence of culturally determined gender stereotypes. We shall now examine some of the important people and institutions that contribute to the adoption of sex-typed characteristics and behavior by girls and boys.

Parents

Parents certainly have a special effect on childhood development. They provide the opportunity for imitation of their own behavior, and they provide differential reinforcements for their children's behavior. Children presumably could imitate any adult to whom they were exposed. Because parents are highly available, nurturant, and powerful, however, they are the models most likely to be copied by children who have them, particularly during the preschool years.[23]

Children are more likely to imitate same-sex models than opposite-sex models because the same-sex models are more similar to themselves. They also are more likely, however, to imitate adult models to whom they are frequently exposed. If they initially spend more time with a mother who displays primarily feminine characteristics, we should expect both boys and girls initially to adopt feminine behaviors. In later years, as boys spend more time with fathers who are predominantly masculine, they should exhibit more masculine behaviors.

Parents' values affect how they raise their children. For example, parents who claim that opportunities for both sexes should be equal in the adult world are more likely to encourage their children to deviate from gender stereotypes than parents who advocate separate roles for women and men.[24] Parents influence their children's behavior by providing differential reinforcements. They base their behavior toward a child according to their conception of what a child of a given sex is likely to be like. Whether innate behavioral differences between the sexes exist or not, many parents believe that they do and act accordingly. Gender stereotypes lead parents to reward boys for being aggressive, competitive, and independent, while girls are rewarded for being compliant, nurturant, and gentle. Thus parents' expectations are likely to be self-fulfilling prophecies. As a result of previous reinforcement patterns, girls and boys typically offer different stimuli to their parents and elicit different responses from them. In this way, children shape their parents' behavior.

Parents encourage their children to develop sex-typed interests through the providing of sex-typed toys, such as playhouses and dolls (including working Barbie dolls) for girls and toy workbenches and guns for boys. More strongly, they discourage their children, particularly their sons, from engaging in activities considered appropriate only for the opposite sex. Other aspects of children's behavior are not seen as relevant to their masculinity and femininity, however, and do not elicit different reactions, even when the sexes actually differ (as in visual-spatial ability).

In summary, differential reinforcement by parents based on the sex of the child and the perceived appropriateness of behaviors for that sex result from parents' beliefs about gender stereotypes and what roles men and women should play. Also, according to Maccoby and Jacklin, boys have more intense socialization experiences than girls. Boys receive more punishment *and* more praise and encouragement from parents. This conveys the message that boys deserve more attention because they are more important. The same theme emerges as we consider school experiences.

School

Once they enter school systems, children are subjected to the influence of authority figures in addition to their parents. They have more adult models from which to choose, and they have more occasion to be rewarded or punished for their own behavior. One of the first messages they receive at school is the sex-typing of positions in the school system itself. Men typically run the system, whereas women work in it. Men hold the majority of administrative jobs, such as superintendent and principal, and women are concentrated in teaching positions, especially in the earlier grades.

Most of today's adults were exposed to teaching materials that depicted girls and boys in exclusively stereotypical ways. School activities were segregated by sex, such as home economics for girls and woodworking for boys. These blatant forms of sex-typing have been reduced sharply in recent years. The subtler forms of socialization pressures remain, however. These originate from the attitudes and behaviors of the teachers themselves.

Marcia Guttentag and Helen Bray reviewed the status of sex-typing in the classroom in the mid-1970s and found that teachers act as powerful mediators of sex role standards. Teachers seldom saw themselves as feeling differently toward girls and boys or treating them differently. Classroom observations, however, revealed considerable differences in teachers' interactions with students. Boys tended to receive more positive and negative attention than girls. They were questioned more, criticized more, and had more ideas accepted and rejected. Girls volunteered more often than boys but were not called upon as often. These trends held at all grade levels and mirrored the parental reactions that give boys more attention than girls. Research conducted in the early 1980s observed the same patterns of teachers' behavior toward their students. In a study of classes in five states, boys still were receiving more attention, encouragement, and "airtime" than girls.[25]

Although male and female teachers usually did not respond differently to students, one study showed that a male *and* a female teacher working together cuts down on the sex-segregating of activities by preschool students. This suggests a possible solution to the problem of teachers' reinforcing of traditional beliefs about gender differences. The problem remains, however: Teachers' greater attention to boys has a significant effect on what girls and boys think of themselves, and on what they learn about how to function in society.

The Mass Media

The mass media, particularly television, influence childhood development by providing opportunities for modeling and information-seeking outside family and school. Americans in all age groups tend to spend more time watching television than any activity other than sleeping. The average American child has been estimated to watch over 20,000 television commercials per year in addition to the commercial programming interspersed between them. In 1985, children two to five years old watched 28 hours of television per week and children six to eleven years old watched 27 hours per week.[26] Thus the messages that television conveys not only represent the culture in which they appear but are also a large part of it.

Stereotypical behavior by females and males characterizes both children's and adult's programming, as well as commercials. For example, a study of Saturday morning children's programs found that 68% of the major characters were male and that male characters engaged in more activity than female characters. Boys thereby had the greater opportunity to imitate same-sex models than girls. Also, the sexes tended to appear in different roles. Females were more often presented in relationships with others such as family or friends, while males were more often portrayed in roles independent of others or at work. In commercials, males were presented as more knowledgeable (e.g., the "Man from Glad") and females as more bewildered (the grateful housewife). Here we see the familiar pattern of males seeming more important, deserving of more attention, and more in command of themselves and the situation. Not surprisingly, both children and adults who watch more television tend to be more aware of gender stereotypes, see themselves in more stereotypical terms, and hold more traditional attitudes toward men's and women's roles.[27]

Magazine advertising has conveyed similar messages. Until recently, ads rarely showed women in working roles and never showed them as executives or professionals. Several stereotypes of women's roles occurred regularly: (a) women's place as in the home; (b) women as not making important decisions; (c) women as dependent and in need of men's protection; and (d) men regarding women as sex objects, not as people. Women most often were portrayed as happy and diligent homemakers, beautiful and dependent social companions, or most concerned with being blond, thin, or having other physical characteristics they did not possess.[28]

Television has made some attempts to adjust to the reality of women in the workplace, but not without difficulty. The *Wall Street Journal* observed in 1984 that, while most advertisers agreed that they should no longer portray mothers as dim-witted housewives aiming to please, they didn't know what should replace that image. As a result, fewer commercials and programs were showing married mothers at all and Dad was instructing the kids about the virtues of toothpaste, instant rice, and the like. Television's stay-at-home mothers have been replaced by single women, divorced mothers, female detectives, mothers with careers, and divorced women sharing homes.[29] These changes suggest that television may contribute less to the formation and reinforcement of gender stereotypes than in the past. It has contributed greatly to gender stereotyping by present-day parents, however, who are passing on what they have learned about male and female roles to their children.

SEX ROLE
ADHERENCE IN ADULTS:
WHAT ARE THE CONSEQUENCES?

Until recently, according to public norms, adherence to traditional sex roles was seen as one of the best routes to happiness and harmony with nature. Now that androgyny has been offered as an alternative, the consequences of fitting the appropriate sex role are no longer so ideologically clear. They may be argued as either positive or negative, depending on one's beliefs about the merits of androgynous people versus masculine men and feminine women.

One way to investigate the results of adherence to sex roles is to examine sex differences in various measures of mental and physical health. We need to proceed with caution in using this approach. When we consider data on differences between females and males, we do not know whether we are examining the effects of biological differences, environmental differences, or cognitive differences. Pressures to conform to sex roles are only one aspect of the environment that could influence behavior and health. Such statistics, however, are likely to provide some indication, if not definitive proof, of the possible consequences of sex roles.

The statistics on women's and men's mortality, health, and health-related actions such as staying in bed during illness, long-term disability, and medical drug use are striking.[30] In 1900, the expectation of longevity at birth was 48.3 years for women and 46.3 years for men. In 1984, it was 78.3 years for women and 71.1 years for men. Life expectancy increased by more than 25 years for both women and men during this period, but the difference favoring women increased from 2.0 to 7.2 years.[31] Males die at a higher rate than females for all age groups, ranging from less than 4 years old to greater than 85 years old. Males also suffer higher death rates from all leading causes, including heart diseases, cancer, accidents, cerebrovascular diseases, pulmonary diseases, liver diseases, suicide, homicide, pneumonia, and diabetes.

Health statistics are considerably different. Even when illnesses due to reproductive functions are excluded, women suffer more from acute conditions and nonfatal chronic conditions than men. Women report more depression and are treated more for mental illness. They report a greater amount of minor physical ailments such as headaches, dizziness, and stomach upsets. Women use more prescription medicines and over-the-counter drugs than men. They restrict their activities due to health problems about 25% more days per year than men, and they spend about 40% more days per year in bed.

In contrast, men suffer more from major physical ailments. They suffer 50% to 60% more injuries at ages 17 to 44. They suffer more visual and hearing problems and paralysis than women at all ages. They have a higher rate of problem drinking and exhibit more stress-related disorders such as cirrhosis of the liver and suicide. They are more likely to exhibit the type A behavior pattern—characterized by extreme amounts of competitiveness, striving for achievement, aggressiveness, haste, impatience, and feelings of being under pressures of time and responsibility—which contributes to coronary heart disease.[32] They also suffer more from life-threatening diseases such as atherosclerosis and emphysema. They experience more overall long-term disability due to chronic health problems than women.

Moreover, husbands and wives affect each other's health. Several studies have shown that wives' employment can have a negative impact on their husbands' mental health. Husbands of wives working full-time tend to feel less adequate as breadwinners than husbands of housewives do, and this leads to their feeling less satisfied with their jobs and lives in general. Although not examined, this effect is probably greatest for husbands with more traditional attitudes toward male and female roles. On the other hand, husbands' employment can have a negative impact on their wives' health. Another study found that the wives of husbands in more stressful occupations had shorter life expectancies. We would expect this effect also to work in reverse, with husbands of wives in more stressful occupations having shorter life expectancies.[33]

In summary, women experience more frequent illness and short-term disability, but their problems typically do not endanger their lives. In contrast, men suffer from more life-threatening diseases that cause more permanent disability and earlier death for them. Women are "sicker" in the short run, but men are sicker in the long run. Spouses also affect the health of each other.

The data on mortality, health, and health actions can be interpreted in a number of ways. The feminine sex role places a much greater emphasis on self-awareness and the expression of feelings, including admission of difficulties, than the masculine sex role. It also encourages dependency on others. Therefore, women could be more inclined than men to report symptoms of mental illness and to make use of or be committed to mental health facilities, even if they were no worse off in mental health. Women, however, are also more inclined to admit that they are experiencing ill health and to take appropriate coping actions, which reduce the likelihood of their illnesses becoming major.

The masculine role can be particularly hazardous to health. Three-fourths of the sex difference in life expectancy may be attributed to sex-role-related factors, with the remaining difference being due to purely biological factors. Aggressiveness and competitiveness can cause men to put themselves in dangerous situations, thereby leading them to suffer more accidents. Emotional inexpressiveness causes psychosomatic and other health problems. Lack of self-awareness keeps men from being sensitive to signals that all is not well for them. The male role encourages the taking of risks that endanger health and discourages men from taking adequate medical care of themselves. In response to women's redefinitions of their own role, a "modern male role" has emerged that encourages men to use their interpersonal and emotional capabilities in two ways: to promote smooth collaboration with others toward achievement (such as by being managers), and within heterosexual relationships. Staying emotionally "cool" else-where, however, remains a major value associated with the male role that contributes to a shorter life span for men.[34]

The different measures of health that have been considered reveal the limitations of both the masculine and the feminine roles. Adherence to the feminine role means surrendering of control over many aspects of one's life to others. This lack of control contributes to feelings of depression, which, in their extreme form, lead to treatment in mental health facilities. On the other hand, adherence to the masculine role means suppression of one's feelings and always striving (or pretending) to be in control of one's own life. The effects of this unbridled push for dominance are seen in mortality rates, type A behavior, coronary heart disease rates, and other symptoms of ill health. These effects are often found in management ranks, suggesting that the managerial role too has its risks.

This analysis suggests that, for women and men to lead healthy and long lives (aside from having a spouse who is conducive to health), it is indeed desirable for them to experience the "best of both worlds." They benefit from having the ability to be aware of and express their feelings and to form empathic relationships with others associated with the feminine stereotype, combined with the ability to be in control and free of excessive dependence on others associated with the masculine stereotype. While we work toward a society that is free of a dependence on gender as the primary means for categorizing people, androgyny seems to offer a healthier standard of living than gender stereotypes.

IMPLICATIONS FOR MANAGEMENT

We began this chapter by posing several questions about sex differences, gender differences, and their general effects. Before we move on, it is appropriate to explore the initial implications of the answers provided to these questions for the practice of management.

Maccoby and Jacklin found three major sex differences: boys' greater mathematical and visual-spatial ability, girls' greater verbal ability, and boys' greater aggression. The first difference and possibly the second could influence the kinds of occupations that boys and girls choose. Some traditionally male occupations such as accounting and engineering particularly call for mathematical or visual-spatial ability. Traditionally female occupations such as nursing or clerical/secretarial work, however, do not seem particularly to call for verbal ability.

Aggression and concern for dominance may have a more immediate impact on managerial behavior and performance. Aggression could be exhibited, for example, in a tendency verbally or physically to attack (or defend) subordinates, peers, or superiors in organizations. Eventually, the aggressive individual may experience negative repercussions, ranging from reprimands to perceptions of poor performance. Aggression also could be channeled into more positive forms of behavior, however, such as an eagerness to "attack" challenging assignments. High aggressiveness in itself does not make a person more, or less, likely to be a good manager.[35]

Maccoby and Jacklin also found a sex difference in self-concept, with college women possessing lower self-esteem than college men. Although of short duration, this difference during such a critical period of time could affect career choices by women and men who attended college and contribute to sex differences in the composition of managerial ranks. Other research on sex differences since Maccoby and Jacklin's review has found that women are more susceptible to influence attempts and more adept at nonverbal communication than men. The first difference suggests that women might be more passive members of work groups and organizations. If this were true, it would certainly hinder their work performance. Women's greater nonverbal abilities, however, would have a positive effect on their communication with coworkers.

Beliefs about sex differences include a much wider range of characteristics than actual sex differences. These beliefs also have a much larger effect than sex differences, as seen in a range of evaluative activities and organizational situations. Recruiters and other organizational representatives evaluate the suitability of applicants for employment. Managers evaluate the performance of their subordinates, who in turn evaluate the kind of leadership demonstrated by their managers. Work group members evaluate the contributions of other members. Promotion decisions are based on evaluations of the past performance and future potential of candidates for promotion. In each of these situations, others' evaluations of an individual materially affect the effectiveness and progress of that individual in the organization. These evaluations are based on beliefs about what the individual is like, which are influenced by whether the individual is male or female. Thus stereotypical beliefs that women are more nurturant or that men are better leaders have an influence on evaluations far beyond what the actual facts may dictate.

Androgyny has been presented not so much as a belief about what individuals are like but as a prescription advocated by some for what individuals should be like. In particular, it has been offered as a model for the effective manager. We shall discuss the merits of this prescription at length in Chapter 5. The long-term benefits of androgyny for individuals in general remain to be seen. They are difficult to determine at this point, because androgyny has not been studied for very long.

Important influences on childhood development such as parents, school, and television have their own organizational analogues. Individuals may react to authority figures in organizations based on how their parents treated them earlier in life and their reactions to the treatment. Early school experiences also are likely to condition responses to authority. Television has provided numerous models for leadership, ranging from Captain James Kirk of *Star Trek* to Wonder Woman, and we can expect it to continue to provide models that influence both children and adults.

The implications of health data for adults on the practice of management are disturbing. Managers occupy a high-stress role that contributes to many symptoms of ill health including coronary heart disease and dependence on alcohol and other drugs. We will more fully discuss how the managerial role contributes to stress, what makes some managerial jobs more stressful than others, and whether female and male managers differ in their experiences with or responses to stress.

We are left wondering what the short-term and long-term effects of a working Barbie doll will be, if any. Unless sex differences in toys— as seen in choices made by children and their parents—disappear, girls will be more exposed to the doll than boys. Thus any direct effect the doll has on attitudes or expectations about the workplace will be seen in girls and not in boys. Girls exposed to the doll could expect to see a more sex-integrated workplace, whereas boys could have less reason to expect the same. These girls, however, could indirectly affect boys' expectations through their contacts with them in the classroom, schoolyard, and home.

What might cause a comparable direct effect on boys' attitudes and expectations about the workplace? Electronic sports games (football, basketball, baseball, and so on) with coed teams? *Real* professional and college sports with coed teams? What could cause changes for both girls and boys? A female president of the United States? A female Lee Iacocca? It will be interesting to find out, if we get the chance.

Gender stereotypes are mostly out of touch with facts about sex differences, are strongly held by many people, and are under attack by others. Given these conflicts, it will be interesting to see how the standards of behavior for "being good girls and boys" continue to evolve. Meanwhile, we shall next consider how the early experiences of girls and boys are translated into decisions, made either by them or for them, about the pursuit of occupations.

NOTES

1. Reprinted from the March 4, 1985, issue of *Business Week* by special permission, © 1985 by McGraw-Hill, Inc.

2. C. W. Sherif, "Needed Concepts in the Study of Gender Identity," *Psychology of Women Quarterly* 6 (1982): 375-98; R. K. Unger, "Toward a Redefinition of Sex and Gender," *American Psychologist* 34 (1979): 1085-94.

3. I. K. Broverman, S. R. Vogel, D. M. Broverman, F. E. Clarkson, and P. S. Rosenkrantz, "Sex Role Stereotypes: A Current Appraisal," *Journal of Social Issues* 28, no. 2 (1972): 59-78.

4. E. E. Maccoby and C. N. Jacklin, *The Psychology of Sex Differences* (Stanford, CA: Stanford University Press, 1974).

5. K. Deaux, "Sex and Gender," *Annual Review of Psychology* 36 (1985): 49-81.

6. S.M.J. Towson and M. P. Zanna, "Toward a Situational Analysis of Gender Differences in Aggression," *Sex Roles* 8 (1982): 903-14; A. Frodi, J. Macaulay, and P. R. Thome, "Are Women Always Less Aggressive Than Men? A Review of the Experimental Literature," *Psychological Bulletin* 84 (1977): 634-60.

7. A. H. Eagly and W. Wood, "Gender and Influenceability: Stereotype Versus Behavior," in *Women, Gender, and Social Psychology*, ed. V. E. O'Leary, R. K. Unger, and B. S. Wallston (Hillsdale, NJ: Erlbaum, 1985); A. H. Eagly, "Gender and Social Influence: A Social Psychological Analysis," *American Psychologist* 38 (1983): 971-81.

8. J. A. Hall, "On Explaining Gender Differences: The Case of Nonverbal Communication," in *Sex and Gender: Review of Personality and Social Psychology*, vol. 7, ed. P. Shaver and C. Hendrick (Newbury Park, CA: Sage, 1987).

9. C. H. Doering, H.K.H. Brodie, H. Kraemer, H. Becker, and D. A. Hamburg, "Plasma Testosterone Levels and Psychologic Measures in Men over a Two-Month Period," in *Sex Differences in Behavior*, ed. R. C. Friedman and R. M. Richart (New York: John Wiley, 1974); A. S. Phillips and A. G. Bedeian, "PMS and the Workplace" (Paper delivered at the Annual Meeting of the Academy of Management, New Orleans, 1987).

10. K. Deaux, "From Individual Differences to Social Categories: Analysis of a Decade's Research on Gender," *American Psychologist* 39 (1984): 105-16.

11. L. Larwood and M. M. Wood, Chapter 2, "Women and Management: Culturally Biased Perspectives," in *Women in Management* (Lexington, MA: Lexington Books, 1977), used by permission.

12. Broverman et al., "Sex Role Stereotypes."

13. J. T. Spence, R. L. Helmreich, and J. Stapp, "Ratings of Self and Peers on Sex Role Attributes and Their Relation to Self-Esteem and Conceptions of Masculinity and Femininity," *Journal of Personality and Social Psychology* 32 (1975): 29-39.

14. D. N. Ruble and T. L. Ruble, "Sex Stereotypes," in *In the Eye of the Beholder: Contemporary Issues in Stereotyping*, ed. A. G. Miller (New York: Praeger, 1982).

15. S. L. Bem, "The Measurement of Psychological Androgyny," *Journal of Consulting and Clinical Psychology* 42 (1974): 155-62; J. T. Spence and R. L. Helmreich, *Masculinity and Femininity: Their Psychological Dimensions, Correlates, and Antecedents* (Austin: University of Texas Press, 1978); J. I. Berzins, M. A. Welling, and R. E. Wetter, "A New Measure of Psychological Androgyny Based on the Personality Research Form," *Journal of Consulting and Clinical Psychology* 46 (1978): 126-38.

16. S. L. Bem, "On the Utility of Alternative Procedures for Assessing Psychological Androgyny," *Journal of Consulting and Clinical Psychology* 45 (1977): 196-205.

17. E. Lenney, "Androgyny: Some Audacious Assertions Toward Its Coming of Age," *Sex Roles* 5 (1979): 703-19.

18. E. J. Pedhazur and T. J. Tetenbaum, "Bem Sex Role Inventory: A Theoretical and Methodological Critique," *Journal of Personality and Social Psychology* 37 (1979): 996-1016; S. L. Bem, *Bem Sex-Role Inventory: Professional Manual* (Palo Alto, CA: Consulting Psychologists Press, 1981).

19. M. C. Taylor and J. A. Hall, "Psychological Androgyny: Theories, Methods, and Conclusions," *Psychological Bulletin* 92 (1982): 347-66; W. H. Jones, M. E. Chernovetz, and R. O. Hansson, "The Enigma of Androgyny: Differential Implications for Males and Females?" *Journal of Consulting and Clinical Psychology* 46 (1978): 298-313; B. E. Whitley, "Sex Role Orientation and Self-Esteem: A Critical Meta-Analytic Review," *Journal of Personality and Social Psychology* 44 (1983): 765-78.

20. S. L. Bem, "Gender Schema Theory: A Cognitive Account of Sex Typing," *Psychological Review* 88 (1981): 354-64.

21. M. Lewis and M. Weinraub, "Origins of Early Sex-Role Development," *Sex Roles* 5 (1979) 135-53.

22. T. J. Berndt and K. A. Heller, "Gender Stereotypes and Social Inferences: A Developmental Study," *Journal of Personality and Social Psychology* 50 (1986): 889-98.

23. Maccoby and Jacklin, *The Psychology of Sex Differences*, Chapter 8, "Sex Typing and the Role of Modeling," and Chapter 9, "Differential Socialization of Boys and Girls."

24. J. K. Antill, "Parents' Beliefs and Values About Sex Roles, Sex Differences, and Sexuality: Their Sources and Implications," in *Sex and Gender: Review of Personality and Social Psychology*, vol. 7, ed. P. Shaver and C. Hendrick (Newbury Park, CA: Sage, 1987).

25. M. Guttentag and H. Bray, "Teachers as Mediators of Sex-Role Standards," in *Beyond Sex Roles*, ed. A. G. Sargent (St. Paul: West, 1977); M. Sadker and D. Sadker, "Sexism in the Schoolroom of the '80's," *Psychology Today* 19, no. 3 (March 1985): 54-57.

26. *Neilsen Report on Television Annual* (1985).

27. P. E. McGhee and T. Frueh, "Television Viewing and the Learning of Sex-Role Stereotypes," *Sex Roles* 6 (1980): 179-88; L. Z. McArthur and S. V. Eisen, "Television and Sex-Role Stereotyping," *Journal of Applied Social Psychology* 6 (1976): 329-51; M. Morgan, "Television and Adolescents' Sex Role Stereotypes: A Longitudinal Study," *Journal of Personality and Social Psychology* 43 (1982): 947-55; L. Ross, D. R. Anderson, and P. A. Wisocki, "Television Viewing and Adult Sex-Role Attitudes," *Sex Roles* 8 (1982): 589-92.

28. D. E. Sexton and P. Haberman, "Women in Magazine Advertisements," *Journal of Advertising Research* 14, no. 4 (August 1974): 41-46.

29. B. Abrams, "TV Ads, Shows Struggle to Replace Bygone Images of Today's Mothers," *Wall Street Journal* 204, no. 68 (5 October 1984): 27, 41.

30. The data on sex differences in health that follow are primarily from L. M. Verbugge, "Gender and Health: An Update of Hypotheses and Evidence," *Journal of Health and Social Behavior* 26 (1985): 156-82.

31. U.S. Department of Commerce, Bureau of the Census, *Statistical Abstract of the United States*, 106th ed. (Washington, DC: Government Printing Office, 1986), p. 68, table 106.

32. M. Friedman and R. Rosenman, *Type A Behavior and Your Heart* (Greenwich, CT: Fawcett, 1974).

33. G. L. Staines, K. J. Pottick, and D. A. Fudge, "Wives' Employment and Husbands' Attitudes Toward Work and Life," *Journal of Applied Psychology* 71 (1986): 118-28; B. C. Fletcher, "Marital Relationships as a Cause of Death: An Analysis of Occupational Mortality and the Hidden Consequences of Marriage—Some U.K. Data," *Human Relations* 36 (1983): 123-34.

34. J. Harrison, "Warning: The Male Sex Role May Be Dangerous to Your Health," *Journal of Social Issues* 34, no. 1 (1978): 65-86; I. Waldron, "Why Do Women Live Longer Than Men?" *Journal of Human Stress* 2 (1976): 1-13; S. M. Jourard, "Some Lethal Aspects of the Male Role," in *The Transparent Self* (New York: Van Nostrand, 1971); J. H. Pleck, *The Myth of Masculinity* (Cambridge: MIT Press, 1981).

35. C. N. Jacklin and E. E. Maccoby, "Sex Differences and Their Implications for Management," in *Bringing Women into Management*, ed. F. E. Gordon and M. H. Strober (New York: McGraw-Hill, 1975).

3

Entering the World of Work

I'm Gonna Be an Engineer

When I went to school I learned to write and how to read
Some history, geography, and home economy,
And typing is a skill that every girl is sure to need,
To while away the extra time until the time to breed
And then they have the nerve to ask, "What would I like to be?"
I says, "I'm gonna be an engineer!"
"No, you only need to learn to be a lady
The duty isn't yours, for to try and run the world
An engineer could never have a baby
Remember, dear, that you're a girl."

Individuals make their own decisions about whether to work, and what kind of work they will do. No one is forced into one type of work or blocked from another. We live in a free country where individuals have the liberty to choose the role, if any, they wish to play in the economy. Right?

Right only in a restricted sense. Americans *are* free to direct their own lives. The government doesn't assign jobs to people; they choose jobs for themselves. People, however, are influenced in their decisions about work by several factors aside from their own interests and capabilities. First, they are influenced by society's norms about who should or should not work. American society generally frowns on welfare if people are capable of working. According to traditional norms, however, women have been discouraged from entering the workplace. Second, people are influenced by others' expectations of their interests and capabilities. Third, they are influenced by the choices that the marketplace presents as they consider various occupations. Fourth, they are influenced by the decisions made by organizations about their applications for employment.

We have already examined general beliefs regarding sex differences and their influence on how children are brought up. Now we will get more specific and look at the choices that individuals make, both about whether or not to work and about the occupations they pursue if they decide to work. Choices are influenced by the perceived characteristics of occupations, which make them seem to welcome certain types of workers and not others. Choices also are influenced by the personal characteristics, backgrounds, and life situations of the individuals themselves, and by the decision-making processes used by recruiters and other organizational representatives, which lead them to hire certain applicants and not others. Let's begin by examining the occupational choices available to individuals as they contemplate entering the world of work.

THE CHOICES AVAILABLE: SEX SEGREGATION IN THE WORKPLACE

If the workplace were completely integrated with regard to sex, the percentages of the male and female labor force in each of the occupations in which people work would be equal. For example, if 5% of all males were engineers, 5% of all females would be engineers, and the same would hold true for all occupations. As one sex increased in proportion in the labor force relative to the other, the percentages of members of that sex in different occupations would remain equal to the equivalent percentages for the other sex. Sex segregation exists when females and males are *not* similarly distributed across occupations.

The extent of sex segregation in the workplace at any time may be measured by a "segregation index." The index is calculated as follows:

$$S = \frac{1}{2} \sum_i \left| m_i - f_i \right|$$

where m_i = the percentage of the male labor force employed in occupation i and f_i = the percentage of the female labor force employed in occupation i. An index value of zero indicates complete sex integration, whereas an index value of 100 indicates complete sex segregation.[1] Table 3.1 shows an example of how the index works.

The segregation index value of 35% means that 35% of the male labor force would have to change occupations for the distribution of males across occupations to match that of females, or vice versa. For example, if 10% of the males shifted from Occupation 1 to Occupation 4, 10% shifted from Occupation 1 to Occupation 3, and 15% shifted from Occupation 2 to Occupation 3, the distributions for males and females would be equal and a total of 35% of the males would have changed occupations.

According to the segregation index values in Table 3.2, sex segregation has been a remarkably stable feature of the American workplace during this century. The index varied between 65.6% and 69.0% between 1900 and 1960, and dropped from 68.3% to 61.7% between 1972 and 1981. The index took its sharpest drop of the century between 1972 and 1981 and achieved its lowest value. This decrease was primarily due to the increased number of females in male-dominated occupations, particularly at the managerial and professional levels. Nonetheless, the segregation index was still very high in 1981. Over 60% of the male or female labor force would have

TABLE 3.1
Example of Sex Segregation Index

Occupation	Percentage of Male Labor Force	Percentage of Female Labor Force	Absolute Difference
1	40	20	20
2	25	10	15
3	15	40	25
4	20	30	10
Total	100%	100%	70%

NOTE: Segregation index = sum of absolute differences/2 = 35%.

TABLE 3.2
Sex Segregation Index Values

Year	Sex Segregation Index Value (percent)
1900	66.9
1910	69.0
1920	65.7
1930	68.4
1940	69.0
1950	65.6
1960	68.4
1972	68.3
1977	64.7
1981	61.7

SOURCE: 1900-1960: E. Gross, "Plus ça Change . . . ? The Sexual Structure of Occupations over Time," *Social Problems* 16 (1968): 202; 1972-1981: A.H. Beller, "Trends in Occupational Segregation by Sex and Race, 1960-1981," in *Sex Segregation in the Workplace: Trends, Explanations, Remedies,* ed. B.F. Reskin (Washington, DC: National Academy Press, 1984), p. 14.
NOTE: The index represents the percentage of females or males who would have to change their occupation for the distributions of males and females in occupations to be the same.

had to change jobs at that time for sex segregation to be eliminated completely.[2]

The extent of sex segregation in the workplace can be seen in greater detail by examining the employment of women and men in specific occupational categories. Table 3.3 summarizes the most recent employment data available. It is not as detailed as the data on which segregation indices are calculated, which have encompassed from 250 to 400 occupations at different times of assessment. It is detailed enough, however, to give us an idea of how men and women differ in the jobs they presently hold.

Occupations are classified in Table 3.3 as male-intensive, female-intensive, or neutral according to a spread around the female (or male) proportion of the work force. We are using a conservative spread of 20 percentage points.[3] In May 1987, 44.7% of all jobs in the labor force were held by women. Therefore, male-intensive occupations are defined as those in which 24.7% or less of the work force was female. Female-intensive occupations are defined as those in which 64.7% or more of the work force was female. The remaining occupations, in which 24.8% to 64.6% of the workers were female, are defined as neutral.

According to Table 3.3, over half of all women (55.3%) were working in female-intensive occupations, while almost half of all men (49.3%) worked in male-intensive occupations. Almost 30% of the female labor force was in the "administrative support, including clerical" occupations, whereas only 6% of the male labor force was employed in these areas. Women also dominated most of the service occupations. In contrast, 41% of the male labor force was employed in the "precision production, craft, and repair" and "operators, fabricators, and laborers" occupations, while only 11% of the female labor force worked in the same occupations. Farming, forestry, and fishing were also dominated by men.

Professional, technical, and sales occupations were male-intensive, female-intensive, or neutral according to the particular occupation being considered. Only 8% of all engineers were women, which gives us a clue as to why the singer of "I'm Gonna Be an Engineer" was being discouraged by others from entering the profession. Health-diagnosing (e.g., medicine) and the legal professions were also male-intensive. Health assessment and treating (e.g., nursing) and teaching except at the college and university level were female-intensive, while other professions were neutral. Technical occupations in the health area were female-intensive, whereas those in engineering and science were male-intensive. The sale of commodities was a male-intensive occupation, while retail sales and the sale of personal services were female-intensive. Sales supervisors and proprietors and the sale of financial and business services were neutral occupations.

Table 3.3 suggests that the greatest disparities in female and male employment were occurring outside of the executive, administrative, and managerial occupations. These occupations, which had been male-intensive by the same 20-point-spread criterion until the mid-1970s, were now neutral in their overall composition. The percentages of female workers in the occupational categories shown do not tell the entire story, however. Women managers are employed to a far greater extent at the lower managerial levels than they are in top management positions. Korn/Ferry International found that only 2% of the top executives it surveyed in 1985 were women. Women have made little progress toward achieving top management positions in some of the more visible *Fortune* 500 companies. For example, in 1985, 7% of the top 6700 managers at IBM were women; 3% of the top 880 executives at

TABLE 3.3

Employment of Women and Men in Occupations: May 1987

Occupation	Percentage of Male Labor Force	Percentage of Female Labor Force	Percentage of Female Workers in Occupation	Occupation Type
Total	100.0	100.0	44.7	
Executive, administrative, & managerial	13.1	9.9	38.0	
officials & administrators, public administrators	.5	.4	41.6	
other executives, administrators, & managerial	9.7	6.2	34.1	
management-related occupations	2.9	3.3	47.7	
Professional specialty	11.5	14.5	50.6	
engineers	2.5	.2	7.7	M
math. & computer scientists	.8	.4	31.6	
natural scientists	.4	.2	23.8	M
health diagnosing occupations	1.0	.2	15.0	M
health assessment & treating occupations	.5	3.7	86.6	F
teachers, college & university	.7	.5	33.8	
teachers, except college & university	1.7	5.5	72.1	F
lawyers & judges	.9	.3	21.0	M
other professional specialties	3.0	3.5	48.7	
Technicians & related support	2.7	3.2	49.1	
health technologists & technicians	.3	1.9	84.6	F
engineering & science technicians	1.4	.4	20.4	M
other technicians	1.0	.9	41.2	

Sales occupations	11.4	12.7	47.4	
supervisors & proprietors	3.9	2.1	30.3	
sales representatives, financial & business services	2.2	2.0	42.4	
sales representatives, commodities	2.1	.5	16.9	M
sales workers, retail & personal services	3.2	8.0	67.3	F
sales-related occupations	.0	.1	56.1	
Administrative support, including clerical	5.8	29.0	80.3	F
supervisors	.5	.8	58.2	
computer equipment operators	.5	1.3	67.3	F
secretaries, stenographers, & typists	.1	9.8	98.2	F
financial records processing	.4	4.5	91.0	F
mail & message distributing	1.0	.6	33.6	
other administrative support, including clerical	3.3	12.0	74.5	F
Service occupations	9.5	18.3	60.9	
private household	.1	1.7	96.8	F
protective service	2.6	.5	13.1	M
food service	3.2	6.8	63.2	
health service	.3	3.3	89.3	F
cleaning & building service	2.6	2.4	42.4	
personal service	.7	3.6	81.5	F
Precision production, craft, & repair	19.8	2.3	8.6	M
mechanics & repairers	6.7	.3	3.5	M
construction trades	7.9	.2	1.8	M
other precision production, craft, & repair	5.2	1.8	22.0	M

(continued)

TABLE 3.3 Continued

Occupation	Percentage of Male Labor Force	Percentage of Female Labor Force	Percentage of Female Workers in Occupation	Occupation Type
Operators, fabricators, & laborers	20.8	8.3	24.9	
machine operators, assemblers, & inspectors	7.6	6.5	40.9	
transportation & material moving	6.9	.8	8.6	M
handlers, equipment cleaners, helpers, & laborers	6.3	1.5	16.7	M
Farming, forestry, & fishing	5.4	1.3	16.0	M
farm operators & managers	1.9	.4	14.7	M
other farming, forestry, & fishing	3.5	.9	16.7	M

SOURCE: U.S. Department of Labor, Bureau of Labor Statistics, *Employment and Earnings* 34, no. 6 (June 1987), computed from p. 46, table A-22.
NOTE: Occupation Type equals M for a male-intensive occupation and F for a female-intensive occupation. No symbol indicates a neutral occupation. The table includes both full-time and part-time employees.

American Telephone and Telegraph were women; 3% of the top 4000 positions at General Motors were held by women; and 2% of the managers eligible for bonuses at General Electric were women. Thus, while the lower managerial ranks have become neutral, the top managerial levels remain male-intensive.[4]

So far, we have shown that women tend to work in different occupations than men. Women and men also differ in earnings. The average wage for full-time female workers was 70% of what full-time male workers earned in 1986, up from 64% in 1983, where it had hovered for the previous three decades. The decrease in the earnings gap between men and women in the mid-1980s resulted from the increased employment of women in male-intensive occupations. The gap remains considerable, however. It is primarily due to the low wages earned in female-intensive occupations. In addition, a sex difference in wages exists within almost every occupation, with men tending to hold the higher-paying jobs and to earn more than women for the same job.[5]

Earnings aren't the only indication of the disparity between male-intensive and female-intensive occupations. Women also experience less career mobility than men. Female-intensive occupations typically have few opportunities to move from entry-level to advanced levels of pay and status. Women receive less on-the-job training so they have fewer resources than men to advance their status and wages. In female-intensive occupations, workers achieve their maximum status in a relatively short period of time. As a result, women tend to gain less occupational status over the course of their careers than men. Because women are concentrated in lower-paying occupations and industries that are less likely to provide pension coverage, they also are at a disadvantage at retirement.[6]

We have portrayed a workplace that to a large extent is sex-segregated, generating employment patterns that convey a powerful message to young people as well as adults who are planning to enter or reenter the job market. The message is that, while all occupations are theoretically open to all qualified individuals, (a) the lower-paying, less-valued occupations are more appropriate for females; (b) the higher-paying, more-valued occupations are more appropriate for males; and (c) men's work is often worth more than women's work for the same job.

The sex segregation of occupations, however, does not dictate decisions about employment. Otherwise, change in the proportions of women and men in particular occupations never would have occurred. To understand more about the process by which employment begins for individuals, we need to examine other influences.

DECISIONS BY INDIVIDUALS

Individuals' decisions regarding initial employment are made in three stages. The first stage consists of the formation of occupational aspirations, or preferences for the occupation in which they would like to work, and expectations for the occupation in which they will actually work. The term *occupation* is used broadly here to include nonpaying lines of work (e.g., staying at home to care for one's family) as well as paid employment. The second stage consists of the decision to work or not at a particular point in time. This decision is influenced by occupational aspirations and expectations previously formed and by the individual's current life situation. The third stage consists of the decision to explore some job opportunities and not others, and the decision to choose one job over another if the need for such a choice arises. These latter decisions are influenced more by the characteristics of the jobs under consideration and organizational recruiting practices.

Occupational Aspirations and Expectations

Studies of the occupational aspirations of preschool and elementary school children indicate that sex differences appear at an early age. Children tend to see activities, including work, in sex-appropriate terms, viewing some as appropriate only for females and others as appropriate only for males. Girls' early aspirations often focus on the female-intensive occupations of teacher and nurse. Boys' early aspirations are typically spread over a wider range of occupations, although mostly male-intensive ones.

Margaret Mooney Marini and Mary Brinton found similar sex differences in the occupational aspirations of adolescents. Using data collected from a nationally representative sample in 1979, they calculated a segregation index for the occupational aspirations of youths aged 14 to 22. In this case, the segregation index indicated the proportion of one sex that would have to change occupational aspirations to make the distributions of aspirations for the two sexes equal. The segregation index value was 67.6% for youths aged 14 to 15 and 61.5% for youths aged 20 to 22. According to Table 3.2, the segregation index for the existing work force was probably between 61.7% and 64.7% in 1979, when the survey data were collected. Although the occupational aspirations were slightly less sex-typed for the older youths, the aspirations of the youths as a whole were just as sex-segregated as the occupations held by people who were then employed.[7]

Marini and Brinton further classified the occupational aspirations of the 14- to 22-year-olds according to whether they were for male-intensive, female-intensive, or neutral occupations. Their definitions, slightly different from the ones we used before, were that male-intensive occupations had less than 30% women, female-intensive occupations had 60% or more women, and neutral occupations had 30% to 59% women. Based on these categories, 86% of the males aspired to male-intensive occupations, and only 4% aspired to female-intensive occupations. In contrast, 53% of the females aspired to female-intensive occupations, and 35% aspired to male occupations. Males were more likely than females to prefer occupations dominated by their own sex.

Occupational aspirations represent dreams that girls and boys have of "what they would like to be when they grow up." For example, Peggy Seeger's aspiring engineer has such a dream. Occupational expectations, on the other hand, represent the work individuals actually believe they will do. Expectations take into account perceptions of constraints such as limited opportunities or personal qualifications on the achievement of these dreams. The discrepancy between aspirations and expectations indicates the extent to which individuals believe that such constraints may prevent realization of their aspirations.

Most studies of both aspirations and expectations have concluded that occupational expectations are more sex-typed than occupational aspirations. For example, a study of eleventh-grade students found no difference between the mean percentage of men employed in occupations aspired to (83%) and expected (82%) by boys. The mean percentage of women employed in occupations aspired to by girls (67%), however, was significantly lower than the mean percentage of women employed in occupations in which the girls expected to work

(75%). Girls saw greater constraints on their aspirations than boys, expecting to work in organizations more female-dominated than those that they preferred.[8]

A study in which high-school seniors were given information about the anticipated proportion of women in two male-intensive occupations, architect and lawyer, yielded similar results. Each senior received information about one of the two occupations and was told that its projected proportion of women in 10-15 years was either 10%, 30%, or 50%. The seniors were then asked how interested they were in the occupation and how successful they thought they would be if they chose this occupation as a career goal. Males expressed greater interest in each career when the projected proportion of women was 10% or 30% than when it was 50%. Their expectations of future success at a career were not affected by its projected proportion of women. In contrast, females expressed greater interest in each career, and expected that they would be more successful at it, when the projected proportion of women was 30% or 50% than when it was 10%. The sexual composition of an occupation influenced boys' and girls' interest in it, but only girls' expectations for success at it.[9]

Let's now shift our focus from occupational aspirations in general to managerial aspirations in particular. Several studies have found that females aspire to managerial careers to a lesser degree than males.[10] These studies, however, typically have not examined factors that might contribute to the sex difference in managerial aspirations. Some colleagues and I investigated whether an individual's sex role identity affects his or her level of managerial aspirations.

We asked undergraduate business students at three universities to answer the question, "If you *had* to choose, in which of the following levels of an organization would you most like to work?" The possible responses were top management, middle management, lower management, and rank and file. Less than 5% of the students marked the lower management or rank and file categories, so we used only the top management and middle management categories in our analysis. Students also described themselves on the Bem Sex-Role Inventory and were classified as masculine, feminine, androgynous, or undifferentiated according to their BSRI masculinity and femininity scores (see Chapter 2).[11]

Table 3.4 presents the proportions of individuals who aspired to top management in each of the sex role identity groups for each sample. Results were similar for the three samples. The proportion of

TABLE 3.4
Percentage of Individuals Aspiring to Top Management

Sample/Sex Role Identity Group	Males		Females		Significance of Sex Difference
	N	Percentage	N	Percentage	
University 1					
androgynous	46	73.9	29	51.7	n.s.
masculine	91	83.5	16	81.3	n.s.
feminine	25	60.0	66	45.5	n.s.
undifferentiated	61	62.3	26	57.7	n.s.
total	223	73.1	137	53.3	< .001
University 2					
androgynous	97	76.3	58	60.3	n.s.
masculine	212	78.8	16	87.5	n.s.
feminine	78	56.4	130	46.9	n.s.
undifferentiated	177	63.8	63	47.6	< .05
total	564	70.6	267	52.4	< .001
University 3					
androgynous	39	66.7	31	54.8	n.s.
masculine	49	83.7	14	57.1	n.s.
feminine	14	64.3	50	40.0	n.s.
undifferentiated	34	58.8	26	30.8	n.s.
total	136	70.6	121	43.8	< .001

SOURCE: L.A. Mainiero, G.N. Powell, and D.A. Butterfield, "Sex Role Identity: A Predictor of Managerial Aspirations" (Paper delivered at the Annual Convention of the American Psychological Association, Toronto, 1978).
NOTE: Significance level pertains to the chi-square value for the relationship between managerial aspiration level and sex in each row, degrees of freedom = 1. The symbol n.s. indicates lack of significance at the .05 significance level. The proportion of masculine individuals aspiring to top management is significantly greater than the proportion of feminine individuals aspiring to top management for each sex in each sample at the .05 significance level.

males aspiring to top management was significantly larger than that of females. When males and females with a particular sex role identity were compared, however, sex differences in managerial aspirations disappeared in all cases except one. These results can be explained by examining the sex role identity distributions for males and females. In each sample, the greatest proportion of males was masculine and the greatest proportion of females was feminine. Masculine individuals aspired to top management in greater proportions than feminine individuals. Therefore, males were shown to have higher managerial aspirations. Sex role identity, however, was the real cause of the sex difference in managerial aspirations.

These results suggest that sex role identity, which seems to be more the result of socialization experiences than of basic sex differences, may have a substantial effect on the formation of occupational aspirations and expectations. Whether they are female or male, masculine individuals may aspire to and expect to succeed in more male-intensive occupations, whereas feminine individuals may aspire to and expect to succeed in more female-intensive occupations. The aspirations and expectations of androgynous and undifferentiated individuals may be less affected by the sex segregation of occupations.

In summary, when individuals make choices about the occupations in which they would like to work and expect to work, they are likely to be influenced by the distribution of male and female workers across occupations and by their own socialization experiences. The fact that expectations mirror the sex segregation of occupations more than aspirations, particularly for females, shows the constraining nature of these influences. In turn, such aspirations and expectations act to maintain the existing level of sex segregation. Changes in occupational aspirations are to be expected, as the increased labor force participation of women affects the socialization of children. Aspirations and expectations would have to change considerably, however, for sex differences in them to disappear.

The Decision to Work

The decision to work differs from the formation of occupational aspirations in several ways. First, it takes economic considerations more into account, whereas the choice of aspirations is primarily a psychological process. Second, the decision to work may involve the needs and wishes of a spouse and/or children, whereas the choice of aspirations involves only the needs and wishes of the person making the choice. Third, the decision to work takes job availability into account, whereas aspirations are formed with the assumption that the occupational choice will be available.[12]

Most people work for the money. They need to support themselves in some manner unless they are independently wealthy. When there are two wage earners in a family, it would seem that the economic need to have both working is less severe than the need to have at least one work. As we mentioned in Chapter 1, however, desire for the higher standard of living possible when both work creates the economic need. In any event, a majority of both women and men say that they work out of economic necessity.

Most people also hope that, in the process of working, they will satisfy their needs for accomplishing something, working with friendly coworkers, achieving some level of status and prestige, and the like. Women and men respond similarly to questions about working for noneconomic reasons. A majority of both working women and working men say that they would continue to work if they did not need to. We don't really know if they would act in accordance with these convictions if put to the test, but the statements themselves suggest that both sexes gain nonmonetary pleasures from working.

A small proportion of individuals, when they decide to work, decide to own and operate their own businesses. The percentage of businesses started and operated by women is about 5% but growing. Women-owned businesses are concentrated in the retail and personal service industries and less prevalent in male-intensive fields such as finance, manufacturing, and research and development. Both female and male entrepreneurs, however, tend to differ from the working population at large. They tend to be highly educated, energetic, independent, self-confident, competitive, and goal-oriented. They are likely to have had negative experiences in working for other people, which led them to venture out alone. Female entrepreneurs also tend to be first-born or only children with entrepreneurial fathers, suggesting that they received special attention and opportunities for development of self-confidence and modeling in childhood. Although we will generally be referring to the decision to work for others in this chapter, we should recognize that some people decide to work for themselves.[13]

Our society usually regards males as *not* having a decision to make about whether they work. Of course they work—they are men! The socialization of children, even when both parents work, typically stresses the male's role as the primary wage earner in the family. Whether they are single, married without children, married with children, widowed, separated, or divorced, most men work until they are ready to retire. Statistics on labor force participation according to marital status (see Table 1.4) show that at least two-thirds of the men in each category work. Over 70% of men aged 20-24, over 80% of those aged 25-34, 35-44, and 45-54, and 65% of those aged 55-64 work.[14] Except for the drop in the employment rate of the older group, which is primarily due to earlier retirements, these statistics have changed little over the past 40 years.

Women, on the other hand, have experienced more change in their employment status over the past 40 years. As a result, most of the research conducted on the decision to work has focused on factors that affect women's decisions. These may be divided into personal and situational factors.

The *personal factors* that could affect women's decisions to work include demographic characteristics such as age, race, and education, as well as personality characteristics. Age plays less of a role in determining whether women will work than it did in the past. About 60% of women aged 20-24, 25-34, 35-44, and 45-54 are presently in the work force. A drop-off in employment does not occur until the 55-64 age group, of which about 40% are employed.[15] Racial or ethnic group also plays a diminished role in women's decisions to work. Due to the increased employment of white women, labor force participation rates of white, black, and Hispanic women were within a 5% range in 1981. The kinds of jobs held by women differ according to their racial or ethnic group, with black and Hispanic women concentrated more in lower-paying occupations, but this factor no longer appears to affect their decisions to work. Race has more of an effect on whether men work, with about 10% more white men than black men in the labor force in 1981.

Education plays an important role in women's decisions to work. Women have been attaining higher levels of education. Women have been receiving at least half of the bachelor's degrees awarded since 1982, whereas they received less than one-third of these degrees in 1965 and less than one-quarter in 1950. They also received one-third of the MBA degrees awarded in 1987, up from 12% in 1976 and 2% in 1967. The employment status of women is highly related to their level of educational attainment. The more education a woman has received, the greater the likelihood that she is in the labor force. As a result, more women are in the labor force. Furthermore, the amount of education a woman receives greatly affects the kind of job she can attain. In 1985, 58% of the women employed in managerial or professional occupations had completed four or more years of college, whereas only 13% of those in technical, sales, or administrative support occupations and 4% of those in service occupations had achieved the same level of education. (A similar trend existed for men.) If women's level of educational attainment continues to rise, we can expect to see further changes in the nature of their employment.[16] The effect of personality characteristics on women's decisions to work, on the other hand, has seldom been examined.

Situational factors may also affect women's decisions to work, especially for married women. One group of situational factors concerns the woman's husband: whether he is employed and living with her; what his occupation, income, and attitudes are; and whether he is expected to be geographically mobile. The more positive the husband's attitude toward his wife's working outside the home, the more likely she is to work. If the husband is unemployed or not present, the wife is also more likely to work. The higher the husband's income and the higher the prestige and responsibility associated with his job, the less likely the wife is to work. The woman's decision to work also may be constrained by limited job selection in the location of the husband's job. If she is expected to be ready to move should he be transferred or take a job in another location, she may be less inclined to invest her energies in a career that does not lend itself to relocations.[17]

Another group of situational factors pertains to the woman's children, if there are any: how many, at what ages, and what child care arrangements are available. Children have less of an effect on whether women work than in previous years. Mothers of children under the age of 6, however, are still less likely to work than mothers of children between the ages of 6 and 17 only. Organizations as a whole do little to accommodate the child care needs of working parents, a subject we will return to in Chapter 6. When suitable child care arrangements are not available, it is typically the wife rather than the husband who sacrifices employment to care for children.

In summary, the decision to work is seldom made without consideration given to the economic needs of the household. Women's decisions to work are also influenced by noneconomic factors. Of the various personal factors considered, education has the most positive effect on women's decisions to work. Situational factors pertaining to husband and children affect their decisions to work. Attitudes acquired early in life, such as the attitude toward female employment in general, may also affect these decisions. In contrast, men typically do not consider whether to work, but when to retire.

Decisions About Job Opportunities

Individuals' decisions to pursue particular occupations are influenced primarily by their aspirations and their perceptions of the opportunities currently available in various occupations. Their decisions about particular job opportunities are influenced more by their inclinations to explore actively potential job openings, the characteristics of the jobs they consider, and the recruiting practices used by the organizations that offer these jobs. Sex differences in job search tendencies, preferences for job characteristics, or responses to recruiting practices could lead male and female applicants to take different types of jobs.

Little research has been conducted on the job search process. One interesting study, however, examined differences in males' and females' job search behavior. It presented college seniors interviewing for jobs with five types of responses that employers typically give to letters of inquiry from applicants: no response, a letter indicating no opening but your letter and resumé will be kept on file, a letter indicating that your letter and resumé are being circulated, a letter showing some interest in you by including a job application form and/or requesting further information, and a request for a job interview. The seniors were then asked what each response would mean about the employer's interest in them and what future actions they would take in light of the response, such as writing again, calling, or dropping the company from their job search. There were no sex differences in interpretations of company responses, job search strategies, or attitudes toward the job search process. This limited evidence suggests that, once they decide to look for a job, men and women do not approach the job search process differently.[18]

Women's and men's preferences for job characteristics have long been a subject of debate. Research on the issue began with the distinction between extrinsic and intrinsic characteristics of jobs. Extrinsic characteristics of jobs are provided by sources other than the job itself. Pay, the opportunity for promotion, pleasant working conditions, and recognition for good work are examples of extrinsic job characteristics, all of which are provided by the organization, peers, or supervisors. Intrinsic characteristics pertain more to the nature of the job. Variety, opportunity for achievement and challenge, and level of responsibility are all intrinsic characteristics of jobs that may provide satisfaction separately from their extrinsic characteristics. According to some research, males place greater importance on intrinsic and less importance on extrinsic job characteristics than females. The differences found, however, have been small.[19]

Philip Manhardt provided a possible explanation for these results by relating individuals' preferences for job characteristics to their general commitment to work. Upon studying new college recruits in an insurance company from 1966 to 1970, he discovered that female graduates placed less importance on long-range aspects of a job that are related to career success than male graduates. He also observed, however, that, when the sample of females was restricted to those who rated having a career first among their major life satisfactions, sex differences in importance of job characteristics were almost completely eliminated. Manhardt concluded, "Given equal perceived importance of a career and probability of continued employment, there is no reason to expect that women would not value success in business and show as much 'desire to get ahead' as men." By this reasoning, if females' commitment to work was similar to that of men, we would expect sex differences in preferences for job characteristics to disappear.[20]

Other research supports this speculation and suggests yet other factors that influence preferences for job characteristics. A study of data collected between 1973 and 1980 from national samples of adults revealed similar patterns in men's and women's preferences. Both sexes, when choosing from a list of one intrinsic and four extrinsic characteristics, identified the intrinsic characteristic of meaningfulness of work as most important to them and rank ordered the four extrinsic characteristics of income, opportunity for promotion, job security, and working hours as increasingly less important to them in that sequence. When significant sex differences in preferences occurred, they were in the opposite direction to that predicted by previous research. Women were more likely than men to select meaningfulness of work as their first preference, and men were more likely than women to select job security as their first choice.[21]

Other factors, however, accounted for job attribute preferences to a much greater degree than sex. Similar to earlier results, both a sex difference in general commitment to work and an effect of this commitment on job attribute preferences were found. As many as 74% of the men and 64% of the women said that they would continue to work even if it were economically unnecessary. Unmarried men and women did not differ in their commitment to work, but married men were more likely than married women to indicate that they would continue to work. Members of both sexes with a higher commitment to work, in turn, were more likely to prefer meaningful work and less likely to prefer high income and short working hours. Also, individuals with higher occupational prestige, education, and income were more likely to select meaningfulness of work as their first choice. Individuals with lower occupational prestige, education, and income were more likely to choose income, opportunity for promotion, or job security as their first preference. While there may be some differences in preferences in job characteristics due to sex, differences due to other factors such as education, income, and commitment to work are far greater.

Finally, women and men could differ in their responses to the recruiting practices used by organizations. Most research on recruiting practices has focused on the characteristics of recruiters and their behavior in interviews. Factors such as the recruiter's personality, knowledge of the job opportunity being discussed, ability and willingness to answer questions, and demonstrated interest in the applicant have been shown in some studies to affect applicants' evaluations of job opportunities. Differences in the responses of male and female applicants to recruiter characteristics or their interview behaviors, however, have seldom been found.[22]

Thus men and women do not seem to differ significantly in their job search behavior, preferences for job characteristics, or reactions to organizational recruiting practices. In fact, they respond quite similarly to job opportunities. Men and women differ to a greater extent in their decisions to work, although the gap between the outcomes of their decisions has become smaller in recent years. They differ most in their occupational aspirations and expectations, which reflect the current level of sex segregation in the workplace. Aspirations and expectations affect the jobs for which men and women apply. Once they apply for jobs in a particular occupation, men and women seem to respond similarly to them. If they do not apply for the types of jobs available in similar proportions, however, the balance of women and men in the various occupations is likely to remain skewed according to sex.

Individuals' decisions about work obviously have a great influence on how they begin their work careers. Sex differences in these decisions are primarily attributable to differences in occupational aspirations and expectations, which in turn are influenced by socialization pressures from parents, schools, and the mass media. Organizations' decisions, however, also affect the entry of women and men into the workplace. We shall next examine the decisions made by organizations about individuals who approach them concerning job opportunities.

DECISIONS BY ORGANIZATIONS[23]

Recruiters, personnel officers, and managers have little information on which to base their decisions to hire one applicant for a job over others. Referrals are a major source of applicants; however, the portrayals of individuals conveyed by referrals are invariably glowing. Decisions about which applicants other than walk-ins or referrals to interview are typically based on resumés, which present some information about applicants' backgrounds and experiences but little about their personal qualities. When recruiting is conducted on college campuses, decisions about which applicants to consider further are based on interviews that last no more than 20 to 30 minutes. The recruiter is likely to have read the resumés of up to a dozen applicants in less than an hour at the beginning of the day. As initial screening devices, campus interviews are necessary for organizations to reduce the large number of applicants who could possibly be considered to a select few who receive closer scrutiny. These interviews, however, lead by necessity to quickly formed impressions, which present only a blurred picture of applicants. Follow-up interviews collect more information about applicants, but not enough so that employers can be absolutely sure that they are making the right choice.

When judgments about individuals are based on very little data, as is the case when organizations make hiring decisions, these judgments are likely to be influenced by stereotypes. Gender stereotypes most concern us in this book, but stereotypes may also be based on such factors as age, race, ethnic group, class, religion, and geographical region of origin. Decision makers presented with limited information about competence or specific job requirements tend to make decisions based on gender stereotypes, whereas those presented with more information do not. The best way to prevent gender stereotypes from affecting decisions then is to collect as much information as possible about all applicants. This is a costly solution, however, which organizations are unlikely to embrace. Thus we are left with the fact that, as long as widely accepted gender stereotypes exist, they are likely to affect decisions about applicants in some way.

Gender stereotypes may lead recruiters to favor female or male applicants. Female applicants could be perceived to be more qualified, offered higher starting salaries, given more challenging job assignments, and/or hired more often than male applicants with equivalent credentials, or vice versa. Which sex is likely to receive the preferential treatment depends in large part on the job for which hiring is taking place. Males often receive more favorable evaluations for male-intensive jobs and females for female-intensive jobs. For example, males may be preferred over females for the jobs of engineer (you remember the song), physician, and security guard, whereas females may be preferred over males for the jobs of secretary, nurse, and retail salesperson. This effect may occur because the characteristics seen as necessary for success in such jobs are characterized as either masculine or feminine, therefore, calling for the appropriate sex. On the other hand, it may simply result from a belief that the sex that dominates a job must be better at it. In either case, the effect of the type of job on hiring decisions is to maintain the existing pattern of sex segregation in the workplace.[24]

This effect has particular relevance to hiring for managerial positions. The job of manager at any level has been male-intensive until recently, and the job of manager at upper levels remains highly male-intensive. Thus, if the same effect of type of job were to hold, we should expect to see males receive preferential treatment. In fact, most studies of hiring for managerial jobs have found a preference for male applicants.

Other characteristics of a job may lead employers to prefer one sex over the other. A study of simulated hiring for managerial positions in a branch banking firm found that male applicants were preferred when the work group to be managed was predominantly male and that female applicants were preferred when the group was predominantly female. Another simulation of initial placement decisions for newly hired engineers found that women engineers received less challenging first job assignments than male engineers when they were about to enter an all-male work group, whereas the presence of a competent female engineer in the work group resulted in male and female engineers receiving first job assignments with similar levels of challenge. Thus the sex of the subordinates or coworkers may affect organizations' hiring and placement decisions.[25]

Recruiter characteristics may also have an impact on organizations' decisions about applicants. Recruiter sex apparently does not affect these decisions, as male and female recruiters seldom differ in their responses to applicants. Personality traits and beliefs of recruiters, however, may affect their evaluations. One study found that recruiters who were high in authoritarianism—reflecting a tendency to stress roles of dominance and submission in male-female relationships— preferred male applicants over female applicants for an administrative trainee position; those who were moderate or low in authoritarianism did not differ in their evaluations of male and female applicants. A separate study found that recruiters who tended to believe in gender stereotypes were more likely to discriminate against applicants of the sex seen to be inappropriate for a job than recruiters who did not endorse the stereotypes. These findings suggest that organizations need to be careful in their selection of recruiters if they are to avoid hiring decisions based more on gender stereotypes than on applicants' actual qualifications.[26]

Applicants' characteristics other than their biological sex also may influence organizations' decisions about them. For example, hiring decisions could be affected by traditional notions concerning the commitment of women to family responsibilities as opposed to those associated with a career. Married women could be regarded as less suitable than married men or single workers for a position that called for extensive travel. We do not know, however, how prevalent this effect is.

There does seem to be an effect of applicants' appearance on hiring decisions. Applicants who are judged as attractive have an advantage over other applicants when they are applying for positions seen as appropriate for their own sex. This effect puts women at a disadvantage when they are applying for managerial positions. Whereas attractive males have been shown to be favored over unattractive males for such positions, unattractive females have been favored over attractive females for them. A possible explanation for this result is that attractiveness leads others to judge an individual more in accordance with gender stereotypes, that is, an attractive woman is seen as more feminine and an attractive man as more masculine than their less attractive counterparts. Attractiveness would then tend to enhance a male's credentials and diminish a female's credentials for a male-intensive job such as manager. Such findings are disturbing, because they place an emphasis on how people look rather than on how qualified they are and because people have little control over their basic attractiveness to others.[27]

Applicants' manner of dress also may affect recruiters' decisions about their suitability for managerial positions. A study of female applicants found that those with more masculine dress (i.e., emphasis on vertical and angular lines, straight silhouettes, large-scale details, dark colors, and heavy textures) received more favorable hiring recommendations than those with more feminine dress (e.g., emphasis on horizontal and curved lines, rounded silhouettes, small-scale details, light colors, and soft, delicate textures). Female applicants, however, could be perceived as "too masculine" in dress; the most favorable recommendations were achieved by those with moderately masculine attire. Others have reported that male applicants for professional positions who wear ill-fitting suits, unironed shirts, ties that are too short, or tacky tie clips create negative impressions. Socks that are white, beige, brightly colored, or large-patterned, and shoes that are sloppy or do not convey a professional image (such as saddle shoes) are also out for males. These findings are only slightly less disturbing than those concerning the effect of attractiveness. Applicants have more control over their dress than their basic appearance, but dress still seems a frivolous basis for deciding whom to hire for a managerial position. Some executives claim that, however, if an applicant wears an outfit judged by others to be inappropriate to an employment interview, he or she probably doesn't understand the realities of the work world and would be an ineffective performer.[28]

The biases that have been described operate most often at an unconscious level. Recruiters who are high in authoritarianism or belief in gender stereotypes do not say to themselves, "I am high in authoritarianism/belief in gender stereotypes, and I will take this into account in evaluating applicants." And recruiters who are presented with an attractive female applicant and an attractive male applicant for the same managerial job hopefully do not think, "Wow! What an attractive woman! That rules her out for this position. The attractive man will be much better in it." Some organizational decision makers, however, consciously use what they believe are other people's biases as the basis for decisions about applicants. If they believe, for example, that their employees or customers will feel uncomfortable with a female manager or engineer or a male secretary or receptionist, they may go along with the expected wishes of others in their hiring decisions even if they have no personal objections to hiring a member of the sex deemed inappropriate for the position. For example, a study of law firms in the early 1980s found that many were reluctant to hire female attorneys due to the expected loss of clients who they believed preferred males in these positions.[29]

So far, we have presented a gloomy picture of how organizations make decisions about applicants. Things may not be as bad as this picture suggests, however. Almost all of the research studies described have had participants, who were either organizational recruiters or college students, evaluate either fictitious resumés or hypothetical applicants seen in videotaped mock interviews. Such studies deliberately keep the amount of information about applicants small, so that the effect of the variable under investigation can be most readily identified. Hardly any studies have been conducted of decisions made about real applicants.

The few studies of actual employment interviews that have been conducted have generally not found an effect of applicant sex on recruiters' decisions. For example, Laura Graves and I recently examined the effects of several variables aside from applicant sex on recruiters' evaluations of applicants in campus interviews. We found that the applicant's subjectively measured qualifications, such as communications ability, knowledge of the job being applied for, and initiative, had the greatest effect on recruiters' evaluations, whereas applicant sex did not affect these evaluations at all. Recruiters tended to see stronger subjective qualifications in applicants with high grade-point averages whom they viewed as similar to themselves and whom they liked. These results support the point made earlier that, when more information is available about applicants, applicant sex has less of an effect on decisions and other factors have more of a effect.[30]

Thus organizations have considerable opportunity to discriminate between male and female applicants in their hiring decisions. They may do so because of the unconscious biases of organizational recruiters, or because of conscious beliefs about the biases of others. Given that so little information is available when decisions are made, the biases described probably affect decisions to some extent. To what extent is unknown. Further research on actual decisions about applicants is necessary to determine the size of this effect. We know enough, however, to conclude that organizations need to guard against possible biases in their decisions about applicants if they are to prevent sex discrimination from taking place.

IMPLICATIONS FOR MANAGEMENT

We shall examine the management implications of the research results presented in this chapter in two ways. First, we will consider the management of recruitment activities, including the way organizations present themselves to applicants (or to the outside world) and the way they decide which applicants to hire. Second, we will consider the effects of the decision-making processes that individuals and organizations use on the composition of managerial ranks.

Occupational aspirations and expectations, which begin being formed by individuals at very early ages, are the characteristics of individuals most responsible for maintaining the sex segregation of occupations. The differences in boys' and girls' aspirations and expectations mirror the existing level of sex segregation to a large extent. Women and men differ to a lesser extent in their decisions on whether to work, and they differ very little in their decision making about whether to take particular jobs. Thus, if organizations are to strive for a workplace that has less sex segregation, they will have the largest impact if they influence the formation of occupational aspirations and expectations. This suggests that they play more of a conscious role in the socialization of children.

How can organizations best play this role? Many organizations already distribute materials to high school guidance counselors about opportunities in their industries. These materials portray both women and men in the various occupations to a greater extent than ever before. High school is not the place for organizations to start, however, if they expect to have any appreciable impact on the development of occupational aspirations and expectations. Organizations also need to direct activities toward younger children. One way they can do this is to send speakers to elementary schools, Cub Scout and Brownie troops, and other places where young children congregate to talk about the opportunities in their industries and the workplace, stressing that they will be looking for both good women and good men. The best speakers would be members of the sex least represented in the occupations being talked about, or mixed-sex teams to demonstrate that both sexes belong in the occupations. For example, if the singer of "I'm Gonna Be an Engineer" succeeds despite the admonishments of everyone around her, she would be an ideal speaker on opportunities in the engineering professions. Films that are distributed to schools and youth groups can be used to convey similar themes.

Organizations can also use the mass media, especially television, more effectively for the same purpose. The opportunities for organizations to use television to have a positive influence on the aspirations and expectations of children are largely untapped. For example, organizations do very little recruiting of applicants on television. Only one large organization currently recruits via television: the Armed Forces of the United States. We frequently see recruiting advertisements for the military services that portray both sexes as fitting in them. Of course, these advertisements are not too realistic—nobody dies, or even gets their hair messed up—but they do convey the message that both sexes belong in the Armed Forces. These advertisements do more than attract applicants. They also give a message to young children that may influence their occupational aspirations and expectations.

Television ads may be too costly a way for most organizations to solicit applicants. After all, the Armed Forces don't pay for their heavy use of television—*we* do as taxpayers. Organizations, however, can prepare public-service messages for television stressing that both women and men belong in their industries. Organizations also need to monitor the influence of their current uses of television on children's aspirations and expectations. They can discourage reliance on gender stereotypes in advertisements for their products and services and in the programs they support with their advertising.

Organizations also affect children's aspirations and expectations by shaping the environment in which their parents work. Any actions that organizations take to make it easier for both parents to work will not only affect the parents' decisions to work, but also are likely indirectly to affect later decisions made by their children. The best way in which organizations can influence these decisions is to provide more and better day-care facilities, or to provide greater financial support and referral services to assist parents in making their own arrangements for day care. In this way, both children and parents benefit from organizations' actions.

Organizations also need to pay close attention to the selection and training of recruiters and others who make hiring decisions. Screening of applicants for recruiter positions should include assessment of beliefs in gender stereotypes and personality traits such as authoritarianism to determine their ability to make unbiased decisions about applicants. Training for individuals who already hold recruiter positions is also recommended. Over 40% of the recruiters surveyed in one study had received *no* formal training in recruiting from their companies.[31] Organizations can do much more than they are already doing to caution people involved in the recruitment process, whether they are full-time recruiters or managers hiring for their own departments, about the ways in which biases could affect their decisions and how to keep these biases from occurring.

The decisions made by individuals and organizations cumulatively affect the representation of the sexes in managerial positions. Individuals' aspirations and expectations have tended to support the existing sex segregation of occupations. Thus it is not surprising that research has shown that more males aspire to management positions, especially top management, than females. As suggested earlier, individuals' sex role identities may provide the best explanation for sex differences in managerial aspirations. If sex role identity is primarily the result of socialization experiences, the cause of sex differences in managerial aspirations then becomes gender stereotypes and the pressures on boys and girls, and men and women, to conform to them. Thus sex differences in aspirations may not disappear unless sex differences in the socialization experiences that promote traditional sex role identities disappear first.

Decisions by organizational recruiters regarding managerial positions also affect the sex composition of managerial ranks. The job of manager has often been defined as masculine, with men seen as more suited for it than women. Many studies have documented a bias toward hiring of male applicants for managerial positions, even when the qualifications of female and male applicants have been equivalent. These results also reflect the influence of gender stereotypes, which suggest that men are more appropriate for leadership roles than women.

Thus we have the conditions present for a self-fulfilling prophecy: Individuals' and organizations' decisions are affected by and often reinforce the current level of sex segregation in occupations. Given these conditions, it is a wonder that change occurs in the level of sex segregation in any occupation.

Yet, such change has been occurring. The sex segregation index value has been gradually dropping in recent years (see Table 3.2). The managerial ranks, and those of many other professions, have a greater proportion of women than ever before. The forces supporting the status quo, which consist of gender stereotypes and the existing level of sex segregation, may be powerful. The desire for a higher standard of living, which has provided an economic reason for both adult members of a household to work, and the women's movement, which has provided an ideological reason for women to seek to exercise more economic power over their own lives, however, are also powerful forces supporting change in the sex segregation of occupations.

In conclusion, the decisions made by individuals about whether they wish to enter the workplace and in what capacity, and the decisions made by organizations about which applicants they hire to fill job openings, are extremely complex. Both types of decisions are affected by the prevalence of gender stereotypes in our society. These decisions are not fully determined by gender stereotypes, however. Otherwise, the singer of "I'm Gonna Be an Engineer," and other individuals who aspired to and now work in occupations in which their sex is in the minority, would never have achieved their dreams.

NOTES

1. O. D. Duncan and B. Duncan, "Residential Distribution and Occupational Stratification," *American Journal of Sociology* 60 (1955): 493-503; E. Gross, "Plus ca Change . . .? The Sexual Structure of Occupations over Time," *Social Problems* 16 (1968): 198-208.

2. A. H. Beller, "Trends in Occupational Segregation by Sex and Race, 1960-1981," in *Sex Segregation in the Workplace: Trends, Explanations, Remedies*, ed. B. F. Reskin (Washington, DC: National Academy Press, 1984); B. F. Reskin and H. I. Hartmann, Chapter 2, "Sex Segregation: Extent and Recent Trends," in *Women's Work, Men's Work: Sex Segregation on the Job* (Washington, DC: National Academy Press, 1986).

3. N. F. Rytina and S. M. Bianchi, "Occupational Reclassification and Changes in Distribution by Gender," *Monthly Labor Review* 107, no. 3 (1984): 11-17.

4. C. Hymowitz and T. D. Schellhardt, "The Glass Ceiling," *Wall Street Journal* 207, no. 57 (24 March 1986): 1D-5D; K. Blumenthal, "Room at the Top," *Wall Street Journal* 207, no. 57 (24 March 1986): 7D-9D.

5. U.S. Department of Commerce, Bureau of the Census, "Male-Female Differences in Work Experience, Occupation, and Earnings: 1984," *Current Population Reports*, series P-70, no. 10 (Washington, DC: Government Printing Office, 1987); A. A. Kemp and E. M. Beck, "Equal Work, Unequal Pay: Gender Discrimination Within Work-Similar Occupations," *Work and Occupations* 13 (1986): 324-47; J. O'Neill, "Role Differentiation and the Gender Gap in Wage Rates," in *Women and Work: An Annual Review*, vol. 1, ed. L. Larwood, A. H. Stromberg, and B. A. Gutek (Beverly Hills, CA: Sage, 1985).

6. Reskin and Hartmann, *Women's Work, Men's Work*, Chapter 1, "The Significance of Sex Segregation in the Workplace."

7. M. M. Marini and M. C. Brinton, "Sex Typing in Occupational Socialization," in *Sex Segregation in the Workplace*, ed. Reskin.

8. M. M. Marini and E. Greenberger, "Sex Differences in Occupational Aspirations and Expectations," *Sociology of Work and Occupations* 5 (1968): 147-78.

9. M. E. Heilman, "High School Students' Occupational Interest as a Function of Projected Sex Ratios in Male-Dominated Occupations," *Journal of Applied Psychology* 64 (1979): 275-79.

10. M. D. Fottler and T. Bain, "Sex Differences in Occupational Aspirations," *Academy of Management Journal* 23 (1980): 144-49.

11. L. A. Mainiero, G. N. Powell, and D. A. Butterfield, "Sex Role Identity: A Predictor of Managerial Aspirations" (Paper delivered at the Annual Convention of the American Psychological Association, Toronto, 1978).

12. V. F. Nieva and B. A. Gutek, Chapter 3, "Factors Affecting Women's Decision to Work," in *Women and Work: A Psychological Perspective* (New York: Praeger, 1981).

13. R. D. Hisrich and C. G. Brush, Chapter 1, "A Historical Perspective," in *The Woman Entrepreneur* (Lexington, MA: Lexington Books, 1986); D. D. Bowen and R. D. Hisrich, "The Female Entrepreneur: A Career Development Perspective," *Academy of Management Review* 11 (1986): 393-407.

14. U.S. Department of Labor, Bureau of Labor Statistics, *Handbook of Labor Statistics* (Washington, DC: Government Printing Office, 1985), pp. 44-47, table 16.

15. Ibid.

16. U.S. Department of Commerce, Bureau of the Census, *Statistical Abstract of the United States*, 106th ed. (Washington, DC: Government Printing Office, 1986), computed from p. 149, table 249, and p. 401, table 678.

17. Nieva and Gutek, *Women and Work*, Chapter 3, "Factors Affecting Women's Decision to Work."

18. B. Z. Posner, J. Schmidt-Posner, and W. A. Randolph, "Can Applicants' Characteristics Explain the Sex Structuring of Organizations?" *Psychological Reports* 56 (1986): 343-50.

19. O. C. Brenner and J. Tomkiewicz, "Job Orientation of Males and Females: Are Sex Differences Declining?" *Personnel Psychology* 32 (1979): 741-50; K. M. Bartol and P. J. Manhardt, "Sex Differences in Job Outcome Preferences: Trends Among Newly Hired College Graduates," *Journal of Applied Psychology* 64 (1979): 477-82; F. Herzberg, B. Mausner, R. O. Peterson, and D. F. Capwell, *Job Attitudes: Review of Research and Opinion* (Pittsburgh: Psychological Service of Pittsburgh, 1957).

20. P. J. Manhardt, "Job Orientation of Male and Female College Graduates in Business," *Personnel Psychology* 25 (1972): 361-68.

21. W. B. Lacy, J. L. Bokemeier, and J. M. Shepard, "Job Attribute Preferences and Work Commitment for Men and Women in the United States," *Personnel Psychology* 36 (1983): 315-29.

22. N. Schmitt and B. W. Coyle, "Applicant Decisions in the Employment Interview," *Journal of Applied Psychology* 61 (1976): 184-92; G. N. Powell, "Effects of Job Attributes and Recruiting Practices on Applicant Decisions: A Comparison," *Personnel Psychology* 37 (1984): 721-32; M. S. Taylor and T. Bergmann, "Sex of Recruiter Effects on Applicant Reactions" (Paper delivered at the Annual Meeting of the Academy of Management, Boston, 1984).

23. This section of the chapter is primarily based on research reviewed in G. N. Powell, "The Effects of Sex and Gender on Recruitment," *Academy of Management Review* 12 (1987): 731-43.

24. M. E. Heilman, "Sex Bias in Work Settings: The Lack of Fit Model," in *Research in Organizational Behavior*, vol. 5, ed. L. L. Cummings and B. M. Staw (Greenwich, CT: JAI, 1983).

25. G. L. Rose and P. Andiappan, "Sex Effects on Managerial Hiring Decisions," *Academy of Management Journal* 21 (1978): 104-12; M. S. Taylor and D. R. Ilgen, "Sex Discrimination Against Women in Initial Placement Decisions: A Laboratory Investigation," *Academy of Management Journal* 24 (1981): 859-65.

26. K. Simas and M. McCarrey, "Impact of Recruiter Authoritarianism and Applicant Sex on Evaluation and Selection Decisions in a Recruitment Interview Analogue Study," *Journal of Applied Psychology* 64 (1979): 483-91; C. Sharp and R. Post, "Evaluation of Male and Female Applicants for Sex-Congruent and Sex-Incongruent Jobs," *Sex Roles* 6 (1980): 391-401.

27. M. E. Heilman and L. R. Saruwatari, "When Beauty Is Beastly: The Effects of Appearance and Sex on Evaluations of Job Applicants for Managerial and Non-managerial Jobs," *Organizational Behavior and Human Performance* 23 (1979): 360-72; T. F. Cash, B. Gillen, and D. S. Burns, "Sexism and 'Beautyism' in Personnel Consultant Decision Making," *Journal of Applied Psychology* 62 (1977): 301-10.

28. S. Forsythe, M. F. Drake, and C. E. Cox, "Influence of Applicant's Dress on Interviewer's Selection Decisions," *Journal of Applied Psychology* 70 (1985): 374-78; K. A. Hughes, "Businesswomen's Broader Latitude in Dress Codes Goes Just so Far; Male Executives Also Suffer for Their Sartorial Mistakes," *Wall Street Journal* 210, no. 45 (1 September 1987): 33.

29. C. F. Epstein, *Women in Law* (New York: Basic Books, 1981).

30. L. M. Graves and G. N. Powell, "An Investigation of Sex Discrimination in Recruiters' Evaluations of Actual Applicants," *Journal of Applied Psychology* (in press).

31. B. Z. Posner, "Comparing Recruiter, Student, and Faculty Perceptions of Important Applicant and Job Characteristics," *Personnel Psychology* 34 (1981): 329-39.

4

Working with People

Impressions from an Office

The family picture is on HIS desk.
—Ah, a solid, responsible family man.
> The family picture is on HER desk.
> —Umm, her family will come before her career.

HIS desk is cluttered.
—He's obviously a hard worker and a busy man.
> HER desk is cluttered.
> —She's obviously a disorganized scatterbrain.

HE is talking with his co-workers.
—He must be discussing the latest deal.
> SHE is talking with her co-workers.
> —She must be gossiping.

HE'S not at his desk.
—He must be at a meeting.
> SHE'S not at her desk.
> —She must be in the ladies' room.

HE'S not in the office.
—He's meeting customers.
> SHE'S not in the office.
> —She must be out shopping.

HE'S having lunch with the boss.
—He's on the way up.
> SHE'S having lunch with the boss.
> —They must be having an affair.

The boss criticized HIM.
—He'll improve his performance.
> The boss criticized HER.
> —She'll be very upset.

HE got an unfair deal.
—Did he get angry?
> SHE got an unfair deal.
> —Did she cry?

HE'S getting married.
—He'll get more settled.
                         SHE'S getting married.
                         —She'll get pregnant and leave.
HE'S having a baby.
—He'll need a raise.
                         SHE'S having a baby.
                         —She'll cost the company money in maternity
                         benefits.
HE'S going on a business trip.
—It's good for his career.
                         SHE'S going on a business trip.
                         —What will her husband say?
HE'S leaving for a better job.
—He knows how to recognize a good opportunity.
                         SHE'S leaving for a better job.
                         —Women are not dependable.

                         —Natasha Josefowitz, 1983[1]

In her poem, "Impressions from an Office," Josefowitz describes gender stereotypes of women and men in office environments. The distinctions that are drawn are exaggerated and not necessarily true, of course. Whether the distinctions are true or not, however, people frequently use gender stereotypes to estimate their own capabilities and those of others, and to evaluate their own performance and that of others. Their responses to coworkers are heavily influenced by the stereotypes that they employ to interpret the coworkers' behavior.

Does gender stereotyping belong in the workplace? Are there any real differences between female and male peers, that is, individuals who hold the same types of jobs or work at the same level? If so, what are the differences, and when are they most often exhibited? If not, why do men and women in some situations feel awkward and uncomfortable in working together, and in other situations act as if each other's sex makes no difference at all?

In this chapter, we shall address issues pertaining to gender stereotyping of workplace peers. First, we shall consider whether gender stereotypes have any relation to actual sex differences exhibited at work. Although few basic sex differences have been found, female and male peers could differ in ways that affect their work relationships. By reviewing research on task-oriented groups, we shall reach a conclusion about the extent of sex differences between women and men peers.

Second, we shall examine the conditions under which gender stereotypes such as those portrayed in the poem come into play. Some characteristics of individuals lead them to believe in gender stereotypes and apply the stereotypes in their work relationships more than other individuals. Also, some characteristics of work situations lead individuals in them to make more use of gender stereotypes than individuals in other situations. We shall describe the personal and situational factors that contribute to gender stereotyping in groups.

Third, we shall explore the ways in which gender stereotyping influences the interactions between peers in skewed groups, that is, groups in which the ratio of females to males is either very high or very low. In particular, we shall examine the effects of groups possessing "token" members of one sex on interactions between the tokens and the more dominant sex. Tokens frequently receive special attention from dominants in ways that hinder their performance and make them feel uncomfortable.

Finally, we shall examine issues pertaining to the expression of sexuality in the workplace. Sexual harassment, or the directing of unwelcome sexual attention by one member of an organization toward another, is a matter of considerable public concern with legal ramifications for the organization. Organizational romances, or the sharing of welcome sexual attention by two members of the organization, have more recently been debated: How should participants and their organizations handle them? Even if they are not the participants, men and women in organizations frequently have to deal with the intermingling of work roles and sexual roles by other employees.

DO FEMALE AND MALE
PEERS DIFFER?

In our examination of behavior related to entry into the workplace, we found that, the closer individuals get to making decisions about particular jobs, the less they differ according to sex. There are large sex differences in early occupational aspirations and expectations, smaller sex differences in decisions to work, and minimal sex differences in decisions about job opportunities. If the same pattern of diminishing sex differences were to hold after individuals entered the workplace, we would expect negligible sex differences in peers' behavioral tendencies and responses to work situations. To investigate whether this expectation is warranted, we shall review research on a variety of topics related to behavior in task-oriented groups.[2]

For many years, women were regarded as the "social specialists" or more expressive members in task-oriented groups and men as the "task specialists" or more instrumental group members. Recent research suggests that this distinction applies mostly to newly formed groups in which members have little information about each other's competence. In such groups, men tend to be initially perceived by themselves and other group members to be more competent than women. When the group has some history and members have gained information about each other's competence, however, members who are seen as higher in competence, regardless of whether they are women or men, tend to engage in more task behavior and less social behavior than group members who are seen as less competent. Sex differences in task versus social roles played in newly formed groups seem to result from group members' belief in gender stereotypes, particularly that males are more competent at tasks than females. Once group members have experience in working with each other, these sex differences tend to disappear.[3]

One of the sentiments not expressed in Josefowitz's poem is that women also have been regarded by many people as possessing a special ability to sense the feelings and thoughts of others ("women's intuition"). Although Maccoby and Jacklin concluded in their exhaustive review of research on sex differences that women and men do not differ in their sensitivity to others, other researchers reached a different conclusion. A recent study investigated task-oriented dyads (pairs) to determine whether the role that an individual plays as leader or subordinate affects his or her level of sensitivity. In this study, women had no advantage over men in sensitivity to others. Instead, individuals in the subordinate role, regardless of sex, were more sensitive to leaders than leaders were to subordinates. Because women have been in the subordinate role in our society more frequently than men, what has been called "women's intuition" might more appropriately be called "subordinates' intuition." These results suggest that the assigning of roles to group members may override any potential sex difference in their sensitivity to other members.[4]

"Fear of success" received a great deal of attention in the late 1960s and 1970s as a personality characteristic that was supposed to distinguish between women's and men's responses to task-oriented situations. Matina Horner proposed that women have particular anxieties concerning success, because success is incompatible with the feminine gender stereotype and thereby may lead to rejection by others. As a result, Horner argued, women possess a motive to avoid success that is not present in men. Women could act on this motive by lowering their aspirations for success in groups or by denying responsibility for their success when it occurs.[5]

The concept of fear of success was initially popular because it reinforced different aspects of people's notions regarding the capabilities of the sexes. For some, it meant not that women were incapable but they feared the consequences if they did well and performed to their full capabilities. For others, it justified a belief that women are less equipped than men to deal with situations that call for an achievement orientation.

Horner's theory failed to hold up under scrutiny in later studies. Fear of success appeared in women mostly for activities that were considered appropriate only for men. In activities considered appropriate for women or men, motives for avoiding success showed no sex difference. Apparently individuals of both sexes shy away from success when it will result in social disapproval, while no such avoidance occurs when social approval is likely to accompany success. Thus fear of success seems a legitimate response of individuals to the anticipated reactions of others in special circumstances, rather than a generalized personality trait possessed more by women than men that affects their efforts to be successful in groups.[6]

Given that research has supported the existence of a basic sex difference in aggressiveness, we might expect it to be manifested in task-oriented groups as a sex difference in dominance-related behavior. Evidence suggests that, in groups, men engage in more dominating behavior than women. They express anger, talk frequently, interrupt others, and invade others' personal space.[7] Women as well as men, however, can be high or low in the tendency to dominate. We might expect individuals who are high in the tendency to dominate to emerge as leaders in groups. Because the tendency to dominate is more compatible with the masculine than the feminine gender stereotype, what happens when high-dominance women work with low-dominance men?

Edwin Megargee assigned high-dominance and low-dominance individuals to dyads and asked each dyad to decide upon a leader before they proceeded to work on a task together. In same-sex dyads, individuals who were high in the tendency to dominate tended to be chosen as group leaders as expected. In mixed-sex dyads where the male was high in dominance and the female was low in dominance, the male tended to be chosen as leader. When the female was high in dominance and the male was low in dominance, however, the male still tended to be chosen as leader. The gender stereotype of males as more dominating prevailed over the female's actually greater tendency to dominate.[8]

These results were obtained, however, from newly formed dyads in which members had very little information about each other. In such circumstances, gender stereotypes of men as leaders might be expected to hold most often. To test how well gender stereotypes hold when more information is available about group members, other researchers conducted a variation of Megargee's study. They gave members of dyads information about each other's competence at the task they were about to do prior to the selection of a leader. In dyads where the high-dominance female was also more competent than the low-dominance male, the female tended to be chosen as the leader more than the male. Information about task competence led to the selection of the more competent person, female or male, as leader, rather than the selection of the male on the basis of gender stereotypes.[9]

Rather than sex differences, sex role identity could affect behavior in peer groups. Androgyny is a characteristic that is supposed to give individuals behavioral flexibility, desirable when women and men are required to solve problems together. Androgynous individuals, who are able to play both task and social roles and to lead as well as follow, may tend to share the roles they perform in groups. In contrast, masculine individuals may tend to adopt task roles and act as the leader more than feminine individuals. In groups of masculine men and feminine women, the men may be more likely to lead and the women to follow.

Recent studies of the relationship between sex role identity and behavior in a task-oriented group support such an explanation. One study found that individuals who were high in masculinity, whether they were men or women, performed in a more active, instrumental manner in groups than individuals who were low in masculinity. In another study, androgynous women and men tended to share leadership in mixed-sex task groups, particularly when they had some social support from other group members of their sex who were also androgynous. In groups where men were masculine and women feminine, men tended to dominate the leadership role. Thus the sex role identity of group members appears to have an important effect on their behavior in groups.[10]

We have not reviewed *all* of the research on sex differences in task-oriented groups, as it would be beyond the scope of this book to do so. The research findings presented, however, suggest an explanation for the existence of differences between female and male peers in some group situations but not in others. Sex differences that reflect gender stereotypes typically have been found in laboratory studies that ask strangers to work on a task together. When group members know something about each other or have been assigned a role in the group, sex differences tend to disappear. Men and women appear to adopt stereotypical roles when they are in unfamiliar situations, but drop such roles when the situation is more familiar or they are armed with more than perfunctory information about each other. Sex role identity differences among group members could provide a better explanation for individual differences in behavior. We must also look to other explanations, however, for the prevalence of gender stereotyping in the workplace, aside from the existence of individual differences.

GENDER STEREOTYPING IN GROUPS: THE CONTRIBUTING FACTORS

Gender stereotypes, when applied to workplace peers, bear little relation to the people being stereotyped. They have more to do with the people doing the stereotyping and the situations in which stereotypes are made. Certain characteristics of individuals lead them to stereotype others, and certain characteristics of situations lead individuals involved in them to stereotype others. Both personal and situational factors contribute to gender stereotyping in groups.

Individuals who hold traditional attitudes toward women and their role in society are more likely to see working women and men in stereotypical terms than individuals with less traditional attitudes. In turn, a variety of personal characteristics appear to influence attitudes toward women. For example, one study found that older and more educated individuals had less traditional attitudes toward women. Maturity and education, which broaden a person's knowledge, may allow the individual to distinguish women's actual characteristics from those assigned by the feminine gender stereotype. Also, the more frequently people attended church, the more traditional were their attitudes toward women. People who are not strongly religious may evaluate their experiential information about women on its own merits. Individuals who attend church more may consider and be more influenced by religious teachings about women rather than their own experiences.[11]

Other studies have found that women with high self-esteem hold less traditional attitudes than those with less self-esteem. Perhaps women who are low in self-esteem lack the confidence that is necessary to adopt nontraditional roles in society or to advocate them for other women. Androgynous women and men, who are likely to be high in self-esteem, tend to hold less traditional attitudes toward women. Feminine women and masculine men, however, whose sex role identity agrees with gender stereotypes, tend to hold more traditional attitudes.[12]

Situational characteristics also influence the manifestation of gender stereotypes in work settings. Over time, simply working with members of the opposite sex seems to affect attitudes toward them. In a study of the entry of women to the traditionally male field of fire fighting, the longer men had worked with women fire fighters, the less traditional their attitudes toward women in general and the more positive their evaluation of women fire fighters. Their beliefs concerning preferential treatment for women as a group, however, were unequivocal: While they were ready to accept women as individuals, they insisted that women be treated as individuals. In a similar study at the managerial level in a corporate setting, male managers who had worked with women as peers were less likely to stereotype women as unfit for management than those who had only worked with women as subordinates. Thus male attitudes toward women workers are affected by personal experience with women on the job. Men who have worked with women peers longer are less likely to characterize them according to gender stereotypes.[13]

The sex ratio of a group—that is, its ratio of women to men or vice versa—is another situational factor that affects whether gender stereotyping occurs. Based on her examination of male-female work relationships in a large industrial corporation, Rosabeth Kanter identified four types of groups of varying sex ratio that can exist in work settings. Kanter focused her analysis on small groups, which could be either work groups or groups of individuals who hold the same job such as manager. Her analysis can be extended to groups of all sizes, however. *Uniform* groups, consisting of all males or all females, represent one extreme. There are no male-female issues in uniform groups by definition. *Balanced* groups, consisting of approximately equal numbers of men and women, represent the other extreme. Attributes of individuals other than their sex have the primary influence on how individuals interact in balanced groups.[14]

Between these two extremes are skewed and tilted groups. *Skewed* groups have a ratio of males to females or vice versa ranging from about 85:15 to almost 100:0. Members of the sex in abundance in skewed groups are called "dominants," because they are seen to control the group and its culture, and members of the other sex are called "tokens," because they are more often treated as representatives of their sex rather than as individuals. *Tilted* groups have less of an abundance of one sex over the other, with the ratio of males to females or vice versa ranging from about 65:35 to about 85:15. In tilted groups, dominants become simply a majority and tokens a minority. Minority members may become allies with each other and have more of an effect on group culture in tilted groups than in skewed groups. They are individuals who are distinguishable from each other, as well as a type of individual that is different from the majority type.

In conclusion, several personal and situational factors may influence the tendency for individuals to engage in gender stereotyping of others in work settings. The personal factors that have an effect include personality characteristics such as sex role identity and self-esteem, and demographic characteristics such as age and education. The situational factors that are relevant include the extent of prior experience with opposite-sex peers and the sex ratio of the group.

GENDER STEREOTYPING IN
SKEWED GROUPS:
TOKENS AND DOMINANTS

Let's now turn our attention to the ways in which gender stereotyping affects interactions between peers in skewed groups.

What happens in skewed groups is of particular interest for two reasons. First, the dynamics of the skewed group apply to many of the interactions that occur between women and men in management. Since women have entered the management profession in large numbers, the overall proportions of women and men in managerial ranks have shifted from being skewed to being tilted. The proportion of women to men managers at upper levels and in many organizations, however, remains sharply skewed. To understand these interactions best, we need to examine the properties of skewed groups. Furthermore, much of the work force has experience with either working or having worked in a skewed group. Even if a group currently has a tilted or balanced sex ratio, most of its members are likely to have belonged to a skewed group at one time. To understand the past experience in groups of some workers (which is likely to influence their responses to current work situations) as well as the present experience of many others, we also need to examine the dynamics of skewed groups.

Kanter chose the term *tokens* for the underrepresented members in a skewed group to highlight the special characteristics associated with being in that position. Tokens are not merely people who differ from other group members along some particular dimension; they are people who are categorized on the basis of an easily recognizable characteristic, such as sex, race, ethnic group, or age. This characteristic carries a set of assumptions about the traits and expected behavior of people in the category. Tokens exist only in small numbers, and the rest of the group puts them in the position of representing their category, whether they want to or not. A token rarely becomes "just another member of the group." Although organizations sometimes deliberately set up token or display situations, anytime people are in a group where others of their category are not usually found, they may find themselves tokens.

The special treatment that tokens receive in skewed groups is detrimental to their performance in several ways. First, because they are highly visible, tokens face additional performance pressures. Second, the differences between tokens and dominants tend to be exaggerated. Third, the characteristics of tokens are often distorted or misperceived because of the dominants' tendency to stereotype them. Let's examine each of these, considering the experience of token women in skewed groups as an example.

Tokens are subject to *performance pressures* because they get attention that individual members of the dominant group don't get, simply because they are different. Such attention could be seen as an advantage, and dominants often envy the attention that tokens receive. Many token women have reported, however, that they have to work twice as hard as men in their groups to have their competence recognized. The token woman has no trouble in having her presence noticed, but she does experience difficulty in having her achievements noticed. The organization also may attempt to show its enlightenment by displaying token women in ways that deny their individuality. At such occasions, they are singled out for the fact that they are female rather than for their particular accomplishments. The reaction of tokens to the attention they receive is also noticed. While dominants may display disaffection with the company and get away with it, tokens display disaffection at greater risk.

Token women react to such performance pressures in several different ways. They may try to overachieve relative to their peers. This strategy is unlikely to work, however, for women who are less than exceptional performers. They may also try to capitalize on their rarity as tokens and turn it to their advantage, calling attention to that which gives them notoriety in the group. This strategy is unlikely to succeed because it risks the displeasure of dominants. Finally, they may seek to be "socially invisible" by avoiding events at which they would have high visibility because of their token status and making little attempt to have their accomplishments known. This strategy results in limited recognition of their competence and reduced likelihood of their receiving the rewards that could go with such recognition. No matter what coping strategy they adopt, token women face performance pressures that men in the dominant group do not face.

By their very presence, tokens also make dominants more aware of what they have in common, while at the same time posing a threat to that commonality. For example, if "boys will be boys," dominant males are even more so when token females are present. They may try to highlight what they can do in personal, sexual, and business affairs as men, in contrast to what the women can do. They also do not want women around at all times, choosing to exclude them from certain secretive activities. This process is called *boundary heightening*. It is seen publicly in the existence of exclusive clubs such as the Bohemian Club, which are open only to men and at which boyish locker-room antics are reported to reign supreme. In work organizations, it is seen in male-oriented social functions that the women are expected not to attend.

Token women are left with few choices for responding to boundary heightening activities by men. They may accept isolation, opting for friendly but distant relations with the male members except at times when they are excluded. On the other hand, they may try to become insiders by defining themselves as exceptional members of their sex and turning against other women who attempt to join the group. This would account for the "queen bee syndrome" where women turn against other women in social settings if men are present, which has been reported by some writers.[15]

Token women also risk being classified according to the feminine gender stereotype, whether or not their personal characteristics are consistent with the stereotype. This process is called *role encapsulation*. Dominants' stereotypes of token women force them into playing limited roles. Such roles benefit men by providing them a familiar context for viewing women, thereby allowing them to make use of familiar forms of behavior. For example, when professional women are mistakenly taken to be secretaries, they are stereotyped as conforming to a traditionally subordinate female role. They may be further stereotyped by being assigned secretarylike functions in groups or by being given jobs that reflect their presumed feminine capabilities and concerns, such as equal employment opportunity or corporate social responsibility jobs.

Token women have few options for responding to role encapsulation. They may accept a stereotypical role, which could limit their participation in situations and lead to programmed male responses. If they try to fight being assigned a stereotypical role, they risk being classified as "iron maidens" and face rejection by the group. On the other hand, they may try not to exhibit any characteristics that might support the stereotypes. This strategy takes considerable effort unless their personal characteristics are naturally contrary to the feminine gender stereotype.

Kanter based her conclusions on her analysis of an environment in which men vastly outnumbered women in positions of authority. She assumed that her theories would apply equally well to women in male-dominated groups other than the ranks of management and to men in female-dominated groups. Some studies have supported this conclusion. For example, a study of law students in two schools, one with a tilted sex ratio of students favoring males and the other with a skewed sex ratio favoring males, found that women experienced greater performance pressures, boundary heightening, and role encapsulation in the school with the skewed sex ratio. A study of male nurses in female-dominated work groups reached a similar conclusion. A more recent study of boundary heightening directed toward male tokens in a nursing school found, however, that the males were no more socially isolated than the numerically dominant female students, suggesting that factors other than the sex ratio of a group affect female-male interactions within it.[16]

Several other factors might influence the relationship between tokens and dominants in skewed groups. Tokens are not always powerless in their relationship with dominants and can do much to build their power. For example, they may establish themselves as indispensable to the group in some way. Tokens who develop special areas of expertise are more likely to receive attention because of their competence than because of their token status. They may also cultivate their skills at diagnosing power issues so that they are aware of how they may have the greatest impact on decisions in a given situation. Depending on their diagnosis, they may seek to influence the assumptions and objectives on which decisions are based, the alternatives to be considered, and/or the information available about alternatives. Tokens may also build their power base through the ability to demonstrate self-confidence, take risks, and verbally advance their causes. Although these skills may seem like a lot to require of tokens, they are also required for dominant group members to be successful.[17]

In conclusion, the sex ratio of a group has a powerful effect on the dynamics of work relationships among its members. We have placed special emphasis on the relationship between dominants and tokens in skewed groups, because this relationship is particularly relevant to the experiences of women and men in management. Tokens face a set of work conditions that are different from those of their numerically dominant colleagues. Token or dominant status alone does not determine how one interacts with others. It does have an important influence on interactions between women and men in management ranks and in other types of groups, however.

SEXUAL HARASSMENT

Sexual harassment is a workplace issue that has received considerable public attention. It is primarily directed toward women, but also toward men. A study of over 20,000 federal employees in 1980 found that 42% of female employees and 15% of male employees reported having been harassed in the previous 24 months, with peers representing the most common harassers for both female and male employees. These figures show that the public attention directed toward sexual harassment has been well-deserved.[18]

The Issue of Definition[19]

As a result of this attention, most people now recognize that a line needs to be drawn between acceptable and unacceptable sexually oriented behavior in the workplace. The question remains, however, as to exactly what types of behavior constitute sexual harassment. In other words, where should the line be drawn?

Definitions of sexual harassment used by surveys and government agencies provide some guidance, but nothing definitive. A Cornell University study defined sexual harassment as "any repeated and unwanted sexual comments, looks, suggestions or physical contact that you find objectionable or offensive and causes you discomfort on your job." The U.S. Office of Personnel Management (OPM), in banning sexual harassment within the federal government, defined it as "deliberate or repeated unsolicited verbal comments, gestures, or physical contact of a sexual nature which are unwelcome." This definition was used as the basis for the 1980 study of federal employees. The U.S. Equal Employment Opportunity Commission (EEOC) ruled in 1980 that sexual harassment would be considered an unlawful employment practice under Title VII of the 1964 Civil Rights Act. It defined sexual harassment as "unwelcome sexual advances, requests for favors, and other verbal or physical conduct of a sexual nature" when submission to or rejection of the conduct enters into employment decisions and/or the conduct interferes with work performance or creates a hostile work environment.[20]

These definitions share several key elements. Harassing behavior is regarded as unwelcome and unsolicited, and it can be either verbal or physical. The definitions do not agree, however, on which actions constitute harassment. The Cornell definition includes comments, looks, suggestions, and physical contact. The OPM definition adds gestures to the Cornell definition but leaves out looks (unless they are included with gestures). The EEOC guidelines are the least precise, specifying advances and propositions but leaving all other offending behaviors as "other verbal and physical conduct of a sexual nature." In fact, when it issued its ruling, the EEOC correctly anticipated that its definition of sexual harassment would be regarded by many as too vague and in need of clarification. Organizations and individuals are left to interpret exactly what conduct is meant by it and when such conduct violates the EEOC guidelines. As a result, individuals' own definitions of sexual harassment assume considerable importance in determining the sexually oriented behaviors that they feel entitled to initiate and their responses to behaviors initiated by others.

People vary widely in their personal definitions of sexual harassment. One study found that about 80% of adults thought that requests for dates or sexual activity, coupled with the understanding that denial would hurt the individual's job situation and compliance would help, constituted harassment, but only 20% considered positive comments of a sexual nature (e.g., "You look sexy today") to be harassment. A study that several MBA students and I conducted in 1981 found that a sample of working women included sexual propositions and touching, grabbing, or brushing, but not staring or flirting, in their personal definitions of sexual harassment. The women were evenly divided over whether sexual remarks, suggestive gestures, or sexual relations should be included in a definition of sexual harassment. A later study yielded similarly varied opinions.[21]

These definitions are influenced by both personal and situational factors. The personal characteristic that has the strongest effect is sex: Women consistently see more sexual harassment than men do. Individuals' sex role identity has a minor effect on their definitions of sexual harassment, but not as great as that of sex. Managerial level is a situational factor that influences definitions of sexual harassment. Managers at lower levels are more likely to see sexual harassment as a problem than those at middle levels, and top managers are the most isolated from the rank and file in their perceptions of sexual harassment.[22]

We see ambiguity in the definitions of sexual harassment provided by government agencies and variability in individuals' own definitions of sexual harassment. What is sexual harassment in the eyes of some workers is simply the harmless expression of individuals' basically sexual nature in the eyes of others. Some people are flattered by sexual attention that others find repulsive. In short, drawing a line between acceptable and unacceptable sexually oriented behavior in the workplace is not easy. Differences of opinion over where the line should be drawn make it difficult for òrganizations to carry out their legal obligation to discourage sexual harassment within their boundaries. Compounding the problem, the presence or absence of sexually oriented behaviors directed toward coworkers may affect the productivity of individuals, their work groups, and thereby the organization as a whole. To understand these effects, we will examine some explanations of sexual harassment to see how well they account for men's and women's experiences.

Explanations

Three general models have been offered as explanations for sexual harassment.[23] According to the *sociocultural model*, sexual harassment has little to do with sexuality—it is an expression of power and hostility. In this view, individuals with the least amount of power in society, meaning women in most cultures, are the most likely to be harassed. In a patriarchal society that rewards males for aggressiveness and domineering behavior and females for passivity and compliant behavior, sexual harassment almost may be regarded as a male prerogative. Harassment under such conditions is likely to appear in the form of extreme "do it or else" behavior.

The opposite view of sexual harassment is that it has everything to do with sexuality. Individuals with strong sex drives are sexually aggressive toward others due to biological necessities. Therefore, it should be neither surprising nor of particular concern that individuals exhibit such aggressiveness in work settings as well as elsewhere. It is also assumed that men and women are naturally attracted to each other and like to interact in sexually oriented ways in the workplace. This view, labeled the *natural/biological model* of sexual harrassment, trivializes the issue and claims that sexual harassment represents a harmless behavior to accept, rather than a problem to solve.

A third explanation, labeled the *organizational model*, suggests that certain organizational characteristics can set the stage for sexual harassment. For example, the hierarchical structure of organizations gives some individuals authority over others, granting them the opportunity to use the promise of rewards or the threat of punishments to obtain sexual gratification from their subordinates. Special job assignments or requirements, such as overtime work or business trips, may activate norms associated with leisure that conflict with the typical norms that govern male-female interactions in the workplace. Individuals who have more access to formal grievance procedures or are more capable of obtaining other jobs may be less likely to experience or put up with sexual harassment.

The sex ratio of a group is an organizational characteristic that also may stimulate or inhibit sexual harassment. The term *sex role spillover* refers to the carryover into the workplace of gender-based expectations that are irrelevant or inappropriate at work. Sex role spillover is most likely to occur when the sex ratio of a group is skewed in either direction, making members of the minority sex more noticeable and subject to special attention. As we have seen, women in male-dominated groups and men in female-dominated groups experience sex role spillover because they are assumed to be basically different from members of the dominant sex and, therefore, are treated differently. Sex role spillover is also seen in the carryover of sexual roles into work relationships. Experiences with sexual harassment may vary according to the sex ratio of the group under consideration.[24]

Actually, there are three different sex ratios that are relevant to female-male work relationships. The sex ratio of an occupation is specified by the proportions of men and women who hold jobs in it nationwide. Many occupations have a skewed or tilted sex ratio. The sex ratio of the occupation, however, does not necessarily reflect the sex ratio of the job. Even if the sex ratio of an occupation is skewed or tilted in one direction, the sex ratio of jobs within it in a particular organization could be skewed or tilted in the other direction. For example, there are more waitresses than waiters, but some restaurants hire only waiters. Finally, the sex ratio of the individual's work group, consisting of the people with whom he or she interacts on a daily basis, may differ from the other two sex ratios. The work group may include supervisors, subordinates, and colleagues and does not necessarily consist of people in the same organizational unit.[25]

The sex ratios of the three types of groups differ in the immediacy of their impact on individuals' work experiences. The sex ratio of the occupation has the least impact on daily behavior at work, but it is part of the context in which this behavior occurs. The sex ratio of the job has some impact, but the sex ratio of the work group, the people with whom one interacts with most frequency, has the most immediate effect. In a skewed work group, the greater visibility of tokens, particularly if they are newcomers, may lead to their being scapegoats for the frustration of dominants. If they have peers who resent their presence, tokens may experience sexual harassment as a way to make them feel isolated and uncomfortable enough to resign.

Experiences

Each of these models could provide at least a partial explanation of sexual harassment in the workplace. To understand their relative merits, we need to examine experiences with sexual harassment in a variety of work situations. Data collected by both Gutek and the federal study shed light on the underlying causes and effects of sexual harassment.

Barbara Gutek obtained data from representative samples of adult female and male workers in the Los Angeles area.[26] She concluded that the presence of sex role spillover and the form that it takes if present depend on two factors, whether the person being considered is in the minority or majority and whether the person is female or male. Women in nontraditional occupations and jobs perceive their differential treatment to be harassment when the treatment is sexually oriented. Men in nontraditional occupations and jobs are less likely to see the sexual attention they receive as harassment. Women in traditional occupations and jobs whose work brings them into frequent contact with men report that the sexuality aspect of the female sex role spills over into the work role. They see aspects of sexuality as entering into their jobs, but they are less likely than nontraditionally employed women to see these aspects as harassment. Men in traditional occupations and jobs with female-dominated work groups report the milder types of sexually oriented behavior but not the major types directed toward themselves, perhaps reflecting the fact that they are more likely than the women to be the supervisors in such situations. They also see less harassment in such attention than their female counterparts. Balanced occupations and jobs stimulate less sex role spillover or problems with harassment for individuals than nontraditional work.

The 1980 federal study also compared the experiences of female and male workers.[27] The sex ratios of the employee's occupation, job, or work group were not assessed in this study. Other data were collected, however, on the personal characteristics and work situation of harassers and victims. Peers were the most common harassers for both sexes (65% for female victims, 76% for male victims). Supervisors, however, were 2.5 times more common as harassers of women (37%) than as harassers of men (14%). In contrast, subordinates were 4 times more likely to be the harassers of male victims (16%) than of female victims (4%). (Percentages add to more than 100% because some victims had been harassed by more than one type of individual.) These differences support the organizational model of sexual harassment. The power differential resulting from the relative positions in the organizational hierarchy of the harasser and victim appeared to contribute to the experiences of female victims more than those of male victims.

Women's harassers were most likely to be older, married men, whereas men's harassers were most likely to be younger, single women. This may follow from the fact that females were more likely to be harassed by superiors, who tend to be older than themselves, and that males were more likely to be harassed by subordinates, who tend to be younger than themselves. It may also lead to the male's harasser being more attractive to him than the female's harasser is to her. Very few of the female victims (8%) went along with the sexual attention directed toward them, but 25% of the male victims went along with the attention. These results lend greater support to the natural/biological model when men are the victims (they like the attention more) and to the sociocultural or organizational model when women are the victims.

Other data on the experiences of federal workers do not make a convincing case for the superiority of any of the models of sexual harassment. Single and divorced employees, whether women or men, were more likely to be victims than married employees, supporting the natural/biological model if single and divorced employees are assumed to be the more sexually available. Employees who were dependent on the job were more likely to be victims, supporting the organizational model. Education was positively related to experience with sexual harassment, with employees having less than a high school diploma reporting the least harassment and those with graduate education the most. This could reflect differences in awareness of the issue, work situations, or other factors.

Men and women both define and experience sexual harassment differently. Women are more inclined to see sexually oriented behavior as sexual harassment and to be bothered by it than men. This may be due to the fact that they have somewhat different experiences with harassment than men. When women are harassed, it is more by men who hold organizationally approved power over them. When men are harassed, it is more by women seen as attractive who may be acting on the basis of attraction themselves. The majority of both female and male victims, however, are harassed by their workplace peers.

The sex ratio of the occupation, job, and work group also affect experiences with sexual harassment. Sex role spillover occurs more in skewed groups than in those with a balanced sex ratio. It is seen in the carryover of aspects of sexuality into the job according to the sex of the dominant group. It is also seen in the directing of unwelcome attention of all kinds, including sexual, toward the minority members of groups.

In summary, confusion between the sex role and work role is common in skewed groups, but women and men differ in their feelings about and experiences with sexual harassment at work. As a result, sexual harassment is an issue that sets many male and female peers at odds with each other. In the last section of this chapter, we shall discuss steps that companies can take to try to prevent sexual harassment.

ORGANIZATIONAL ROMANCES

Sexual interest in a coworker is not always unwelcome. In some cases, it is reciprocated and serves as the basis for an organizational romance between two employees. We shall define *organizational romances* as those relationships between women and men working together that are characterized by mutual sexual attraction and made known to others through the participants' actions.[28] They have received less public attention than sexual harassment, for several reasons. While sexual harassment is illegal, there are no laws against organizational romances. Sexual harassment usually victimizes and offends the target person. The "victim" of an organizational romance is less clear, although one or both parties may pay a price in their emotional health, task assignments, or career advancement if others are offended by the romance. In such cases, the participants are seen as bringing on their own troubles rather than being victimized by others.

.

While most people root for lovers in principle, because they like to believe that romantic relationships can have happy endings, organizational romances are a controversial issue. Various observers have sharply disagreed over their merits and how they should be handled. Margaret Mead argued that, much like the taboos against sexual expression in the family that are necessary for children to grow up safely, taboos against sexual involvements at work are necessary for men and women to work together effectively. Some people have recommended that both individuals be fired, or, if the more valuable person can still be effective, the organization should get rid of the other.[29]

Others have argued that people do not need protection or taboos but mutual respect for the freedom and rights of others, including the right to participate in an organizational romance. Mary Cunningham, who resigned from an upper management position due to allegations of her having a romantic involvement with her boss (she subsequently married him) amidst considerable media attention, particularly stressed the value of romances that lead to marriage. She said that when two coworkers cultivate a relationship that eventually leads to marriage, it enhances their creativity as a unit and helps the company's bottom line.[30]

Most individuals have to deal with both the need for intimacy and the need for accomplishment. When the two needs conflict, they must be reconciled. Because the workplace is a particularly convenient setting for meeting attractive people of the opposite sex, individuals are frequently faced with situations where they have to choose which need, if not both, they will fulfill. While recognizing that romantic relationships pose problems for their organizations, they still have their own needs, which may not agree with the needs of the business.

Beliefs

I recently conducted a study to provide insight into the choices that the "managers of tomorrow" might make when it comes to organizational romances. Two groups of students were surveyed, undergraduate business students, most of whom expect to hold full-time jobs, and evening MBA students, most of whom already hold full-time jobs. The study examined individuals' beliefs concerning the positive effects of sexual intimacy, the desirability of managerial actions to discourage it, the acceptability of sexually oriented behavior in general, and whether they would participate in an organizational romance. It also examined the difference between men's and women's beliefs and between the beliefs of undergraduates and evening MBAs.[31]

The results of the survey, summarized in Table 4.1, revealed an uneasy coexistence between sexual intimacy and work. Individuals were low in their endorsement of positive benefits that might arise from sexual intimacy at work. They strongly disagreed with the statement that sexual relations foster better communications and disagreed to a lesser extent with the statement that sexual intimacy makes for a more harmonious work environment. A relationship leading to marriage was regarded more positively, though individuals still disagreed more than they agreed with Mary Cunningham on its benefits.

Respondents believed strongly that management should try to discourage sexual propositions toward coworkers and that supervisors who direct sexual attention toward their subordinates should be reprimanded. They were more neutral about the use of reprimands when any worker, not necessarily a supervisor, directed sexual attention toward another. When sexually oriented behavior did not affect productivity, responses were also close to neutral.

Individuals showed a tolerance for some workplace attempts to satisfy needs for intimacy. Looking for a marriage partner was generally acceptable. Dressing attractively to draw attention from others was more acceptable than unacceptable. Flirting with the supervisor aroused more disapproval. Respondents were disinclined to say "never" about intimate involvements with coworkers themselves. Supervisors, though, were regarded less favorably as sexual partners than coworkers.

Overall, individuals seemed to agree that some forms of sexual intimacy are acceptable in the workplace, as long as they are not extreme and have no adverse effect on productivity. Intimate exchanges between supervisors and subordinates were regarded more negatively than those between coworkers in general. There were considerable differences in the beliefs of female and male respondents, however. Women saw less positive value in sexual intimacy in the workplace, desired more managerial action to discourage sexually oriented behavior, regarded sexually oriented behavior by others as

TABLE 4.1
Beliefs Concerning Sexual Intimacy in the Workplace

	Combined (N = 351)	Male (N = 198)	Female (N = 153)
1. Sexual relations foster better communication between the workers involved.	2.05	2.33	1.68**
2. Some sexual intimacy among coworkers can create a more harmonious work environment.	3.30	3.58	2.95**
3. When two workers cultivate a relationship that eventually leads to marriage, it enhances their creativity as a unit and helps their company's bottom line.	3.51	3.57	3.44
4. Management should take strong steps to discourage sexual propositions toward coworkers.	5.27	4.97	5.64**
5. Supervisors who direct sexual attention toward their subordinates should be reprimanded.	5.71	5.53	5.95*
6. Any worker who directs sexual attention toward another should be reprimanded.	3.83	3.71	3.98
7. Companies ought to ignore sexually oriented behavior among coworkers as long as it doesn't affect productivity.	4.34	4.47	4.17
8. It is all right for someone to look for a marriage partner at work.	5.15	5.22	5.07
9. It is all right for someone to dress attractively to draw the attention of coworkers of the opposite sex.	4.71	4.98	4.37**
10. I would be offended by a coworker flirting with the supervisor.	4.42	4.29	4.59
11. I would never get intimately involved with a coworker.	3.51	3.20	3.91**
12. I would never get intimately involved with my supervisor.	4.43	4.13	4.82**

SOURCE: G. N. Powell, "What Do Tomorrow's Managers Think About Sexual Intimacy in the Workplace?" *Business Horizons* 29, no. 4 (July/August 1986): 32-33.
NOTE: All statements were rated from strongly disagree (1) to strongly agree (7). Mean scores are shown, with the higher scores underlined for significant sex differences.
*p < .01; **p < .001.

less acceptable, and were less inclined than men to get involved in organizational romances themselves. Also, individuals who already held full-time jobs responded more negatively to sexual intimacy in the workplace than those who were not yet in the work force. The undergraduates were more idealistic than the evening MBAs, believing that sexual intimacy and work can be mixed successfully.

Because women are more likely than men to see sexual harassment in the workplace and to be concerned about it, their negative reactions to sexual intimacy in the workplace should not be surprising. Given their historically lower status, women have been the ones who suffered more when sexual liaisons became public knowledge. When decisions are made to fire the least valuable person, that person is more likely to be the woman. Thus it is understandable that women disapprove of sexual intimacy entering the workplace more strongly than men. They rightfully see themselves as having the most to lose if it does.

Explanations and Experiences

Let's distinguish between three types of organizational romances. One type, labeled "true love," involves two people who have a sincere long-term interest in each other and usually leads to marriage. This type of relationship, which Mary Cunningham wrote about, arouses the fewest objections from coworkers, particularly when it occurs between peers. In the second type, the "fling," both participants become deeply excited and involved, but the relationship ends quickly. A fling meets with less approval from coworkers, although they may try to look the other way. A third type, labeled the "utilitarian relationship," involves some trade-off between sexual adventure and ego satisfaction for one participant and job or career advancement for the other. This relationship violates coworkers' sense of equity in the workplace and provokes the most extremely negative reactions.[32]

Most organizational romances have been between higher-status males and lower-status females. For example, a survey of romances in white-collar settings reported that 62% involved a man in a higher position, 30% involved males and females at the same level, and only 8% involved a woman in a higher position. Such figures may result from more men being in management positions, particularly at upper levels. This is not to say that, to quote the poem, when "she's having lunch with the boss, they must be having an affair." A large majority of organizational romances involve a power differential, however, suggesting that the status of participants plays some role in their relationship.[33]

Lisa Mainiero recently summarized research evidence regarding the work conditions that foster romances, the personal risks involved for participants, the internal dynamics of romances, and the effects on and reactions of the work group. Other workplace factors aside from status contribute to the existence of organizational romances. Proximity is an important factor, given that working closely with others fosters interpersonal attraction that may set the stage for a romantic relationship to develop. The intensity of the work relationship, stimulated by the pursuit of similar work goals and performance of similar tasks, may create a feeling of excitement that also fosters interpersonal attraction and leads to romance.[34]

Getting involved in an organizational romance is a risky endeavor for participants. When there are hierarchical differences between the couple, other workers may lose respect for the higher-level participant, feeling that his or her professional judgment has been clouded. The lower-level participant may be faced with lower self-esteem, wondering whether his or her progress in the organization is due to competence or favoritism. Others may wonder the same. The risks to home and family if one or both participants has another romantic commitment are also high. The fear of violating office norms regarding the boundary between personal and private behavior may prompt participants to try to hide their romance, although such attempts are typically futile. Most coworkers are sensitive to even minor changes in behavior and can sense that a romantic relationship exists whether it is publicly announced or not. Because they are more often the lower-status participants, the risks for women are greater than the risks for men.

According to Mainiero, organizational romances invoke issues of power and dependency. The more powerful participant is the one who is giving more than he or she is getting, and therefore is least dependent on the relationship. Different kinds of dependency are at stake, however. One is task dependency, which exists when a worker depends on another to perform his or her function effectively. Another is career dependency, given that individuals who desire advancement in organizations are dependent on the consent of others.

In manager-subordinate relationships, subordinates often exchange working hard (satisfying the manager's task dependency on the subordinate) for the organizational reward of career advancement (for which the subordinate depends on the manager).

In an organizational romance, a personal/sexual dependency is added to an otherwise work-oriented relationship and this threatens the balance between task and career dependencies. This in turn activates a reaction from peers. Other group members, who are blocked from interacting with the two romantic partners in the personal/sexual domain, fear that their interactions with the participants in the task and career domains will be altered because of the romantic relationship. When the partners are at the same level, the effect of the relationship does not seem so troublesome. When they are at different levels, however, others are more upset. They fear that task or career rewards will be handed out in exchange for personal/sexual favors, thereby creating an inequitable situation.

When there is an imbalance of power in a romantic relationship, there is a high potential for exploitation. The higher-level participant can use the personal exchange to force the lower-level participant to increase task performance. On the other hand, the lower-level participant can use the personal exchange to argue for favorable task assignments or work conditions. Whoever is more dependent on the relationship is a candidate for exploitation. Work group members are made uncomfortable by the potential for exploitation in organizational romances. When this potential does not exist, the relationship may provoke gossip but does not jeopardize the task assignments or career advancement of other organizational members. The potential for exploitation is least present when the two participants are at the same organizational level and not dependent on each other for task assignments or career advancement.

This analysis suggests that organizational romances may endanger the careers and self-image of participants or may threaten the morale and productivity of coworkers. The extent of any damage depends on the potential for exploitation in the relationship or on the suggestion or existence of workplace inequities. Organizational romances for utilitarian reasons present the biggest threat to coworkers and the organization. Unconscious biases may influence unintentionally performance evaluations and the rewards that result. When biases become conscious and rewards are deliberately granted on the basis of personal relationships, morale is affected and the organization is rendered less effective. While flings may disturb organizations through their effect on coworkers' perceptions of workplace inequities, these relationships are motivated by infatuation or ego rather than job or power enhancement and pass quickly. Relationships based on true love and long-term interest, particularly between peers, are the least threatening to organizations and may actually contribute to the productivity of the couple.

Gutek's study of workers in the Los Angeles area, which focused primarily on sexual harassment, suggested that the sex ratio of the occupation, job, and/or work group also could influence the tendency for organizational romances to arise. The nature of the work environment, as defined by these three ratios, affected workers' tendencies to direct different types of sexually oriented behaviors toward others, including the milder, more positive types that have the greatest chance of being reciprocated. Physical attractiveness was more important in some work environments than others, such as in female-dominated occupations and jobs with male-dominated work groups, raising the possibility that romances would be more likely to flourish in those environments. Men were more likely than women to say that their organization accepts dating among employees. Given that this sex difference existed even among women and men engaged in the same type of work, it may reveal less about organizational policies than what women and men perceive they would gain or lose from dating a fellow employee.[35]

True love relationships seem the most difficult to maintain in a skewed group. Boundary heightening directed toward tokens by the dominant group makes it difficult for a dominant group member to get personally involved with a token member. Flings would seem more likely to occur in a skewed group, because they are more based on short-term feelings of excitement rather than perceptions of long-term compatibility. Utilitarian relationships could occur in a skewed group if members of the group are at different organizational levels. On the other hand, true love relationships seem more possible in a balanced group, where members are respected more as individuals and are less influenced by gender stereotyping or dominant-token dynamics in their relationships with others.

Whether they stem from long-term interest, short-term excitement, or utilitarian reasons, organizational romances will always be potential problems for the organization. Unless these problems are dealt with, morale and productivity among coworkers are likely to suffer. Organizational romances are also an issue on which women and men have different perspectives. For the time being, we can expect women and men to hold different beliefs about and have different experiences with organizational romances. Given that women still have lower work status than men on the whole, they have the most to lose from organizational romances.

IMPLICATIONS FOR MANAGEMENT

At the beginning of this chapter, we posed the question of why women and men sometimes feel awkward and uncomfortable in working with each other and at other times feel perfectly at ease. Our review suggests three conditions that contribute to awkwardness or discomfort. The first is that gender stereotyping enters into the relationship, due to either personal characteristics of the workers or characteristics of their work situation, such that the male's perception of the female is influenced more by the feminine stereotype than by her actual traits and behaviors and/or the female's perception of the male is influenced more by the masculine stereotype than by his actual traits and behaviors. The second is that either the male or female has directed unwelcome sexual attention toward the other, or unwelcome sexual attention is frequently directed by one coworker toward another in their work environment and individuals fear that they will eventually be on the receiving end of such attention. The third is that either the male or female is a participant in an organizational romance, which leads the other to be concerned about workplace inequities, or one or both fear the potential of mutual sexual attraction entering into their relationship and maintain a distance from the other as a result.

Let's now consider the implications of our answers to the above question, and make recommendations for how organizations and the individuals involved can best deal with the various conditions described. We shall focus in turn on three issues: gender stereotyping, sexual harassment, and organizational romances.

Dealing with Gender Stereotyping

How can organizations reduce the effects of gender stereotyping among peers? One approach would be to rely on the effects of situational factors. In some situations, gender stereotyping diminishes without any managerial action required. This happens when workers gain experience over time in working with opposite-sex peers. It also happens when employees work with greater numbers of opposite-sex peers at a given time. Thus the first token in a skewed group is the one who suffers most from performance pressures, boundary heightening, and role encapsulation, and later tokens in the group suffer less from these types of special treatment. Also, dominants who have been in a skewed group longer are less likely to stereotype tokens than new dominants in the group. So, if the numbers of men and women in a group are shifting in the direction of being more balanced, management may simply wait for the shift to happen.

The opposite approach would be for organizations to seek to prevent the conditions that foster gender stereotyping from occurring, by increasing their equal opportunity efforts at recruiting and promoting individuals for all jobs. A greater balance of women and men in a job may be achieved if the organization refrains from discriminatory recruiting practices and tries to increase the number of applications from members of the minority sex in a job. This balance in turn would lead to a reduction in gender stereotyping.

An intermediate approach would be to have employees attend training programs that help them cope with the gender stereotyping that takes place. Programs to make recruiters aware of the biases that may influence their decisions regarding applicants were recommended in the last chapter. In the same vein, *all* organizational members have something to gain from training programs that help them to identify their own biases. Such programs can encourage men and women to alert each other to stereotypic behavior so that they can serve as "change agents" for each other until there is a greater balance in the sex ratios of jobs and work groups.

It may be tempting for management to claim that gender stereotyping is beyond its control and therefore to do nothing about it. Organizations cannot ban gender stereotyping from the workplace by their own actions. They have too much to lose from the negative effects of gender stereotyping, however, to ignore it altogether. They will gain from taking steps both to reduce the likelihood that gender stereotyping will occur and to alleviate its effects when it does occur.

Dealing with Sexual Harassment

Unless they are very fortunate and no sexual harassment occurs within their boundaries, sexual harassment is a problem that organizations must address in some way. If they don't, they may not only be held in violation of the law but also risk losing productivity and alienating a large portion of their work force. Some writers have suggested a ban on all forms of sexual expression in the workplace. Most employees, however, would not agree with this prescription. Some of the milder forms of sexual expression, such as flirting and dressing attractively to draw attention, are regarded more benignly than the more extreme forms of required dating or sex. Also, potentially harassing forms of behavior are reacted to and experienced differently by women and men and by members of groups with different sex ratios. Managerial action is not required in all cases of sexual expression in the workplace, but it is required in many cases. We shall describe possible actions that can be taken by organizations and by the victims of sexual harassment, and the circumstances under which various actions should be taken.

Organizations begin to combat sexual harassment by issuing strong written policies against it and establishing special grievance procedures to deal with cases of alleged harassment. New employees should be informed of the organizational policy on sexual harassment during their initial orientation. Managers should also be informed in training programs of the reasons for the policy and the variety of forms that sexual harassment can take. The programs should advise managers on what to do if they see or hear about possible cases of harassment. The programs should also make them aware that sexual harassment would be disastrous behavior for themselves and could cost them their careers.[36]

In dealing with cases of alleged harassment, the severity of the action taken should be matched with the severity of the alleged offense and the certainty that an offense was committed. After a complaint of sexual harassment has been directed to a designated party, organizational policy can be effectively implemented by a grievance procedure such as the following:

(1) Interview the complainant, the accused, and possible witnesses.
(2) Check personnel files for evidence that documents prior animosities between the parties, previous complaints against the accused or by the complainant, and/or sudden discrepancies in the work record of the complainant or accused.
(3) Assess the severity of the offense, considering the behavior, intent, and frequency:

(a) Severe—forced sexual relations, sexual propositions, touching, grabbing, or brushing.

(b) Moderate—suggestive gestures, sexual remarks, sexual relations with promise of ensuing rewards.

(c) Mild—staring, flirting.

(4) Assess the certainty that an offense was committed:

(a) High—solid evidence to support the complaint.

(b) Medium—some evidence to support the complaint.

(c) Low—no evidence to support the complaint other than the complainant's word.

(5) Determine appropriate action(s) to be taken. Severe action steps are to be applied when the alleged offense is severe and the certainty that it was committed is high. Mild action steps are to be taken when the alleged offense is mild and the certainty that it was committed is low. Moderate action steps are to be taken in cases which fall between these two extremes. Possible action steps include:

(a) Severe—dismissal, demotion, suspension, or transfer of the accused; restoration of the work record of the complainant when unjustly blemished.

(b) Moderate—warning or disciplinary notice in file of accused with provision for action if subsequent offense (dismissal, demotion, or some other action) and/or provision for removal of the notice if no subsequent offense within a specified period of time.

(c) Mild—no record of complaint in file of accused, or record with annotation that it was found groundless; no dissemination of information about the complaint; letter to the accused stressing organizational policy against sexual harassment; general announcement to all employees reminding them of organizational policy against sexual harassment.[37]

Such a procedure, if well-administered, clearly addresses the issue of sexual harassment. It demonstrates that an organization is willing to take positive action to remove or minimize the incidence and effects of harassment among its employees. It also acknowledges that there are differences of opinion regarding sexual harassment by matching the sanction with the severity of the offense and the certainty that one was committed. When organizations apply such a procedure in a clear and objective way, they both protect themselves from liability and increase the probability that their employees will work in an environment free of harassment.

No matter how well-intentioned a special grievance procedure may be, however, it will have little effect unless individuals who feel that they have been harassed are willing to make formal complaints against their harassers. Many victims prefer instead to deal with the situation themselves. In fact, this may be their only recourse if there is no concrete proof that harassment has taken place.

Mary Rowe recommends that, when verbal requests to stop offensive behavior have been unsuccessful, the victim write a letter to the harasser. The letter should contain (a) a detailed description of the offending behavior, when it occurred, and the circumstances under which it occurred; (b) the feelings of the victim about the behavior and the damage that has been done (e.g., "Your behavior has made me feel uncomfortable about working in this unit," "You have caused me to ask for a change in job"); and (c) what the victim would like to have happen aside from an end to the harassment, such as the rewriting of an unjust evaluation that was prepared after the victim rejected sexual advances. The letter should be delivered in person with a security person or some other witness present. The harasser will usually accept the letter and say nothing. There is rarely a response in writing, and, nearly always, the harassment stops.[38]

Rowe sees the role of the organization as encouraging employees to take such measures as a way of focusing their anger and recognizing that they can take steps to protect themselves. The organization may also wish to initiate its own action if there is significant evidence of wrongdoing, in which case it should provide assurance that people who do not wish to file formal complaints remain anonymous. If individuals feel uncomfortable about writing such a letter, the organization can still assist them by providing the opportunity to discuss the harassment with a psychologist, personnel counselor, or some other person who is known to be discreet and supportive of victims.

We have detailed several kinds of actions that organizations may take to deal with sexual harassment. Organizations should establish firm policies against sexual harassment, set up and administer special grievance procedures, make sure that employees are aware of both policies and procedures, and provide assistance to employees in psychologically coping with harassment and in dealing with it on their own if they so choose. Only when organizations consistently take such actions will they begin to make a dent in the problem of sexual harassment in the workplace.

Dealing with Organizational Romances

What organizations should do about romantic relationships between employees is less clear-cut. There is a wide range of opinions over how organizations should respond to romances, ranging from fostering norms that encourage them to firing one or both participants. A *Business Week* survey found that the written policies of most companies specified only that married couples should not work with or for each other. Unwritten policies were more varied. Some companies looked more disfavorably on extramarital affairs than on other romances, reflecting the values of the dominant people in the company or a concern for possible scandal. From a business point of view, however, extramarital affairs were seen as less worrisome than romances between single employees who also have some work relationship. Most companies transferred one or both participants when they learned of such a relationship. One company took the approach of dealing with the relationship only if sexual harassment or a conflict of interest was involved. If the relationship was seen as having a detrimental effect on productivity or morale, then it was treated as a performance problem requiring some action. Otherwise, the company didn't interfere.[39]

The latter approach seems about as enlightened as we can expect. The primary concern of management ought not to be who is involved with whom, but whether the necessary work is getting done, and done well. A personal relationship that hinders productivity and creates the potential for, if not the reality of, biased professional judgments presents a legitimate threat to the organization and needs to be dealt with in some manner. The customary management action of transferring or firing the lower-status participant, however, is not the best approach to take.

In fact, there is a range of actions from which management may choose in responding to organizational romances. As for cases of alleged sexual harassment, the severity of the action taken should be matched with the severity of the alleged offense and the certainty that an offense was committed. Possible actions range from severe (e.g., dismissal, demotion, or suspension) to mild (e.g., informal counseling of the participants). If there is no actual or potential disruption to the organization's pursuit of its goals, then there is no need for management to take any action. This would apply to romances between individuals who cannot possibly influence each other's task assignments or career advancement.

Relationships in which task-related or career-related decisions could be, but have not been, influenced by personal/sexual considerations present some threat to the work of the organization. In such a case, the relationship causes a problem by leading coworkers to fear its potentially inequitable effect on decisions or to suspect that it is already having an effect. As a result, the morale and productivity of coworkers may suffer. When the two participants have committed no actual workplace offense (assuming that simply being involved in an organizational romance is not such an offense), but the potential for a workplace offense exists, they should be presented with two options. Either they may "cool" the relationship and demonstrate to coworkers that it has been cooled by their subsequent interactions in the presence of others, or they may accept being transferred to equivalent positions elsewhere in the company. Either one or both participants could be transferred, depending on the situation.

Relationships in which task-related and/or career-related decisions definitely have been influenced by personal/sexual considerations are a cause for greater concern. Now, some kind of punitive action against *both* participants is in order. The organizational level of the participants should not be allowed to affect the actions taken. This recommendation runs counter to the practice of many organizations that the lower-status person receive the brunt of punitive action. When both individuals who have harmed the organization through their actions are punished, rather than only the person at the lower level, however, the appearance of an equitable decision will have the most positive effect on the morale and productivity of the organization.

Organizations can also contribute to a satisfactory resolution of issues raised by romances by making counseling available to all individuals involved—the two participants, the managers of work areas that are disrupted by the relationship, and the coworkers in such areas as well. Coworkers need to have a designated party in the organization with whom they can consult about a troublesome romantic relationship. Because their manager may be a participant in the relationship, they need to be able to report it without fear of reprisal to themselves.

Organizational romances present a different kind of threat to organizations than sexual harassment. The legal threat is not the same, but the threat to productivity and morale is similar. We have outlined steps that organizations can take to respond to the negative effects of organizational romances and to help the individuals affected by them to help themselves. In taking such steps, organizations contribute to the creation of a more comfortable, if not entirely asexual, work environment for their employees.

In conclusion, gender stereotyping, sexual harassment, and organizational romances are workplace phenomena that sometimes hinder the working relationships between males and females. Whether they have an effect, and what kind of effect they have, depends on factors such as the personal characteristics of individuals, their experience in working with members of the opposite sex, and the proportions of men and women in occupations, jobs, and work groups. Managers can take actions to prevent the negative effects of these phenomena or to alleviate such effects when they occur.

Individuals, however, have some say about whether such events interfere with their working relationships. Both men and women have the capability of recognizing that they have used gender stereotypes in the past and of discontinuing their further usage. They have the capability of refraining from engaging in token-dominant dynamics. They have the choice of whether to harass other employees or not. They also choose whether or not to act on sexual attraction that they may feel for coworkers, and how they manage the interface between work roles and sexual roles if they act on the attraction. Ultimately, men and women jointly determine whether they are uncomfortable or comfortable in working with each other, and whether they employ stereotypes such as those conveyed in the poem at the beginning of the chapter.

NOTES

1. © 1983 by Natasha Josefowitz. Reprinted with permission by the author from *Is This Where I Was Going*. New York: Warner Books.

2. K. L. Dion, "Sex, Gender, and Groups: Selected Issues," in *Women, Gender, and Social Psychology*, ed. V. E. O'Leary, R. K. Unger, and B. S. Wallston (Hillsdale, NJ: Erlbaum, 1985).

3. W. Wood and S. J. Karten, "Sex Differences in Interaction Style as a Product of Perceived Sex Differences in Competence," *Journal of Personality and Social Psychology* 50 (1986): 341-47; J. A. Piliavin and R. R. Martin, "The Effects of the Sex Composition of Groups on Style of Social Interaction," *Sex Roles* 4 (1978): 281-96; B. F.

Meeker and P. A. Weitzel-O'Neill, "Sex Roles and Interpersonal Behavior in Task-Oriented Groups," *American Sociological Review* 42 (1977): 91-105.

4. S. E. Snodgrass, "Women's Intuition: The Effect of Subordinate Role on Interpersonal Sensitivity," *Journal of Personality and Social Psychology* 49 (1985): 146-55; M. L. Hoffman, "Sex Differences in Empathy and Related Behaviors," *Psychological Bulletin* 84 (1977): 712-22.

5. M. S. Horner, "Sex Differences in Achievement Motivation and Performance in Competitive and Noncompetitive Situations" (Ph.D. diss., University of Michgan, 1968).

6. V. F. Nieva and B. A. Gutek, Chapter 8, "View of Women's Achievements," in *Women and Work: A Psychological Perspective* (New York: Praeger, 1981).

7. C. Radecki and J. Jennings, "Sex as a Status Variable in Work Settings: Female and Male Reports of Dominance Behavior," *Journal of Applied Social Psychology* 10 (1980): 71-85.

8. E. I. Megargee, "Influence of Sex Roles on the Manifestation of Leadership," *Journal of Applied Psychology* 53 (1969): 377-82.

9. R. A. Fleischer and J. M. Chertkoff, "Effects of Dominance and Sex on Leader Selection in Dyadic Work Groups," *Journal of Personality and Social Psychology* 50 (1986): 94-99.

10. J. A. Kelly, H. E. Wildman, and J. R. Urey, "Gender and Sex Role Differences in Group Decision-Making Social Interactions: A Behavioral Analysis," *Journal of Applied Social Psychology* 12 (1982): 112-27; N. Porter, F. L. Geis, E. Cooper, and E. Newman, "Androgyny and Leadership in Mixed-Sex Groups," *Journal of Personality and Social Psychology* 49 (1985): 808-23.

11. D. D. Baker and D. E. Terpstra, "Locus of Control and Self-Esteem Versus Demographic Factors as Predictors of Attitudes Toward Women," *Basic and Applied Social Psychology* 7 (1986): 163-72.

12. B. G. Harrison, R. F. Guy, and S. L. Lupfer, "Locus of Control and Self-Esteem as Correlates of Role Orientation in Traditional and Nontraditional Women," *Sex Roles* 7 (1981): 1175-87; S. J. Motowidlo, "Sex Role Orientation and Behavior in a Work Setting," *Journal of Personality and Social Psychology* 42 (1982): 935-45; M. Collins, L. K. Waters, and C. W. Waters, "Relationships Between Sex-Role Orientation and Attitudes Toward Women as Managers," *Psychological Reports* 45 (1979): 828-30.

13. J. M. Craig and R. R. Jacobs, "The Effect of Working with Women on Male Attitudes Toward Female Firefighters," *Basic and Applied Social Psychology* 6 (1985): 61-74; B. M. Bass, J. Krusell, and R. A. Alexander, "Male Managers' Attitudes Toward Working Women," *American Behavioral Scientist* 15 (1971): 221-36.

14. R. M. Kanter, "Some Effects of Proportions on Group Life: Skewed Sex Ratios and Responses to Token Women," *American Journal of Sociology* 82 (1977): 965-90; R. M. Kanter, Chapter 8, "Numbers: Minorities and Majorities," in *Men and Women of the Corporation* (New York: Basic Books, 1977).

15. G. Staines, C. Tavris, and T. E. Jayaratne, "The Queen Bee Syndrome," *Psychology Today* 7, no. 8 (January 1974): 55-60.

16. E. Spangler, M. A. Gordon, and R. M. Pipkin, "Token Women: An Empirical Test of Kanter's Hypothesis," *American Journal of Sociology* 84 (1978): 160-70; B. E. Segal, "Male Nurses: A Case Study in Status Contradiction and Prestige Loss," *Social Forces* 41, no. 1 (October 1962): 31-38; G. T. Fairhurst and B. K. Snavely, "A Test of the Social Isolation of Male Tokens," *Academy of Management Journal* 26 (1983): 353-61.

17. G. T. Fairhurst and B. K. Snavely, "Majority and Token Minority Group Relationships: Power Acquisition and Communication," *Academy of Management Review* 8 (1983): 292-300.

18. U.S. Merit Systems Protection Board (USMSPB), *Sexual Harassment in the Federal Workforce: Is It a Problem?* (Washington, DC: Government Printing Office, 1981).

19. This section of the chapter is primarily based on G. N. Powell, "Sexual Harassment: Confronting the Issue of Definition," *Business Horizons* 26, no. 4 (July/August 1983): 24-28.

20. L. Farley, *Sexual Shakedown: The Sexual Harassment of Women on the Job* (New York: Warner Books, 1978), p. 39; Office of Personnel Management (Policy statement and definition of sexual harassment, Appendix E2, Washington, DC: USMSPB), p. E-8; Equal Employment Opportunity Commission (Guidelines on discrimination because of sex, Appendix E3, Washington, DC: USMSPB), p. E-10.

21. B.A. Gutek, C. Y. Nakamura, M. Gahart, and I. Handschumacher, "*Sexuality and the Workplace,*" *Basic and Applied Social Psychology* 1 (1980): 255-65; G. N. Powell, C. A. Benzinger, A. A. Bruno, T. N. Gibson, M. L. Pfeiffer, and T. P. Santopietro, "Sexual Harassment as Defined by Working Women" (Paper delivered at the Annual Meeting of the Academy of Management, San Diego, 1981); G. N. Powell, "Effects of Sex Role Identity and Sex on Definitions of Sexual Harassment," *Sex Roles* 14 (1986): 9-19.

22. Gutek et al., "Sexuality and the Workplace"; Powell, "Effects of Sex Role Identity"; E.G.C. Collins and T. B. Blodgett, "Sexual Harassment: Some See It . . . Some Won't," *Harvard Business Review* 59, no. 2 (March/April 1981): 76-95.

23. S. S. Tangri, M. R. Burt, and L. B. Johnson, "Sexual Harassment at Work: Three Explanatory Models," *Journal of Social Issues*, 38, no. 4 (1982): 33-54.

24. Nieva and Gutek, *Women and Work*, Chapter 5, "Integrating Women into the Workplace."

25. B. A. Gutek and B. Morasch, "Sex-Ratios, Sex-Role Spillover, and Sexual Harassment at Work," *Journal of Social Issues* 38, no. 4 (1982): 55-74.

26. B. A. Gutek, Chapter 8, "Explanations for Sexuality in the Workplace: Unequal Sex Ratios and Sex Role Spillover," in *Sex and the Workplace* (San Francisco: Jossey-Bass, 1985).

27. USMSPB, *Sexual Harassment in the Federal Workforce*; Tangri et al., "Sexual Harassment at Work."

28. L. A. Mainiero, "A Review and Analysis of Power Dynamics in Organizational Romances," *Academy of Management Review* 11 (1986): 750-62.

29. M. Mead, "A Proposal: We Need Taboos on Sexuality at Work," in *Sexuality in Organizations*, ed. D. A. Neugarten and J. M. Shafritz (Oak Park, IL: Moore, 1980); E.G.C. Collins, "Managers and Lovers," *Harvard Business Review* 61, no. 5 (September/October 1983): 142-53.

30. P. Horn and J. Horn, *Sex in the Office* (Reading, MA: Addison-Wesley, 1982); Statement by Mary Cunningham, *Hartford Courant* 145, no. 128 (8 May 1982), p. A2.

31. G. N. Powell, "What Do Tomorrow's Managers Think About Sexual Intimacy in the Workplace?" *Business Horizons* 29, no. 4 (July/August 1986): 30-35.

32. R. E. Quinn and P. L. Lees, "Attraction and Harassment: Dynamics of Sexual Politics in the Workplace," *Organizational Dynamics* 13, no. 2 (Autumn 1984): 35-46.

33. C. I. Anderson and P. L. Hunsaker, "Why There's Romancing at the Office and Why It's Everybody's Problem," *Personnel*, 62, no. 2 (February 1985): 57-63.

34. Mainiero, "A Review and Analysis of Power Dynamics."

35. Gutek, *Sex and the Workplace*, Chapter 8.

36. T. L. Leap and E. R. Gray, "Corporate Responsibility in Cases of Sexual Harassment," *Business Horizons* 23, no. 10 (October 1980): 58-65; P. Linenberger and T. J. Keaveny, "Sexual Harassment: The Employer's Legal Obligations," *Personnel* 58, no. 6 (November/December 1981): 60-68; C. Backhouse and L. Cohen, Chapter 10, "Action Plans for Management and Unions," in *Sexual Harassment on the Job* (Englewood Cliffs, NJ: Prentice-Hall, 1981).

37. Powell, "Sexual Harassment."

38. M. P. Rowe, "Dealing with Sexual Harassment," *Harvard Business Review* 59, no. 3 (May/June 1981): 42-46.

39. "Romance in the Workplace: Corporate Rules for the Game of Love," *Business Week*, no. 2847 (18 June 1984): 70-71.

5

Managing People

Executive Opinions

Women have a tendency to sell themselves short. On the other hand, for whatever reasons (ego-defense, etc.), the dozen or so women managers I have known seem hostile and defensive, at times almost paranoid. To sum up, women need higher goals plus better personal adjustment to upward movement.
—"Mr. A," president of retail firm, 1965

> My premise is that a woman conceives her role to be that of helper to an individual—as mother, wife, secretary. To succeed in management, she must substitute for this limited image of herself a vision of her job as potentially helpful to whole segments of the population.
> —"Ms. B," board chairperson of consumer goods firm, 1965

Young and middle-aged men are much more comfortable with women executives. Passage of time will eliminate equality problems.
—"Mr. C," vice president of manufacturing firm, 1985

> When will companies realize that we (women in management) are here to stay and that we, too, have what it takes?
> —"Ms. D," vice president of bank, 1985

—*Harvard Business Review* surveys
[Reprinted by permission of the *Harvard Business Review*.
Excerpts from "Are Women Executives People?"
by G. W. Bowman, N. B. Worthy, & S. A. Greyser (July/August 1965)
and "Executive Women—20 Years Later"
by C. D. Sutton & K. K. Moore (September/October 1985).
© 1965 and 1985 by the President and Fellows of Harvard College;
all rights reserved; reprinted by permission.]

In 1965, *Harvard Business Review*, which then billed itself as "The Magazine of Thoughtful Businessmen," conducted a survey of male and female executives' attitudes toward women in management. The results of the survey were published in an article titled "Are Women Executives People?" The article posed the general questions of whether women executives act like people, whether they think of themselves as people, and whether the business community was treating them like people. These seem to be curious questions from today's vantage, but we must remember that women held a much smaller proportion of management positions at the time. The first two are questions that we might expect dominants to ask about tokens, and the third is about dominant-token relationships.[1]

The survey results suggested that women were saying, "Treat us like people"; men were saying to women, "Act like people"; and successful women were saying to other women, "Think of yourselves as people." Most women executives believed that women should be treated on an individual basis rather than as a uniform group. Although few men (6%) were strongly opposed to women in management, a large proportion (41%), however, regarded the idea with some disfavor. They believed not only that women were special but also that they had a special place, which was outside the ranks of management. Older men tended to be more accepting of women in managerial roles than younger men, and men who had been superiors or peers of women managers thought more favorably of them than men who had only worked for women. Few men thought that they would be comfortable in working for a woman manager, however, and even fewer thought that men in general would be comfortable in such a situation.

Respondents to the survey gave several reasons for the negative attitudes toward female executives. Many men did not want to contend with women as well as other men for the keenly competitive managerial jobs. According to a large proportion of both male and female executives, women themselves were partially responsible for the negative attitudes because they had accepted their exclusion from managerial ranks without major protest. Cultural prejudice against women working outside the home was also cited as a reason. Furthermore, over half of the male executives believed that the rationale for excluding women from management was basically sound. Like "Mr. A," who had known only a dozen women managers but nevertheless felt that he was qualified to judge what all women would be like as managers, men cited deficiencies in women's capabilities to handle managerial jobs. Women executives such as "Ms. B" were more positive in their beliefs about women's capabilities and encouraged them to shed their traditional roles to make use of these capabilities in the workplace.

When women are treated like people, on a case-by-case basis rather than as a category, they are more likely to think of themselves as people, not just as women, and to act naturally. On the other hand, women who act like unique individuals rather than representatives of their sex and ask for no special treatment are more likely to be treated like people. In the opinions of the executives surveyed in 1965, change was needed in how both women and men were thinking and acting for women to be successful in management. Otherwise, women would continue to be at a disadvantage in entering and being promoted within the ranks of management.

In the next 20 years, the composition of the managerial ranks changed considerably. The proportion of female managers more than doubled between 1965 and 1985, increasing from 15% to 36%. Between 1965 and 1985, the number of female managers quadrupled, whereas the number of male managers increased by only one-quarter. Two-thirds of the managers added to the work force since 1965 have been women.

Attitudes about whether women belong in management also changed, particularly among male executives. In a 1985 replication of the 1965 *HBR* survey, only 5% of male executives viewed the idea of women managers with some disfavor. In fact, male executives were more positive about how women executives were being accepted in business than the women themselves. The proportion of men who thought that a woman must be exceptional to succeed in business dropped from 90% in 1965 to 59% in 1985, whereas this proportion remained at about 85% for women. Similarly, the proportion of men who thought that the business community will never wholly accept women executives fell from 61% in 1965 to 20% in 1985, whereas this proportion fell only from 47% to 40% for women. As in 1965, younger male executives expressed less favorable attitudes toward women managers than older male executives. As the quotation from "Mr. C" suggests, however, men thought that women's prospects would inevitably improve with the passage of time. "Ms. D" was wondering exactly when that improvement would take place, if at all. While men reported that things were better for women in management, women executives saw continued resistance to their progress.[2]

The increase in female managers has led to several kinds of situations occurring with greater frequency in organizations. More employees than ever before have had a female boss at some time. Many employees have become used to working for a woman, having had two or more female bosses in their careers. Most middle managers now have female as well as male lower-level managers as their subordinates. At the same time, more lower-level managers than ever before have a female middle manager as their boss. The proportion of women in top management positions remains extremely low, however.

As we see, there has literally been a change in the "face" of management. That face is now female more than one-third of the time. This calls into question the universality of prevailing theories of management. Until recently, most studies of how managers manage and what works well and not so well for them have been based on observations of male managers. Ralph Stogdill's classic 1974 compendium of research results, *Handbook of Leadership*, discovered few studies that exclusively examined female managers or even included female managers in their samples. When female managers were present in organizations being studied, they were usually excluded from the analysis because their inclusion might lead to distorted results. It was as if female managers were less real, or less worthy of observation, than male managers.[3]

Management researchers no longer automatically exclude female managers from their samples. Nonetheless, most of the existing theories of management have been developed with male managers in mind. Do these theories apply equally as well to female managers, or should female managers be described with models of their own? Male and female managers could differ in their basic behavioral tendencies and internal responses to work situations, or they could be quite similar.

The leadership styles of managers are affected by the reactions of their subordinates. Few managers are likely to adopt and maintain a style of leadership that does not yield the desired responses from their employees. Thus subordinates have an influence on the leadership styles of their managers. Subordinates who engage in gender stereotyping are likely to have different expectations of female and male managers and to reinforce different behaviors from them. Aside from examining the behavioral tendencies of female and male managers, we need to examine subordinates' preferences for and responses to female versus male managers.

Managerial stereotypes also need to be reconsidered in light of the changing face of management. Much as the masculine stereotype has provided a model of the "good boy" and the feminine stereotype has provided a model of the "good girl," a managerial stereotype has provided a model of the "good manager." This stereotype has reflected the fact that most managers over time have been male. The overall proportions of female and male managers have changed considerably in recent years, but not so at the upper levels of the managerial ranks. Thus we have reason to wonder whether the stereotypes that people have of good managers have changed or remain the same. We also need to examine the relationship between stereotypes of good managers and what actually makes managers effective.

In this chapter, we shall examine both the stereotypes and the realities of management today. First, we shall examine how stereotypes of managers compare with gender stereotypes and whether they have changed over time. Second, we shall investigate whether female and male managers differ in their own responses to managerial situations or in the responses they elicit from subordinates. Finally, we shall consider whether masculinity is actually associated with more effective management. In so doing, we shall also address the question of whether androgyny should serve as the new model of the effective manager.

MANAGERIAL STEREOTYPES

Studies of the relationship between sex, managerial stereotypes, and gender stereotypes were first conducted in the early 1970s. Virginia Schein compiled a list of 92 characteristics of individuals that differentiated between people's beliefs about women and men, thereby forming the basis for gender stereotypes. She then asked a sample of middle managers to describe how well each of the characteristics fit either women in general, men in general, or successful middle managers. Both female and male executives believed that successful middle managers possessed an abundance of characteristics that were more associated with men in general than with women in general.[4]

Acceptance of the masculine stereotype as a model for success in management was particularly strong for female managers with less than five years of managerial experience and for younger male managers. Once women managers had gained experience and felt more secure in the ranks of management, they may have felt less need to conform to stereotyped beliefs. Younger men may have felt more threatened by the prospect of competing with women for managerial positions and been unable to see them in other than stereotypical terms as a result. Older men who were more established in their managerial careers may have felt less threatened by the entry of women into the ranks of management. Also, older men may have personally experienced their wives' reentry into the work force and thus been forced to modify their beliefs about women's capabilities. A later replication of Schein's studies yielded essentially the same results.[5]

Tony Butterfield and I took a different approach to the analysis of managerial stereotypes in the mid-1970s. The concept of androgyny began receiving attention as a standard of psychological health that was more flexible for both men and women than the double standards of masculinity and femininity. Androgyny and more effective behavior had been linked in a variety of nonwork situations. We reasoned that if the more effective *person* is androgynous, the more effective *manager* might be androgynous as well. Also, the proportion of female managers had risen to 22% in 1977 from a figure of 15% in 1965. As more women became managers, it was possible that traditional masculine standards for management were being replaced with more androgynous standards. Therefore, we hypothesized that the "good manager" would now be seen as androgynous.[6]

In the 1976-1977 academic year, we administered a questionnaire containing the Original Bem Sex-Role Inventory (BSRI) to a sample of undergraduate business students and part-time evening MBA students. As you recall from Chapter 2, the Original BSRI contains 20 masculine items, 20 feminine items, and 20 filler items. Each individual completed the questionnaire twice, describing how much each phrase applied to both him- or herself and to a good manager.

The good-manager descriptions from this study are summarized in the first column of Table 5.1. Contrary to our hypothesis, individuals overwhelmingly preferred a masculine manager. About 70% of both women and men and both graduate and undergraduate students described a good manager in predominantly masculine terms. Less than 20% of all individuals described a good manager as androgynous.

TABLE 5.1
Descriptions of a Good Manager

Questionnaire Date of Data Collection	Original BSRI 1976-1977 (percent)	Short BSRI 1984-1985 (percent)
Undergraduates:		
Males		
androgynous	16	25
masculine	70	69
feminine	1	1
undifferentiated	13	5
Females		
androgynous	18	20
masculine	67	76
feminine	2	2
undifferentiated	13	2
Part-Time Graduates:		
Males		
androgynous	21	19
masculine	72	67
feminine	2	1
undifferentiated	5	13
Females		
androgynous	10	25
masculine	80	67
feminine	0	0
undifferentiated	10	8
Totals:		
androgynous	16	22
masculine	72	70
feminine	1	1
undifferentiated	11	7

SOURCE: G.N. Powell and G.N. Butterfield, "The 'Good Manager': Does Androgyny Fare Better in the 1980's?" (Paper delivered at the Annual Meeting of the Academy of Management, Chicago, 1986).
NOTE: The totals were obtained by weighting undergraduate males, undergraduate females, part-time graduate males, and part-time graduate females equally.

Virtually no one preferred a feminine good manager. Men and women did not significantly differ in their descriptions of a good manager.

Two developments in subsequent years led us to believe that we might obtain different results if we conducted our study again. Sandra Bem released a "new, improved" BSRI, called the Short BSRI. It contained half as many items as before and no longer included the highly undesirable feminine characteristics of the Original BSRI. We expected that individuals would rate the good manager as no different in masculinity but much higher in femininity on the new instrument, thereby leading to a more androgynous view of the good manager. The other development was that the proportion of women in management positions had continued to rise, reaching 34% by 1984. In Rosabeth Kanter's terms, this proportion had shifted from skewed in 1965 to tilted in 1977 to on the borderline of being balanced in 1984. We thought that with women constituting more than one-third of all managers, the image of good managers as masculine may have finally been dispelled.

Consequently, we conducted a replication of the original study eight years later, during the 1984-1985 academic year, using the Short BSRI with a new sample of undergraduate business students and part-time evening MBA students. Once again, we hypothesized that the good manager would be seen as androgynous. And, once again, our hypothesis was rejected. As we see in the second column of Table 5.1, approximately two-thirds of both women and men and both graduate and undergraduate students again described a good manager in predominantly masculine terms. Even when we reanalyzed our original data using only the items on the Short BSRI, over 60% of all students still saw a good manager as masculine.[7]

In summary, despite the increase in female managers and no matter what questionnaire or study design has been used to investigate stereotypes of managers, people have described men as more like good managers than women, and good managers as higher in stereotypically masculine traits than stereotypically feminine traits. Men and women at all career stages examined, including practicing managers, part-time MBA students on the verge of careers as managers, and undergraduate business students, share the same biases about management.

These results, however, raise as many questions as they answer. The first question pertains to their dependence on sex ratios in the management ranks. If the proportion of women managers continues to rise, will there be some point at which stereotypes of managers no longer agree with the masculine gender stereotype? Not necessarily. Our review of gender stereotypes showed that, even though they have been demonstrated repeatedly to have little to do with actual sex differences, support for them has diminished little over time. Managerial stereotypes have stayed essentially the same despite the considerable increase in women managers in recent years. We have little reason to believe that the stereotypes will change if even more women become managers. In addition, the upper levels of management remain a male bastion despite the overall increase in the proportion of women managers. If stereotypes of managers are influenced at all by sex ratios, they may be influenced most by the sex ratio of top executives. Unless this sex ratio changes, the stereotypes may remain the same. Furthermore, women may bring similar qualities to the managerial job as men and thereby not necessitate a change in managerial stereotypes.

A second question raised by managerial stereotypes pertains to the nature of their effect. Should we be concerned with managerial stereotypes at all, or should we be concerned only with the reality of what makes a manager good or bad? Our answer to this question is that the stereotypes as well as the realities of management are important. Further results that Tony Butterfield and I obtained shed light on the possible effects of managerial stereotypes.

In both our 1976-1977 and 1984-1985 studies, we found that undergraduate business students exhibited stereotypical sex differences in their self-descriptions, with males seeing themselves as higher in masculinity and lower in femininity than females. Female and male undergraduates agreed on a description of the good manager as highly masculine. As a result, the undergraduate women saw effective managers as most unlike themselves. Given this perception, these women may hold back the most in developing their management skills and in seeking managerial positions. Such actions on their part would help to perpetuate the belief that men or masculine characteristics are best suited for management.

In contrast, there were few sex differences in the self-descriptions of part-time evening MBA students. Male MBAs described themselves in similar terms as male undergraduates. Female MBAs, however, saw themselves as more masculine and less feminine, and thereby more like a good manager, than female undergraduates. Why do women's self-descriptions, but not those of men, differ according to student status? As we stated in the last paragraph, the undergraduate women who least fit the stereotype of a good manager may be diverted from the pursuit of managerial careers. Women who most fit the stereotype may be the ones who apply for admission to graduate business programs. They may also be the ones who are most likely to be accepted by the programs. In addition, many organizations exert strong pressures on their members to conform to ways acceptable to other members, particularly those in power. As long as women remain in the minority in management circles, they may be expected to behave in the same way as men. Thus a masculine stereotype of the good manager is self-reinforcing and inhibits the expression of femininity by women in or aspiring to management positions. On the other hand, males are more socialized from the onset to fit the stereotype of a good manager. Men who are close to attaining management positions are unlikely to differ substantially from those who are at earlier stages in their careers.

The third and final question raised by managerial stereotypes pertains to their applicability to the practice of management. Stereotypes are known to die hard, even when facts do not substantiate them, but they are not necessarily wrong. Do the stereotypes that men are better managers and that better managers are masculine accurately reflect what makes for a good manager, or do these stereotypes only reflect the facts that most managers have been men and that most men have been expected to live up to the masculine stereotype?

The remainder of the chapter shall be devoted to this question. First, we need to examine whether sex differences are actually exhibited within the ranks of management. If men and women behave similarly once they become managers, even if they differed beforehand, the stereotype that men make better managers would not be supported. Subordinates could differ in their responses to female and male managers, however, thereby influencing their managers' overall effectiveness. Thus we also need to examine subordinates' responses to female and male managers.

DO FEMALE AND MALE
MANAGERS DIFFER?

This question is not as easy to answer as it may seem. Men and women differ in the extent to which they have achieved success in the ranks of management. For example, male managers tend to have more managerial experience, hold higher managerial levels, and receive higher salaries than female managers. This, however, may be due simply to the fact that the average male manager is older than the average female manager rather than to any essential sex difference. The influx of women managers has most occurred in the lower age brackets, in which individuals are least likely to hold high managerial levels or receive high salaries.[8]

Hardly any recent writers have advocated the existence of biologically based sex differences that affect the capability of women versus men to manage effectively. Instead, most writers now focus on differences in the early socialization experiences of females and males that set up expectations for participation in the work force. They reach very different conclusions, however, about whether or how sex differences in socialization experiences contribute to sex differences in the managerial ranks.

Some writers conclude that women who pursue the nontraditional career of manager reject their gender stereotype and have needs, motives, and values similar to those of men who pursue managerial careers. This may be due to self-selection, with men and women who decide upon managerial careers sharing similar traits and behavioral tendencies. It may also be due to a similarity in experiences within the managerial role.[9]

Other writers conclude that female and male managers differ in the ways predicted by gender stereotypes as a result of their different socialization experiences. For example, in a best-selling book in the 1970s, Margaret Hennig and Anne Jardim advocated that men are better prepared to be managers because of such factors as their greater participation in team sports during their formative years. They concluded that men "bring to the management setting a clearer, stronger and more definite understanding of where they see themselves going, what they will have to do, how they will have to act, and what they must take into account if they are to achieve the objectives they set for themselves." Although Hennig and Jardim saw women as lacking essential managerial skills and traits coming out of childhood, they believed that women could still be successful as managers and compete on an equal footing with men if they developed the skills they had not developed in earlier years.[10]

Still other writers conclude that female and male managers differ in ways opposite to gender stereotypes because women managers have had to be exceptional to compensate for the early socialization experiences that are different from those of men. For example, a survey of American Management Association (AMA) members found that female managers were more committed to their careers, as opposed to their family or home lives, than male managers with equivalent ages, salaries, educations, and managerial levels. These findings were believed to reflect a reaction to traditional beliefs that the appropriate role for the man is at work and for the woman at home. To hold managerial positions, women were viewed as having greater barriers to overcome than men, both in their internal predispositions and in others' expectations for them. A female manager with a position and background equivalent to a male manager may have had to have a greater commitment to her career to overcome such barriers. Men, on the other hand, who have greater sex role expectations for success than women, could find themselves in managerial jobs in response to such pressures even if they possessed less of a career orientation than women in equivalent positions.[11]

We shall review the extent of support for each of these competing points of view. In so doing, we shall consider four types of differences that may exist between female and male managers. One type pertains to their behavioral responses to others, particularly their subordinates. The second type pertains to their internal motivation and commitment to their jobs, organizations, and careers. The third type pertains to their experiences with stress. The fourth type pertains to subordinates' responses to female and male managers. Let's begin our analysis by examining sex differences in managerial behavior.

Managerial Behavior

Many studies of leadership have concluded that managers vary in two critical types of leader behavior, initiating structure and consideration. *Initiating structure* refers to the extent to which the manager initiates activity in the group, organizes it, and defines the way work is to be done. It includes such behavior as insisting on standards and deadlines and deciding in detail what will be done by subordinates and how it will be done. For example, a newly appointed manager who reorganizes a department, develops a description of the function of each department member, formulates department and individual goals, assigns projects, and gives details on how projects should be conducted would be very high in initiating structure behavior.

Consideration behavior, on the other hand, refers to the extent to which the manager exhibits concern for the welfare of group members. Consideration-oriented managers express appreciation for work performed well, devote attention to subordinates' satisfaction, seek to build their self-esteem by treating them as equals, try to make them feel at ease, take their ideas into account, and seek their approval before proceeding with important matters that affect them. For example, a manager who organizes an office party to celebrate the marriage of a group member, asks for input into the layout and decoration of the office area, or reschedules meetings that conflict with a subordinate's appointment with a doctor is very high in consideration behavior.[12]

A recent compilation of research results concluded that male and female leaders do not exhibit different amounts of initiating structure or consideration behavior in their jobs. Also, male leaders were found to be more effective than female leaders in laboratory experiments, but leader sex did not influence effectiveness when real leaders were the object of investigation. Given that laboratory-based studies provide only a limited amount of information about managers, they are more likely to elicit results that support managerial stereotypes than studies conducted in the "real world." Thus these results suggest the lack of a sex difference in the effectiveness of actual leaders.[13]

In a comprehensive study of managers along several dimensions of behavior, Susan Donnell and Jay Hall similarly found that female and male managers did not differ in task-oriented or people-oriented behavior toward subordinates. They also examined managers' use of the behavioral processes of exposure and feedback. Exposure consists of open and candid sharing of feelings and information, whereas feedback consists of the active solicitation of feelings and information from others. Use of exposure and feedback by female and male managers with each of three groups—superiors, colleagues, and subordinates—was assessed, resulting in six comparisons. Female managers were found to be less open and candid with their colleagues than male managers, possibly reflecting feelings of social isolation. The other five comparisons did not yield sex differences, however.[14]

Initiating structure, consideration, exposure, and feedback represent global measures of managerial behavior. Even if female and male leaders generally did not differ in behavior according to these measures, they could differ in their responses to specific situations. One such situation is when the manager is confronted with a poorly performing subordinate. A two-step process occurs when leaders are confronted with poor performers. First, they attribute the poor performance to one of four causes: lack of ability, lack of effort, a difficult task, or bad luck. Second, they decide upon corrective action based on their causal attributions. People often differ in their causal attributions for the performance of women and men, however, with attributions ranging from "what's skill for the male is luck for the female" to "those who are number two (i.e., the women) try harder."[15]

Male and female leaders may differ in their responses to poor performers. In some studies, male leaders' responses were based more on a norm of equity. They were inclined to punish subordinates who performed poorly because of lack of effort and to provide extra training to subordinates who performed poorly because of lack of ability. In contrast, the responses of female leaders were based more on a norm of equality. They were equally likely to punish or to train subordinates who performed poorly regardless of whether the performance was attributed to lack of effort or lack of ability. Their responses were sometimes affected by the subordinate's sex, however, typically being less punitive and more supportive of female subordinates. Male leaders may have preferred an equity orientation because they were socialized to value achievement, performance, and contributions to team accomplishment. Female leaders may have preferred an equality orientation because they were socialized to minimize status differences and to strive for group harmony.[16]

These studies established consistent differences between the responses of female and male leaders to a particular situation—the poorly performing subordinate. The results may have been affected by personal characteristics of the leaders, however, such as their self-esteem and self-confidence. Other researchers investigated the effect of self-confidence and leader sex on the selection of general influence strategies used to direct and facilitate the work of subordinates. Managers may use positive strategies emphasizing praise and rewards, negative strategies emphasizing criticism and threats, or neutral strategies emphasizing information and general interest in workers and their performance. A leader who is high in consideration behavior would be expected to use more positive than negative influence strategies. A leader who is high in initiating structure, however, could favor any of these strategies.[17]

Women tended to make fewer attempts to influence subordinates' performance, to use a more limited range of influence strategies, to use fewer positive strategies, and to use more negative strategies than men. Women, however, also exhibited lower levels of self-confidence than men. While the self-confidence of males was not affected by prior supervisory experience, the self-confidence of women was very much related to their prior experience as managers. Females reported levels of self-confidence commensurate with their experience, whereas males reported that they felt capable of being effective supervisors regardless of their previous experience at it. Women with high self-confidence differed less from men in their use of influence strategies than women with low self-confidence. These results suggest that sex differences in influence strategies may disappear as women gain experience and thereby self-confidence in managerial positions.

Other sex differences in managerial behavior also may reflect differences in self-confidence or self-esteem. For example, direct observations of managers at all levels in one study revealed that female managers were twice as accessible to others as their male counterparts. Criteria for accessibility included open and closed office door policies, use of secretaries to screen out potential interruptions, and encouragement of telephoning at home on evenings and weekends. Women managers experienced greater difficulty in saying no to others, possibly stemming from a fear of being seen as rejecting the person making the request. Most female managers rarely if ever closed their office doors, while most men closed their doors when they needed to work. Compared with the men, the women may have undervalued themselves and the importance of their own time. Accessibility is not good or bad in itself. Managers can contribute to their subordinates' satisfaction and growth by being truly accessible and gaining rapport with them, but the need to say no to subordinates' requests for time when appropriate and the importance of one's own time are also important considerations. The sex difference in accessibility, however, is worthy of note.[18]

These results portray a mixed pattern of sex differences in managerial behavior. Sex differences are not evident in global dimensions of behavior such as initiating structure and consideration. Sex differences in specific behaviors, such as responses to poorly performing subordinates, influence strategies, and accessibility to others, that support the influence of gender stereotypes are more evident. These differences, however, could reflect differences in self-confidence or self-esteem of women versus men managers. When women managers are tokens in their work environments, their treatment by dominants does not give them reason to feel self-confident. As male dominants become more comfortable with female tokens or as women move from having token status to occupying a larger proportion of managerial positions, women managers as a group have their competence doubted less and probably gain in self-confidence. The research on influence strategies suggests that, as women managers gain managerial experience and grow in self-confidence, they become more similar to males in their responses to subordinates.

Managerial Motivation and Commitment

Several conceptual schemes have been proposed for the kinds of motives that people have and how the motives interact. In one of the most popular schemes, Abraham Maslow proposed that individuals have a hierarchy of needs with successively higher-order needs motivating individuals once lower-order needs have been satisfied. The needs in Maslow's hierarchy range from physiological needs at the lower end to safety, social, ego, and then self-actualization needs at the higher end. A simpler scheme proposes three types of needs that individuals may seek to satisfy without positioning them in a hierarchy. These are the need for achievement, satisfied by having challenging assignments in which success is neither guaranteed nor precluded; the need for power, satisfied by having influence and control over the activities of others; and the need for affiliation, satisfied by having warm and friendly relationships. The need for power may be subdivided into the need for socialized power, satisfied through serving the organization or others, and the need for personalized power, satisfied through controlling and exploiting others.[19]

Early motivation research, conducted primarily on male managers, concluded that motivation is critical to the success or failure of managers. The needs that entrepreneurs seek to satisfy have a strong influence on the fate of their businesses, with the need for achievement being the primary motivator for successful entrepreneurs. Possession of a high need for power has been seen as more conducive to the success of managers who work for others. The power motivation of managers is more beneficial, however, when it consists of the need for socialized power rather than personalized power.[20]

With their greater numbers, women managers are now considered worthy of inclusion in studies of managerial motivation. Women have been found to be as highly motivated to manage as men. Moreover, the motivation of women and men changes similarly with training and experience. Some, but not all, researchers have found that women and men managers score essentially the same on psychological tests of needs and motives that are supposed to predict managerial success.[21]

When differences have been found in the relative strength of motives possessed by female and male managers, the differences have generally favored women and been contrary to gender stereotypes. In one study, women managers had a higher need for achievement, a higher need for power, and a not significantly different need for affiliation than men managers. When the need for socialized power was separated from the need for personalized power, women managers were higher than men managers in the more desirable need for socialized power and at the same level in the less desirable need for personalized power. Also, Donnell and Hall found that women managers reported lower basic needs and higher needs for self-actualization. Compared with males, female managers were more concerned with opportunities for growth, autonomy, and challenge and less concerned with work environment and pay. The women managers exhibited a more mature and higher-achieving motivational profile than the male managers.[22]

These results support the notion that women managers possess traits superior to those of their male counterparts. Because they have had to overcome stereotypical attitudes about their unsuitability for management, women who have successfully gained managerial positions may have been motivated by a higher need for achievement and self-actualization than male managers. Women with a high need for socialized power may have once looked elsewhere such as to teaching careers to fulfill that need, but now look to managerial opportunities, which are more open to them. The results suggest that female managers conform more closely than male managers to the ideal motivational profile originally developed with male managers in mind.

Having the right motivational profile is not the only desirable characteristic for a manager. The sense of commitment that managers bring to their work is also important, at least as far as their organizations are concerned. Commitment to job, work, organization, and career versus home or family life have all been examined in research studies. We shall simply talk about commitment in general, because each suggests a greater involvement in work in spite of fine differences among them. More committed managers might be expected to work longer hours when the need arises, to relocate when the organization wishes, and to place a greater importance on the interests of the organization than on personal interests when the two are in conflict. Managers who are less committed will be more likely to emphasize their family-related and leisure interests, believe that "a job is a job," and balk when they are asked to do anything that is outside of their normal routines. Excessive commitment could result in overzealous or unethical behavior. In general, however, when managers are more committed to the organization, the organization itself is likely to be more effective. Clearly, it is desirable for organizations to identify, hire, promote, and otherwise reward more committed managers.[23]

Thus the question of whether female or male managers, or neither, are the more committed managers is of considerable interest. Gender stereotypes suggest that women are lacking in the qualities that are essential for a successful managerial career, such as the inclination to be committed to their jobs, organizations, and careers. The research evidence, however, does not give a clear indication of the relationship between sex and managerial commitment. Some studies have found that women are more committed as a group than males; other studies have found that women are less committed; and still other studies have found no sex difference in commitment.[24]

Commitment may best be explained by variables other than a person's sex. For example, the personal influences of age, education, and the possession of needs at the upper end of Maslow's hierarchy of needs have been positively linked to commitment. Favorable job circumstances such as higher job satisfaction, more meaningful work, and greater utilization of skills are also positively related to commitment.[25]

Family characteristics such as being married and having children could contribute to a sex difference in managerial commitment. Although the commitment of working men in general does not appear to be affected by family considerations, the commitment of working women in general is more affected by family considerations. This effect may be small among managers, however, because fewer female managers than male managers are married or have children. In 1986, 75% of all male managers were married; 10% were widowed, separated, or divorced; and 15% had never been married. In contrast, 58% of all female managers were married; 20% were widowed, separated, or divorced; and 22% had never married. Looking at the ranks of top management, a 1982 survey of female senior executives found that 52% had never married or were widowed, separated, or divorced, and that 61% had no children. A similar study of male senior executives in 1979 found that only 5% of the men were unmarried and only 3% had no children. The marital status of female and male executives in both the 1965 and the 1985 *Harvard Business Review* surveys differed in similar fashion.[26]

The degree of sex role conflict felt by the woman manager, which is influenced by family variables but not fully determined by them, seems more important than the family situation itself in determining her level of commitment. Sex role conflict can be caused by pressures from others as well as an overload from family responsibilities. Working women as a whole feel a greater degree of sex role conflict than working men. In turn, individuals who feel a greater degree of sex role conflict are less committed to their jobs, organizations, and careers. Married working women with nontraditional attitudes toward sex roles, however, are more committed to their jobs than those with traditional attitudes. Women managers definitely have nontraditional attitudes toward sex roles, as demonstrated by the fact that they have rejected the prescriptions of others in assuming leadership roles in organizations. The results of the AMA survey described earlier suggest that they may be less inclined to feel sex role conflict than other women. This could be because women managers are less affected by family considerations than other women, or because they have worked hard to overcome such conflict. The excitement of their jobs may stimulate a strong sense of commitment that overrides the negative effect of sex role conflict.[27]

Rather than concluding that there are sex differences in commitment, it is more appropriate to conclude that the commitment of male and female managers is affected by the same set of variables. Variables such as family characteristics and sex role conflict could lead to a sex difference in managerial commitment. Managers are more likely to have their level of commitment influenced, however, by job circumstances and personal factors other than their sex.

Managerial Stress

Early studies of stress in managers as well as people in other occupations were conducted using male subjects. These studies found that individuals who held more taxing jobs, such as that of manager, were particularly prone to type A behavior. As you recall, type A behavior was described in Chapter 2 as consisting of extreme levels of competitiveness, aggressiveness, striving for achievement, haste, impatience, and pressures of time and responsibility. Type A behavior increases the risk of coronary heart disease. Male managers also were found to engage in high consumption of alcohol, tranquilizers, and sleeping pills and to experience exhaustion, to be overweight, to lack exercise, to have high blood pressure, and to have family problems.[28]

More recent research using female subjects has similarly shown that those with higher occupational levels and more demanding jobs than other women are more prone to type A behavior and suffer from the same symptoms of stress as male managers. A study of top female executives in the United Kingdom found that the women generally did not report high incidence of physical ill health, although a quarter of them experienced migraine headaches. They more reported having experienced psychological maladies, with tiredness, irritation, and anxiety being experienced by over half of the executives. Behavioral manifestations of stress included high rates of smoking and consumption of stress-relieving drugs and alcohol. Similar to male managers, most of the female executives did not like to admit that they suffered from some form of stress-related illness and attempted to hide it from colleagues. They felt that they could not afford to be ill.[29]

Managerial work is stressful. Managers frequently experience work overload, both in qualitative terms by having difficult work to do, not having the necessary training, or having to meet performance standards that are too high, and in quantitative terms by having too much work to do, too many different things to do, or insufficient time to complete their work. They are responsible for many decisions but often have little latitude in making them. They have to deal with competing pressures that cannot all be satisfied, insecurity about their career progress, and ambiguity about their roles, objectives, and scope of responsibilities. Having responsibility for people versus responsibility for things is also a source of managerial stress. Because managers gain a large portion of their self-satisfaction and their identity in work, their work and nonwork lives become interdependent. Stress experienced on the job spills over into nonwork life and may contribute to stress in it as well. The stress caused by having an unsatisfactory home life may in turn contribute to the level of stress felt in the managerial role. As a result, managers often experience a vicious cycle of escalating stress in all areas of life once major stress is experienced in one area.[30]

Stress is a negative by-product of both commitment and motivation. Managers who feel a high degree of commitment work extra hours, relocate when their organization wishes, and make other personal adjustments that are more in the organization's best interest than their own. This pattern of putting the organization first takes its toll in the form of added stress. Both female and male managers who are more committed to their jobs are more likely to exhibit type A behavior. A high need for power, seen as preferable for managers in general, has also been linked to type A behavior in women but not in men.[31]

Although women and men are affected by common stressors such as the demands of the managerial job, women have to deal with a unique set of stressors that men encounter less often. These include discrimination, gender stereotyping, social isolation, and the conflicting demands of family and work life. Discrimination is a major obstacle to their advancement and thereby a key source of stress. Although women managers have not let gender stereotyping keep them from attaining management positions, they still have to deal with individuals whose reactions to them are influenced by the stereotypes and may feel stress as a result. Social isolation resulting from being placed in the token category also contributes to stress. The conflicting demands of family and career cause stress when the woman is expected to provide the primary care for her children while pursuing her career. The husband's supportiveness of the woman's career and equal participation in child care and household duties can help to alleviate this stress. In reaction to gender stereotypes, however, the managerial mother may still feel sex role conflict about not spending more time with her children. Of course, these conflicting demands are not present for the single woman manager with no children.[32]

Men seldom experience conflicting demands of career and family life because they traditionally have not been expected to stay at home with their families. Nonetheless, men could experience unique stress from trying to live up to the demands of the masculine stereotype. For example, they could feel stress caused by role overload from trying to maintain their image as successful achievers and providers, pressure and conflict from attempts to exercise leadership, and frustration and dissatisfaction if they are not progressing as rapidly as expected in their roles as "breadwinners." The consequence of male managers' trying to live up to the masculine stereotype is seen in their tendency to physical illness and nonwork problems, however, rather than in their career progress. The masculine stereotype does not place as great a constraint on men's careers and achievements as the feminine stereotype places on those of women.[33]

Due to the difficulty of obtaining access to appropriate samples, the stress-related experiences of female and male managers have seldom been examined in the same study. Thus we do not know with certainty whether female and male managers experience different levels of suffering from stress symptoms. Female and male managers could differ, however, in their exposure to stressors and in their coping responses to stress. Female managers could experience greater stressors than male managers but not show it. As women in general take more health actions that could prevent major illnesses from occurring than men in general, women managers could compensate for experiencing greater stressors by taking better care of themselves than men managers. The research evidence is also inconclusive on this point. It is not clear whether there are differences in the ways in which women and men cope with stress or in the effects of their coping strategies.[34]

It is clear, however, that the managerial role tends to promote type A behavior in both women and men, and that women and men managers exhibit many of the same symptoms of stress. Thus the attaining of a managerial position seems to be a mixed blessing. The managerial role may be a source of considerable satisfaction for its male and female occupants, but it is also a source of considerable stress.

Subordinates' Responses

Even if male and female leaders did not differ in any respect, subordinates could still respond to them differently or have different preferences for working with them. In Chapter 4, we discussed differences in individuals' tendencies to see women and men in terms of gender stereotypes. Subordinates who make heavy use of gender stereotypes may prefer their managers to be men. In the 1965 and 1985 *Harvard Business Review* surveys, support for the statement "I would feel comfortable working for a woman" increased from 27% to 47% for male executives and from 75% to 82% for female executives. Given that individuals were not asked how comfortable they would feel working for a man, it should not be assumed that they felt totally comfortable with that prospect either. Nonetheless, it was striking that over half of male executives and almost one-fifth of female executives surveyed in 1985 reported anticipated discomfort at the prospect of working for a woman. Such individuals may be particularly prone to being influenced by gender stereotypes. Discomfort in working for women reflects fear of the unknown as well as traditional attitudes and is likely to be alleviated by the actual experience of being managed by a woman.[35]

Laboratory studies of subordinates' responses to female and male managers have typically found that male managers are judged more favorably when their behavior fits the masculine stereotype and that female managers are judged more favorably when their behavior fits the feminine stereotype. For example, female managers who used a consideration leadership style were rated more highly than male managers who used that style; and male managers who were high in initiating structure were rated more highly than female managers using that style. Thus effective managerial behavior for a woman was considered to be quite different from effective managerial behavior for a man. In contrast, studies of actual managers and their subordinates have typically found that subordinates respond similarly to male and female managers.[36]

A comparison of two studies conducted at the United States Military Academy at West Point, one "in the laboratory" and the other "in the field," vividly demonstrates how conclusions can differ according to the method of study. In one study, randomly selected cadets worked in groups on tasks that were obviously designed for the purpose of a behavioral experiment. Half of the groups had male leaders and half had female leaders; otherwise, leaders were randomly chosen from the participating cadets. Also, half of the groups had male followers with more traditional attitudes toward women and half had male followers with more liberal attitudes toward women.

(Female cadets were scarce at West Point at the time.) After the experiment was completed, followers evaluated their leader's performance, group performance, and group morale. In the other study, conducted two years later, male and female cadets completed a questionnaire assessing their attitudes toward women in a new-cadet orientation program. After later completing a six-week summer training program, they similarly evaluated the performance of their squad or platoon leader as well as group performance and morale: 11% of the cadets had a female leader.[37]

The two studies yielded substantially different results. In the laboratory study, groups with male leaders performed more effectively than groups with female leaders. Followers who held more traditional attitudes toward women made less favorable judgments about female leaders than male leaders, and followers with more liberal attitudes toward women made more favorable judgments about female leaders than male leaders. In the field study, male and female leaders were seen as similar in effectiveness by their followers. Also, followers did not differ in their judgments of male or female leaders depending on whether they possessed traditional or liberal attitudes toward women. Thus the laboratory study yielded results supporting followers' use of gender stereotypes in responding to their leaders, whereas the field study did not obtain such results.

Upon completing the field study, the researchers concluded,

> The long term duration and intensity of leader-follower interactions may be a key difference accounting for the results of the present study and prior laboratory research. In the present study, leaders and followers interacted on a 24-hour per day basis over a period of several weeks; they got to know one another quite well. In contrast, the previous studies yielding bias effects have been based on either short term laboratory interactions or totally hypothetical situations in which subjects responded to written scenarios concerning the actions of male or female managers. [The effect of gender stereotypes] may wane over time as people are compelled to judge women based on long-term performance and face-to-face interaction.[38]

Less research has been conducted on the effect of the sex of subordinates on their responses to leaders. A small amount of evidence suggests that females give more positive ratings of leader behavior than males, regardless of the situation. This could result from female subordinates receiving more favorable treatment from leaders than male subordinates, with their generally favorable evaluations of leaders reflecting this preferential treatment. On the other hand, female subordinates could use different standards than male subordinates in evaluating leaders. The greater amount of evidence indicates, however, that male and female subordinates do not differ in their responses to male or female leaders.[39]

Overall, subordinates do not appear to respond differently to male and female leaders for whom they have actually worked. Results supporting the influence of gender stereotypes on subordinates' responses to leaders have been obtained primarily from laboratory studies but not from field studies. Once subordinates have experienced both female and male managers, the effects of gender stereotypes tend to disappear and managers are treated more as individuals than as representatives of their sex.

Conclusion

The title of this section of the chapter posed the question, "Do female and male managers differ?" The research evidence answers, "They differ in some ways and at some times, but, for the most part, they do not differ."

Sex differences have generally not been found in global measures of managerial behavior. Specific behavioral differences, such as response to poorly performing subordinates or influence strategies, tend to favor male managers. As one study suggested, however, these differences may be caused by the initially lower self-confidence of women managers and alleviated by the acquisition of management experience. On the other hand, sex differences in motivational profiles consistently favor female managers. There is no clear-cut sex difference in managerial commitment or in symptoms of stress experienced. Female managers appear to be faced with greater stressors, but they may cope with stressors better than male managers. Male and female managers also provoke similar responses in subordinates. Overall, the sex differences that have been found are few and tend to cancel each other out.

We are left with little reason to believe that either female managers or male managers are superior in executing, involving themselves in, or personally coping with the responsibilities of their jobs. The only meaningful difference between managerial men and women may be in the environments in which they operate, with imbalanced sex ratios—particularly at the top management levels—contributing to stereotype-driven perceptions and unrealistic expectations for managerial women.[40] The stereotype that men make better managers is simply not true.

IMPLICATIONS FOR MANAGEMENT: ARE BETTER MANAGERS MASCULINE?

The other stereotype about management that warrants our attention is that better managers are masculine. Unlike the stereotype that men make better managers, this stereotype has received little critical examination because management research has generally been blind to issues regarding the socialization of managers. Until recently, virtually all theories of effective management have been based on observations of male managers. These theories make judgments about which managerial behaviors are more effective and which are less effective. They typically do not, however, recognize that men, who still constitute the majority of managers, are also judged in our society according to their adherence to the masculine gender stereotype. Thus it is not surprising that masculinity remains prevalent in the ranks of management.

The fact that managers tend to be masculine does not necessarily mean that *better* managers are masculine. Management theories have varied over the years, and no universal agreement has been reached on which theory is best. Most theories, however, have made reference to feminine as well as masculine characteristics. Let's briefly review some of the major theories of management, leading up to the only theory that has been based on an analysis of the appropriateness of gender stereotypes in our society, that of androgynous management.

Great-man theories were among the earliest management theories. They were developed in the belief that knowledge about the personalities of individuals who have influenced the course of Western civilization provides insight into what makes a great leader. The leaders typically examined were men such as Winston Churchill, Thomas Jefferson, and Alexander the Great. The bias of these theories is captured best by their label. Women such as Joan of Arc, Queen Elizabeth I, and Catherine the Great who also have strongly influenced Western civilization were ignored in the development of these theories. These theories receive little attention today.[41]

Trait theories of leadership assume that effective leaders are endowed with personal qualities that differentiate them from their followers and can be applied to any situation. Given that all individuals do not have these qualities, only those who actually possess them are fit to be leaders. These qualities include characteristics associated with the masculine gender stereotype such as initiative, decisiveness, and self-confidence, characteristics associated with the feminine stereotype such as sociability, tactfulness, and nurturance, and characteristics not associated with either stereotype such as intelligence, physical energy, and fluency of speech. Studies that have attempted to identify the set of traits best suited for leaders, however, have yielded few consistent findings. As a result, theories stressing universal traits of leadership have been deemphasized in recent years.[42]

Behavioral theories of leadership are the theories that currently receive the greatest amount of attention. In contrast to trait theories, behavioral theories focus on the specific behaviors used by managers to influence their subordinates' actions. We have already discussed sex differences in types of managerial behavior such as initiating structure and consideration. Most behavioral theories propose two types of managerial behavior that resemble initiating structure and consideration, although their labels vary (e.g., autocratic and democratic leadership, boss-centered and subordinate-centered leadership, concern for production and concern for people). Behavioral theories differ in whether they regard these types of behavior as independent dimensions, with an individual being able to be high or low in each, or as opposite poles along the same dimension of behavior. Some behavioral theories regard one type or combination of behaviors as best in all situations. Other behavioral theories, also called *situational theories*, regard different types of behavior as appropriate for different situations. Task-oriented and people-oriented types of behavior, however, form the basis for most behavioral theories.

The linkage between gender stereotypes and behavioral theories of leadership is obvious. Task-oriented behaviors by the leader such as initiating structure, setting goals, and making decisions are those most associated with the masculine stereotype. People-oriented behaviors by the leader such as showing consideration toward subordinates, soliciting of subordinates' ideas, and demonstrating concern for subordinates' satisfaction are those most associated with the feminine stereotype.

Specific behavioral theories vary in prescribing when these behaviors should be used. For example, the Managerial Grid theory proposes that the best manager is one who is high in both task-oriented and people-oriented behavior in all situations. Bob Tannenbaum and Warren Schmidt say that managers should decide to be more task-oriented or people-oriented depending on their evaluation of factors such as their own knowledge and values, subordinates' motivational needs and previous experiences with managers, and situational factors such as time pressure and the organization's climate. Paul Hersey and Ken Blanchard say that the manager should adopt high-task/low-people, high-task/high-people, low-task/high-people, and low-task/low-people behavioral styles in that order as subordinates move from low to high in maturity.[43]

None of the behavioral theories suggests that better managers are masculine (i.e., mostly task-oriented) or that better managers are feminine (i.e., mostly people-oriented) except in special situations. The Managerial Grid theory suggests that better managers are androgynous by advocating a combination of task-oriented and people-oriented behavior. Although they did not offer their own theory of leadership, Donnell and Hall reached the same conclusion. Managers in their study who were high achievers successfully integrated their concerns for task and people, average achievers concentrated on the task at the expense of the people performing it, and low achievers showed little concern for either task or people. To paraphrase their results in sex role identity terms, high achievers were androgynous, average achievers were masculine, and low achievers were undifferentiated. Donnell and Hall may have provided an explanation for why the ranks of management are filled with individuals who exhibit predominantly masculine behaviors, even though such behaviors are seldom exclusively recommended. These individuals may be the organization's average managers, who perform well enough to retain their positions but not well enough to be considered excellent performers.[44]

When a high-task/high-people behavioral style has been advocated for managers, the rationale has usually been that subordinates need both their work structured for them and concern shown for their feelings, ideas, and job satisfaction. *Androgynous management,* defined by Alice Sargent as "a style that blends behaviors previously deemed to belong exclusively to men or women," has been proposed for somewhat different reasons. Sargent offers several reasons why managers should be androgynous. One reason is that women, who are assumed to have different qualities than men, are entering the profession of management in increasing numbers. Therefore, management theory and practice should expand its definition of what makes a good manager beyond the masculine behaviors preferred by males to include the feminine behaviors exhibited by the newest members of the managerial ranks. This reason relies on assumptions about the applicability of gender stereotypes to male and female managers, which we have already rejected.[45]

A second reason offered in support of androgynous management is that androgyny is the best route to fulfillment in men's and women's personal lives and makes them happier people. If androgyny is also adopted as a standard for managerial behavior, androgynous managers will be better able to integrate their personal and professional lives. We reviewed the controversy over the advantages of androgyny for individuals in Chapter 2. Sargent takes a valid position about the merits of androgyny, but it is still uncertain as to whether androgynous individuals are truly better off in life.

A third reason offered for androgynous management is that it is particularly appropriate for the climate in which organizations currently operate. Sargent argues that workers increasingly seek fulfillment rather than just a paycheck from their work and that more motivated and committed employees are needed to take advantage of improved technology. Also, in a low-growth economy with shrinking or unchanging capital resources, organizations must focus on the contributions of their human resources if they are to improve their efficiency and work output. Behavioral theories of leadership also offer this reasoning to justify managers' showing concern for people as well as concern for the task, but it is the sole justification for androgynous management that has widespread support.

Little research has been conducted on whether androgynous individuals actually are superior managers. A strong case can be made for androgynous management, however, if we adopt a broad interpretation of what is meant by *androgynous*. Sandra Bem came to measure androgyny as a propensity to describe oneself as high in both feminine and masculine characteristics. An androgynous behavioral style may be inferred from this, as we have inferred up to this point, to mean the exhibiting of high amounts of both feminine and masculine behaviors. Bem found, however, that androgynous individuals were actually high in behavioral flexibility and adaptability. They were capable of exhibiting exclusively masculine behaviors, exclusively feminine behaviors, or whatever combination of masculine and feminine behaviors a situation called for. Androgynous individuals were less locked into a rigid set of behaviors dictated by gender stereotypes than masculine men or feminine women. The description of the androgynous individual that emerged from studies by Bem and others has been summarized as follows: "Because androgyny is defined in terms of a balance of masculine- and feminine-typed characteristics, the androgynous person has both forms of responses in his or her repertoire and presumably derives adaptive behavioral flexibility from this array of options."[46]

Several management theories, including all of the situational theories, advocate the same type of behavioral flexibility in responding to management situations. If an androgynous manager is defined as one who has the capability to be either high or low in both task-oriented and people-oriented behavior, most management theorists would agree that better managers are androgynous. This view certainly has greater support than the view that better managers are masculine, which is advocated only for special situations such as when subordinates are extremely immature.

Thus we reject another managerial stereotype. It makes no more sense for us to believe that better managers are masculine than it does to believe that men make better managers. The androgynous manager, who is flexible in his or her responses to managerial situations, seems preferable to the masculine manager. Neither managerial stereotype is warranted, if either ever was.

As we pointed out before, stereotypes are not necessarily wrong. Stereotypes are resistant to change, however, even when they are not substantiated by facts. We should all hope that the stereotypes that have been perpetuated about management die soon. Women do not deserve the burden of having to prove that members of their sex belong as managers. Neither women nor men deserve the burden of having to live up to the masculine stereotype in their managerial roles, nor do they deserve the symptoms of stress that accompany excessive masculinity. Everyone who works in organizations will gain if men and women in management positions are encouraged to exhibit the behavioral flexibility of androgynous managers.

NOTES

1. G. W. Bowman, N. B. Worthy, and S. A. Greyser, "Are Women Executives People?" *Harvard Business Review* 43, no. 4 (July/August 1965): 15-28, 164-78.

2. C. D. Sutton and K. K. Moore, "Executive Women—20 Years Later." *Harvard Business Review* 63, no. 5 (September/October 1985): 43-66.

3. R. M. Stogdill, *Handbook of Leadership* (New York: Free Press, 1974).

4. V. E. Schein, "The Relationship Between Sex Role Stereotypes and Requisite Management Characteristics," *Journal of Applied Psychology* 57 (1973): 95-100; V. E. Schein, "Relationship Between Sex Role Stereotypes and Requisite Management Characteristics Among Female Managers," *Journal of Applied Psychology* 60 (1975): 340-44.

5. D. Massengill and N. Di Marco, "Sex-Role Stereotypes and Requisite Management Characteristics: A Current Replication," *Sex Roles* 5 (1979): 561-70.

6. G. N. Powell and D. A. Butterfield, "The 'Good Manager': Masculine or Androgynous?" *Academy of Management Journal* 22 (1979): 395-403.

7. G. N. Powell and D. A. Butterfield, "The 'Good Manager': Does Androgyny Fare Better in the 1980's?" (Paper delivered at the Annual Meeting of the Academy of Management, Chicago, 1986).

8. G. N. Powell, B. Z. Posner, and W. H. Schmidt, "Sex Effects in Managerial Value Systems," *Human Relations* 37 (1984): 909-21; U.S. Department of Labor, Bureau of Labor Statistics (Unpublished tabulation from the *Current Population Survey*, Annual average industry and occupation tables for year ending December 1986, 1986), table 4.

9. J. R. Terborg, "Women in Management: A Research Review," *Journal of Applied Psychology* 62 (1977): 647-64.

10. M. Hennig and A. Jardim, Chapter 2, "Patterns of Difference and Their Implications," in *The Managerial Woman* (New York: Anchor Press/Doubleday, 1977), p. 63.

11. Powell et al., "Sex Effects in Managerial Value Systems."

12. B. M. Bass, Chapter 21, "Consideration and Initiating Structure," in *Stogdill's Handbook of Leadership* (New York: Free Press, 1981); K. M. Bartol and D. A. Butterfield, "Sex Effects in Evaluating Leaders," *Journal of Applied Psychology* 61 (1976): 446-54.

13. G. H. Dobbins and S. J. Platz, "Sex Differences in Leadership: How Real Are They?" *Academy of Management Review* 11 (1986): 118-27; K. M. Bartol, "The Sex Structuring of Organizations: A Search for Possible Causes," *Academy of Management Review* 3 (1980): 805-15; Bass, Chapter 30, "Women and Leadership," in *Stogdill's Handbook of Leadership*.

14. S. M. Donnell and J. Hall, "Men and Women as Managers: A Significant Case of No Significant Difference," *Organizational Dynamics* 8 (1980): 60-77.

15. S. G. Green and T. R. Mitchell, "Attributional Processes of Leaders in Leader-Member Interaction," *Organizational Behavior and Human Performance* 23 (1979): 429-58; K. Deaux and T. Emswiller, "Explanations of Successful Performance on Sex-Linked Tasks: What's Skill for the Male Is Luck for the Female," *Journal of Personality and Social Psychology* 29 (1974): 80-85; J. Feldman-Summers and J. B.

Kiesler, "Those Who Are Number Two Try Harder: The Effect of Sex on Attributions of Causality," *Journal of Personality and Social Psychology* 30 (1974): 846-55.

16. G. H. Dobbins, "Effects of Gender on Leaders' Responses to Poor Performers: An Attributional Interpretation," *Academy of Management Journal* 28 (1985): 587-98; G. H. Dobbins, "Equity vs. Equality: Sex Differences in Leadership," *Sex Roles* 15 (1986): 513-25; G. H. Dobbins, E. C. Pence, J. A. Orban, and J. A. Sgro, "The Effects of Sex of the Leader and Sex of the Subordinate on the Use of Organizational Control Policy," *Organizational Behavior and Human Performance* 32 (1983): 325-43.

17. D. Instone, B. Major, and B. B. Bunker, "Gender, Self Confidence, and Social Influence Strategies: An Organizational Simulation," *Journal of Personality and Social Psychology* 44 (1983): 322-33.

18. N. Josefowitz, "Management Men and Women: Closed vs. Open Doors," *Harvard Business Review* 58, no. 4 (September/October 1980): 57-62.

19. A. H. Maslow, *Motivation and Personality* (New York: Harper & Row, 1954); J. W. Atkinson, *An Introduction to Motivation* (New York: Van Nostrand, 1964); D. C. McClelland, *The Achieving Society* (Princeton, NJ: Van Nostrand, 1961); D. C. McClelland, "The Two Faces of Power," *Journal of International Affairs* 24 (1970): 31.

20. McClelland, *The Achieving Society*; D. C. McClelland and D. H. Burnham, "Power Is the Great Motivator," *Harvard Business Review* 54, no. 2 (March/April 1976): 100-110.

21. J. B. Miner, "Motivation to Manage Among Women: Studies of Business Managers and Educational Administrators," *Journal of Vocational Behavior* 5 (1974): 197-208; J. B. Miner, *Studies in Management Education* (New York: Springer, 1965); A. Harlan and C. Weiss, *Moving Up: Women in Managerial Careers*, working paper no. 86 (Wellesley, MA: Wellesley College, Center for Research on Women, 1981).

22. Chusmir, L. H. "Motivation of Managers: Is Gender a Factor?" *Psychology of Women Quarterly* 9 (1985): 153-59; L. H. Chusmir, "Dimensions of Need for Power: Personalized vs. Socialized Power in Female and Male Managers," *Sex Roles* 11 (1984): 759-69; Donnell and Hall, "Men and Women as Managers."

23. G. N. Powell, B. Z. Posner, and W. H. Schmidt, "Women: The More Committed Managers?" *Management Review* 74, no. 6 (June 1985): 43-45; D. M. Crandall, "Commitment and the Organization: The Organization Man Revisited," *Academy of Management Review* 12 (1987): 460-71.

24. R. T. Mowday, L. W. Porter, and R. M. Steers, *Employee-Organization Linkages* (New York: Academic Press, 1982); N. S. Bruning and R. A. Snyder, "Sex and Position as Predictors of Organizational Commitment," *Academy of Management Journal* 26 (1983): 485-91; R. Fuchs, "Different Meanings of Employment for Women," *Human Relations* 24 (1971): 495-99; J. M. Stevens, J. M. Beyer, and H. M. Trice, "Assessing Personal, Role, and Organizational Predictors of Managerial Commitment," *Academy of Management Journal* 21 (1978): 380-96.

25. L. H. Chusmir, "Job Commitment and the Organizational Woman," *Academy of Management Review* 7 (1982): 595-602; L. H. Chusmir, "Organizational Commitment and the Organizational Woman" (Unpublished manuscript, University of Colorado, Denver, 1986).

26. M. Kim and C. Cammann, "Effects of Family-Related Variables and Sex Differences on Job Involvement" (Paper delivered at the Annual Meeting of the Academy of Management, Chicago, 1986); U.S. Department of Labor, Bureau of Labor Statistics (Unpublished tabulation from the March 1986 Supplement to the *Current*

Population Survey, 1986), table 12; Korn/Ferry International, *Profile of Women Senior Executives* (New York: Korn/Ferry International, 1982).

27. Chusmir, "Job Commitment and the Organizational Woman"; Kim and Cammann, "Effects of Family-Related Variables"; Powell et al., "Sex Effects in Managerial Value Systems."

28. R. J. Burke and T. Weir, "The Type A Experience: Occupational and Life Demands, Satisfaction and Well Being," *Journal of Human Stress* 6, no. 4 (1980): 28-38; C. L. Cooper and M. J. Davidson, "The High Cost of Stress on Women Managers," *Organizational Dynamics* 10, no. 4 (1982): 44-53.

29. K. E. Kelly and B. K. Houston, "Type A Behavior in Employed Women: Relation to Work, Marital, and Leisure Variables, Social Support, Stress, Tension, and Health," *Journal of Personality and Social Psychology* 49 (1985): 1067-79; Cooper and Davidson, "The High Cost of Stress."

30. J. M. Ivancevich and M. T. Matteson, Chapter 1, "The Nature of Stress," and Chapter 5, "Physical Environment and Individual Level Stressors," in *Stress and Work: A Managerial Perspective* (Dallas: Scott, Foresman, 1980).

31. J. A. Hood and L. H. Chusmir, "Factors Determining Type A Behavior Among Employed Women and Men" (Paper delivered at the Annual Meeting of the Academy of Management, Chicago, 1986).

32. D. L. Nelson and J. C. Quick, "Professional Women: Are Distress and Disease Inevitable?" *Academy of Management Review* 10 (1985): 206-18.

33. A. P. Brief, R. S. Schuler, and M. Van Sell, Chapter 7, "Working Women and Stress," in *Managing Job Stress* (Boston: Little, Brown, 1981).

34. T. D. Jick and L. F. Mitz, "Sex Differences in Work Stress," *Academy of Management Review* 10 (1985): 408-20.

35. H. F. Ezell, C. A. Odewahn, and J. D. Sherman, "The Effects of Having Been Supervised by a Woman on Perceptions of Female Managerial Competence," *Personnel Psychology* 34 (1981): 291-99.

36. Bartol and Butterfield, "Sex Effects in Evaluating Leaders"; B. Rosen and T. H. Jerdee, "The Influence of Sex-Role Stereotypes on Evaluations of Male and Female Supervisory Behavior," *Journal of Applied Psychology* 57 (1973): 44-48; M. B. Jacobson and J. Effertz, "Sex Roles and Leadership: Perceptions of the Leaders and the Led," *Organizational Behavior and Human Performance* 12 (1974): 383-96; R. N. Osborn and W. M. Vicars, "Sex Stereotypes: An Artifact in Leader Behavior and Subordinate Satisfaction Analysis?" *Academy of Management Journal* 19 (1976): 439-49; Dobbins and Platz, "Sex Differences in Leadership."

37. R. W. Rice, L. R. Bender, and A. G. Vitters, "Leader Sex, Follower Attitudes Toward Women, and Leadership Effectiveness: A Laboratory Experiment," *Organizational Behavior and Human Performance* 25 (1980): 46-78; J. Adams, R. W. Rice, and D. Instone, "Follower Attitudes Toward Women and Judgments Concerning Performance by Female and Male Leaders," *Academy of Management Journal* 27 (1984): 636-43.

38. Adams, Rice, and Instone, "Follower Attitudes Toward Women," pp. 641-42.

39. R. W. Rice, D. Instone, and J. Adams, "Leader Sex, Leader Success, and Leadership Process: Two Field Studies," *Journal of Applied Psychology* 69 (1984): 12-31; D. A. Butterfield and G. N. Powell, "Effect of Group Performance, Leader Sex, and Rater Sex on Ratings of Leader Behavior," *Organizational Behavior and Group Performance* 28 (1981): 129-41; V. F. Nieva and B. A. Gutek, Chapter 7, "Women and

Leadership," in *Women and Work: A Psychological Perspective* (New York: Praeger, 1981).

40. A. M. Morrison, R. P. White, E. Van Velsor, and the Center for Creative Leadership, Chapter 3, "Perception Is Reality: The Narrow Band of Acceptable Behavior," in *Breaking the Glass Ceiling* (Reading, MA: Addison-Wesley, 1987).

41. Bass, Chapter 3, "An Introduction to Theories and Models of Leadership," in *Stogdill's Handbook of Leadership*.

42. Bass, Chapter 5, "Traits of Leadership: A Followup to 1970," in *Stogdill's Handbook of Leadership*.

43. R. R. Blake and J. S. Mouton, *The Managerial Grid* (Houston: Gulf, 1964); R. Tannenbaum and W. H. Schmidt, "How to Choose a Leadership Pattern," *Harvard Business Review* 36, no. 2 (March/April 1958): 95-102; P. Hersey and K. H. Blanchard, *Management of Organizational Behavior: Utilizing Human Resources*, 4th ed. (Englewood Cliffs, NJ: Prentice-Hall, 1982).

44. Donnell and Hall, "Men and Women as Managers."

45. A. G. Sargent, "Prologue" and Chapter 6, "New Models of Effective Managers in the 1980's," in *The Androgynous Manager* (New York: AMACOM, 1981), p. 2.

46. S. L. Bem, "Sex Role Adaptability: One Consequence of Psychological Androgyny," *Journal of Personality and Social Psychology* 31 (1975): 634-43; J. A. Kelly and J. Worell, "New Formulations of Sex Roles and Androgyny: A Critical Review," *Journal of Consulting and Clinical Psychology* 45 (1977): 1101-15, p. 1102.

6

Getting Ahead

The Two-Career Carousel

Imagine that three of America's beloved old sitcoms were modernized to reflect the predicaments facing today's urban young professionals. In the 1980s versions, Ozzie and Harriet Nelson [*The Adventures of Ozzie and Harriet*], Ward and June Cleaver [*Leave It to Beaver*], and Jim and Margaret Anderson [*Father Knows Best*] would be newly married yuppies. The wives, of course, would have careers outside the home.

Harriet would have an MBA degree and would be employed in the marketing division of a *Fortune* 500 corporation; June would have a law degree and would be an associate with a large law firm; and Margaret would be a field producer with a television news program.

Instead of hilarious situations about a casserole that burns the evening the boss is coming to dinner or tiffs with the neighbors, the new plots would deal with Ozzie's reaction to Harriet's bigger salary, June's insistence that she postpone having children until she becomes a partner in the firm, and Margaret's disruptive transfer to London.

The new reality also means extinction for one of the most enduring domestic scenes in middle-class mythology:

The big guy comes home after a hard day at the office. Exhausted, he collapses in his favorite chair. The little woman, who much earlier completed her housewifely duties and is refreshed and attentive, gives him an adoring kiss, mixes him a drink, brings him the newspaper— pipe and slippers are optional—and asks him how his day was. Sometimes, she surprises him by putting the kids to bed early and preparing a romantic, candlelight dinner for the two of them.

Fade out and flash forward. Now, they *both* are wiped out from work, although it is unlikely that they arrive at the apartment at the same time. He is probably working late on a report, and she may be flying to

Seattle on business. If they are both in town, chances are they will take a brief nap, jog or visit the health club, then eat at a trendy neighborhood restaurant—taking recreational drugs or talking shop to keep from falling asleep at the table—before heading home and crashing to Johnny Carson's monologue.

—Paul Galloway, 1985[1]

Galloway's humor conveys what may be called the old and new stereotypes of women's and men's careers. Women and men had vastly different career patterns under the old stereotype: women were homemakers and men were breadwinners. The new stereotype portrays women and men as having similar career patterns: both members of a couple "win bread" and, with the help of the baby-sitter or day-care program, also "make home" in their spare time. We know that the old stereotype is no longer appropriate, but should it be replaced with the new stereotype? Are there no longer any differences between men's and women's career patterns, or do some differences remain? If there still are sex differences in career patterns, what are they?

Unfortunately, we cannot rely upon theories of career development that have been proposed in the management literature for answers to these questions. Similar to theories of what makes for an effective manager, most theories of how individuals' careers evolve and what helps or hinders them in getting ahead in organizations have been derived from observations of men. If data on women's and men's careers had been compared, there would be some concrete basis for describing their career patterns as similar or different. Such comparisons have seldom been made, however, rendering most conclusions about sex differences in career patterns speculative rather than factual.

The overemphasis on men's careers is not as easily remedied as the overemphasis on men's management styles. Managerial behavior yields a variety of short-term results that may be measured and evaluated, enabling researchers to reach conclusions about the effectiveness of female and male managers fairly easily. Careers, on the other hand, may cover a span of over 60 years from childhood's first impressions of occupations and developing aspirations to retirement. To establish whether men and women differ in their basic career patterns, we would need to compare their career decisions, strategies, and progress over time. Such research would yield meaningful results only if the necessary data were available and if the external factors that affected individuals' careers either remained constant over the duration of careers or changed in a manner that similarly affected women and men. Neither of these conditions, however, has been met during the last 60 years.

Until the 1970s, researchers were rarely interested in women's careers, so there is little data that can be used to compare the full careers of older men and women. Even if researchers had been inclined to collect the necessary data, few women were in the ranks of management before the 1970s, rendering statistical comparison of the careers of successful women and men impractical. Furthermore, social and governmental pressures forced many organizations beginning in the late 1960s to initiate affirmative action programs. Proportions of women and men in various jobs became closely monitored rather than ignored or taken for granted as before, and corrective actions were often attempted, though they were seldom entirely successful. As a result, the forces that influenced the development of men's and women's careers changed.

Thus it has been nearly impossible in recent years for anyone to discover whether women's and men's careers are best described by the same or by separate theories and concepts. Longitudinal studies, more difficult to conduct than studies with shorter time perspectives, are essential for reaching definitive conclusions about the patterns of women's and men's careers. The relative lack of social changes that differentially affected the sexes over the course of these studies would also contribute to the usefulness of their results. In the meantime, what is available for us to consider is a small amount of research evidence and a large amount of conjecture and speculation based on limited observations over a narrow period of time.

In this chapter, we shall review both the speculation and the facts about women's and men's careers. First, we shall examine the ways in which various theories of career development have addressed the topic of sex differences. Second, we shall examine the research evidence concerning sex differences in career development. Third, we shall identify the necessary ingredients for a model of women's and men's career development, including the societal, individual, and organizational factors that may affect career patterns. Finally, we shall examine the implications of our review for organizations in aiding their employees' pursuit of careers and for individuals in pursuing their own careers.

THEORIES OF CAREER DEVELOPMENT

Most theories of career development specify stages in individuals' careers, the ages at which individuals typically occupy the stages, and the developmental tasks associated with each stage that individuals must work through before advancing fully to the next stage. For example, Edgar Schein identified the stages of the career cycle as growth, fantasy, and exploration (age 0 to 21), entry into the world of work (16 to 25), basic training (16 to 25), full membership in early career (17 to 30), full membership in midcareer (25+), midcareer crisis (35 to 45), late career in nonleadership role (40 to retirement) or leadership role (unspecified), decline and disengagement (40 to retirement), and retirement. Schein listed general issues to be confronted and specific tasks to be completed for each stage. Douglas Hall classified career stages more simply as early career, middle career, and late career, and suggested that individuals try to satisfy different task needs and socioemotional needs in each career stage.[2]

Most theories also raise and address, even if only in passing, the question of whether or how women's careers differ from men's. Women's careers are typically depicted as vastly different, although reasons for the perceived sex differences depend on whether the theorist has been more interested in women's or men's careers. Some theorists have argued that men's and women's abilities, interests, and proper roles in society are basically different. Others have argued that the life experiences that shape women's and men's careers are basically different. Still others have argued that, while the career development of women is not fundamentally different from the career development of men, women's careers are a great deal more complex.[3]

Theories Emphasizing Men's Careers

Donald Super, author of one of the first formal theories of career development, regarded woman's role as homemaker as a biological and social necessity. He argued that women's careers, career orientations, and career motivations are fundamentally different from those of men because the woman's role as childbearer makes her the focal point of the home and gives homemaking a central place in her career. In support of this argument, he quoted Kate Meuller, author of the 1954 book *Educating Women for a Changing World*:

> Girls will be girls, or at least 90 percent of them will be girls, and the other 10 percent may find themselves in Who's Who ... The significant thing is the far more uniform and standardized pattern of feminine interests than of masculine. John may want to be a lawyer, physician, engineer, farmer, statistician, radio announcer, but Mary, nine times out of ten, can see no further than her marriage. She wants a little job that will put her immediately into the company of men.[4]

Meuller's argument was strongly rooted in gender stereotypes. The notion that being in *Who's Who* and being female are incompatible was a direct reflection of gender stereotypes. Meuller distinguished between masculine and feminine interests rather than the interests of boys and girls, failing to separate the person from the gender stereotype. The statement that girls want a "little" job to place themselves in the company of marriageable men trivializes their occupational aspirations and is not supported by research.

Super proposed four career patterns for men and seven career patterns for women. The career patterns for men were (a) *stable*, life-long occupation begun immediately after schooling; (b) *conventional*, a progression from initial to trial to stable employment; (c) *unstable*, failure to establish stable employment at first attempt and change to a career in which the individual may or may not permanently establish himself; and (d) *multiple-trial*, frequent change of employment with no one type sufficiently prolonged to justify calling the person established in a career. The career patterns for women included (a) *stable homemaking*, marriage at the completion of schooling or shortly thereafter with no significant work experience; (b) *conventional*, marriage and full-time homemaking ends what starts as the conventional career pattern for men; (c) *stable working*, work as the life career in lieu of marriage (followed by Meuller's 10% of women); (d) *double-track*, continuing to work after marriage—a "double career"; (e) *interrupted*, a sequence of working, homemaking, and then working while or instead of homemaking; (f) *unstable*, irregular switching between working and homemaking; and (g) *multiple-trial*, a pattern of unrelated jobs as for men.

Super assumed that the same theory of career development was applicable to both sexes when modified by childbearing and homemaking tasks for women. He deserves some credit for recognizing that women as well as men had careers outside the home, at a time when the media conveyed an image of women as exclusiv ly homemakers. He also deserves credit for acknowledging that he did not have data on women's careers and was, therefore, speculating. He reflected the prevailing bias of his times, however, a bias that many people still hold, that women's central role as homemaker is based on a biological fact. Although society prescribed this role for women for a long time, no biological fact stops the husband from being a full-time homemaker and the wife from pursuing a full-time career. Thus Super's theory of the difference between women's and men's careers was primarily based on gender stereotypes.

Other models of career development proposed at about the same time conveyed a similar bias. For example, in investigating individuals' occupational choices, Eli Ginzberg and his colleagues restricted their primary sample to males because

> in our society the role of work has heightened significance for the male members. This does not deny that many women have strong occupational drives, but it [the decision to study males only] was based on the assumption that for most women marriage, rather than a job, forms the center of life.

Sons within upper-middle-class families who were either Protestant or Catholic, had both parents alive and living together, and judged to be free of any physical, emotional, or intellectual handicap were chosen to be interviewed for the study, because such boys were felt to have minimum constraints on their occupational choices. To offer some comparison with the males, ten female college students were also interviewed. These were hardly representative samples of either males or females.[5]

Nonetheless, the researchers concluded that their assumptions about women's versus men's career interests were supported by their study. The males considered marriage an eventuality that did not affect their choice of occupation. In contrast, the females were reported not to have any clear picture of the type of life they would lead because it would be largely determined by whether they married, when they married, whom they married, when they had children and how many, and the attitudes of their husbands toward their working.

Three types of female career patterns were identified: work-oriented, marriage-oriented, and a combination of work and marriage in which marriage dominated although individuals also had some desire to express themselves through work. In contrast, males were depicted as solely work-oriented. As Super had done, Ginzberg et al. concluded that the career development process of women and men was equivalent except that marriage was more important than work in the career planning of most women.

More recent theories of career development have not been as obvious in their endorsement of gender stereotypes. Nevertheless, many allegedly general theories of career development have still been consciously or unconsciously based on data about men's career patterns, with women's career patterns treated as special cases to which theories should be carefully applied. For example, Schein's discussion of the similarity or difference between men's and women's careers was limited to one sentence: "Since much of the research has been done on men, there is likely to be some male-oriented bias in the stages and crises which have been identified." He then identified what were first called "stages and tasks of the (male) biosocial cycle" and then simply "stages and tasks of the biosocial cycle." The only other specific mention women received was as contributing to the increase in dual-career families through their increased participation in the work force, with dual-career issues seen as calling for some form of accommodation by one or both job holders. We shall discuss these issues at length later in the chapter.[6]

Daniel Levinson, in *The Seasons of a Man's Life*, presented a theory of adult development that received considerable attention in the 1970s. He decided to base his theory-building effort on in-depth interviews with a sample of 40 men, describing his rationale for including only men as follows:

> Ultimately, it is essential to study the adult development of both genders if we are to understand either. The challenge of development is at least as great for women as for men. . . . Despite my strong desire to include women, I decided finally against it. A study of twenty men and twenty women would do justice to neither group. The differences between women and men are sufficiently great so that they would have to become a major focus of analysis. . . . In all candor, however, I must admit to a more personal reason for the choice: I chose men partly because I wanted so deeply to understand my own adult development.[7]

Hence the familiar bias of a male researcher toward examining only men's careers, but this time justified for personal reasons.

Theories Emphasizing Women's Careers

In contrast, some career theorists, primarily seeking to understand the careers of women, have paid more attention to the effects of such factors as socialization experiences and the sex segregation of occupations. They have not agreed among themselves as to whether the same theory can adequately describe both men's and women's careers or whether separate theories are needed. They have generally included the same types of variables in their theories, however.

Helen Astin, for example, assumed that work motivation was the same for men and women but that they make different career choices, including whether to work at all, because of their different socialization experiences and the opportunities that are made available to them. Socialization experiences differ as described in Chapter 2. Opportunities were seen as differing according to sex due to such factors as the sex segregation of occupations and discriminatory hiring decisions.[8]

In Astin's model, socialization experiences and opportunity combine to shape individuals' work expectations, or their perceptions of what types of work are accessible and can best satisfy their needs. Expectations in turn contribute to shaping career choices. If socialization experiences, workplace opportunities, and perceptions of workplace opportunities were to become equal for girls and boys, sex differences in work expectations and thus career choices would disappear. The model could account for how reduced discrimination against women in some male-dominated professions has led their expectations for progressing in these professions to be greater than before and their choices to pursue careers in the professions to be more frequent. Astin's model was criticized by some scholars for not being well-grounded in previous research, and revisions in its relationships between major variables were recommended. The model was generally applauded, however, as a major step forward in understanding women's careers—by others particularly concerned with women's careers. It has received little attention from researchers who have been more concerned with men's careers.

Barbara Gutek and Laurie Larwood took a different approach, arguing that a theory of women's career development must be separate from theories of men's career development:

> At one time it was believed that if women's careers were ever found to be important, the theories and research into men's careers would undoubtedly fit them. It is important to realize, however, that the modal pattern of men's careers is unlikely ever to provide a good fit for the modal pattern of women's careers. This is not to say that women's career achievements are likely to be any less than those of men or that some women do not fit the male model. Nonetheless, women on the whole face a somewhat different set of opportunities and problems that those seen by most men.[9]

According to Gutek and Larwood, women's careers are different and likely to remain different from men's careers for several reasons. Men and women have different expectations regarding the appropriateness of jobs for them. Women are faced with more constraints in the workplace, particularly the use of gender stereotypes in hiring and promotion decisions and in performance evaluations. Family life is often treated as an external irrelevancy in models of men's careers, whereas it is an important consideration in women's careers. Husbands and wives are seen as not accommodating themselves to each other's careers to the same extent, with wives generally more willing to move or otherwise adapt themselves to their husbands' careers than vice versa. Also, as commonly defined by individuals, the mother role requires more time and effort than the father role. By way of comparison, Astin's model explicitly included differential expectations and constraints/opportunities but not family or parental roles.

Gutek and Larwood addressed the need for a theory of women's career development, perhaps for similar reasons as Levinson but also because of the increased status of women in the workplace. While not proposing a formal theory, they identified five elements that it should possess: career preparation, opportunities available, marriage, pregnancy and children, and timing. The situation seen as most likely to lead to career success is one in which the woman is prepared in adolescence to anticipate a career, finds that opportunities necessary for her career are available, embarks on her career at the same age as a man, remains committed to working whether or not she marries or has children, and returns to her career as rapidly as possible if she has children. The traditional situation for women was seen as the exact opposite. In this situation, the adolescent does not anticipate a career, sees few interesting career possibilities available, and psychologically prepares for being a housewife. If she holds a job at the time of marriage, it is one that is started and ended easily and requires little training. She leaves the job after marriage if her husband's income is sufficient, or after pregnancy for as long as economically possible. If she reenters the work force, it is when she is older and is at a disadvantage because of both her age and her lack of prior job experience.

In summary, we have seen a shift away from a reliance on gender stereotypes in theories of career development. Super and Ginzberg presented stereotypes as facts. In the case of Super, the "fact" that women's careers were centered on homemaking was based on his general observations and opinions. In the case of Ginzberg, the "fact" that most women placed marriage before career was initially stated as an assumption and then as supported by interviews with only ten college women. Thus this aspect of both Super's and Ginzberg's theories was based more on gender stereotypes than on actual data about women's and men's careers. Later theorists have not reached the same stereotypical conclusions about women's and men's careers. When they have proposed any sex difference in career patterns at all, they have referred to the effects of such factors as differential socialization experiences, family variables, and workplace opportunities rather than as gender stereotypes. Supposedly general theories of career development such as Schein's, however, still have been primarily based on observations of men.

There is little common ground among the theorists reviewed except that they would agree that men's and women's career patterns tend to be strikingly different. Early theorists such as Super and Ginzberg defended this proposition by citing women's natural inclination toward homemaking as their primary vocation. Later theorists such as Astin defended the same proposition by citing a difference in the social forces and opportunities that shape women's and men's careers. A comprehensive theory that explains both women's and men's career development has yet to be proposed and fully accepted.

THE RESEARCH EVIDENCE

The limited research evidence available supports the proposition that women's and men's career patterns are different. For example, separate studies have found that women managers tend to receive more promotions and larger merit increases but not advance as far in the organizational hierarchy as their male counterparts.[10]

The difference in women's and men's career patterns is accounted for in part by their basic career plans and tactics. One study found that female and male managers differed in the advice they would give to a young person starting a career. This advice was assumed to be based on individuals' experiences in planning their own careers and what they had seen as working well for others whom they felt were successful. Men tended to adopt a "plan ahead" approach in their advice, advocating the early development of skills in anticipation of future career needs. In contrast, women tended to emphasize the importance of proving one's ability by doing a good job. Women's advice to others could be summarized in Horatio Alger-like terms: "Work hard and someday you will be rewarded for your efforts."[11]

Another study found that female and male managers differed somewhat in the tactics that they regarded as most important in attaining career advancements. The most striking sex difference was that women saw tactics involving sex role as more important than men. These included close contacts with female personnel, appearing as feminine as possible, learning from male models, and learning from female models. These results suggested that women were more conscious of factors related to their sex and traditional sex roles than men. This consciousness, however, did not appear to have affected their career success to date.[12]

Other research has shown that some career tactics, particularly having a mentor, have been more available to and used by men than women. Mentors play important developmental roles for individuals:

Mentors provide young adults with career-enhancing functions, such as sponsorship, coaching, facilitating exposure and visibility, and offering challenging work or protection, all of which help the younger person to establish a role in the organization, learn the ropes, and prepare for advancement. In the psychosocial sphere, the mentor offers role modeling, counseling, confirmation, and friendship, which help the young adult to develop a sense of professional identity and competence.[13]

Most corporate presidents, who have been primarily males, have had mentors who were critical to their success. Levinson's theory of career development portrayed young men as seeking a mentor early in their careers and seeking to play the mentor role for younger men later in their careers. Mentorship is equally important for the career success of women. Most top female executives have also had mentors who were vital to their success. Women, however, have had more difficulty in finding suitable mentors than men because of the limited number of highly placed, older female managers. Also, mentors have less of an impact on women who begin their careers later in life after raising children than on women who begin their careers at the same time as men.[14]

The difference in women's and men's career patterns is also caused by the actions of their coworkers and organizations. We have previously reviewed the effects of gender stereotyping, the relative proportions of women and men in groups, and sex discrimination in initial hiring decisions on the treatment of individuals. Sex discrimination also has been found in promotion decisions and in the setting of wage levels by organizations. Such research demonstrates that individuals' career patterns are influenced by the actions of others, not merely their own.

There is also persuasive evidence, however, that, as Galloway's "The Two-Career Carousel" suggests, sex differences in career patterns are diminishing. Laurie Larwood and Urs Gattiker examined age differences as well as sex differences in the career paths of successful men and women. "Successful" individuals were selected by personnel officers in 17 major corporations, with the stipulation that approximately equal numbers of women and men, line and staff personnel, and younger (under age 40) and older individuals were to be chosen. The career patterns of younger women, younger men, older women, and older men were then compared.[15]

The researchers hypothesized that career patterns would show the effects of social change. Women still were expected to have experienced delays in their career development relative to men due to the effects of gender stereotypes. Younger men were expected to follow essentially the same career paths as older men, but their levels of success were expected to be lower because they had not progressed as far in their careers. Women's career paths, however, were expected to be less consistent. First, older and younger women were expected to have been similarly affected by the attempts at equal opportunity by organizations that previously had been discriminating against them, but at different stages in their careers. Second, the relationship between work experience and career success was expected to be less smooth for women than for men. If organizations had moved women along quickly in response to equal opportunity regulations, the women who had been moved along may not have obtained the same background experiences as men. This would make it more difficult to describe the career path of a successful woman than that of a successful man.

Larwood and Gattiker found that their expectations were largely confirmed. For both women and men, the earlier an individual attained professional status and reached the upper level of a line department, the more likely he or she was to rise in the organization's hierarchy. The route to success, however, was more varied for women than for men. It was possible to track the progress in men's careers, showing how first jobs related to later success, but it was more difficult to describe the route to success for women.

Overall, men more often had professional status, were in line rather than staff positions, and occupied higher positions in their departments than women. This effect was primarily confined to older rather than younger individuals, however. The careers of the younger men lagged behind those of the older men in rising within their organization's hierarchy and in attaining officer or director status, whereas younger women and older women had experienced approximately the same level of success by these measures. Looking at these results another way, older women had experienced significantly less success than older men, whereas the success of younger women was not significantly different from that of younger men.

Larwood and Gattiker's study demonstrated that societal changes can affect the career development of women and men. Whether due to conscious efforts by organizations to provide equal opportunities for men and women, a reduced effect of gender stereotypes over time, or a change in the career orientation or qualifications of younger women versus older women, the differences between the career paths of younger women and younger men were less than those between the career paths of older women and older men.

TOWARD A GENERAL THEORY OF
CAREER DEVELOPMENT

In order to understand the current nature of women's and men's careers, we need a theory that can account for the ways in which women's and men's career patterns are similar, different, and becoming more alike. A career pattern may be considered the cumulative result of the positions held by an individual, including nonwork activities, and the transitions made from one position to another. If there were sex differences in career patterns, we would expect to find them in the effects of various factors on the positions held and transitions made by men and women. As a means of working toward a theory of career development, let's more closely examine the factors that appear likely to influence the shape of individuals' career patterns. Figure 6.1 presents the factors to be considered.

Figure 6.1 depicts individuals and organizations as influenced by societal factors, as influencing each other, and as combining to influence career patterns. Career patterns are most determined by the actions of individuals about which career opportunities to pursue and how to prepare themselves for these opportunities, and by the decisions of organizations about them. Career patterns are influenced indirectly by organizational practices and by personal and family factors, which in turn are influenced by societal factors. Each of these types of factors may contribute to or alleviate a sex difference in career patterns. The factors are also likely to differ in the stage of career at which they have the greatest influence. For example, occupational aspirations developed during adolescence are likely to have their greatest effect at the time of initial entry to the workplace, with individuals' work experiences having a greater effect on later transitions. Similarly, the career strategy of relying on a mentor is more beneficial for individuals in the early and middle stages of their careers than in later stages, when their early mentors have typically moved out of the organization.

You have probably noticed that Figure 6.1 suggests the ingredients

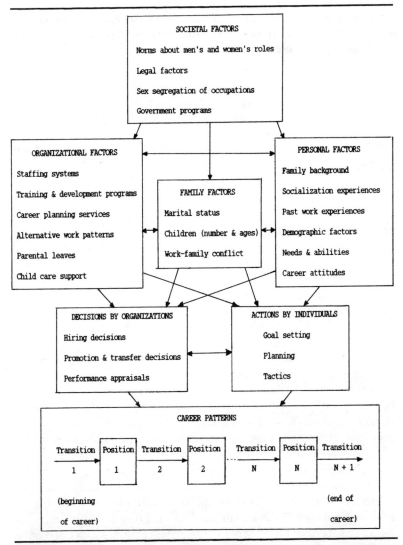

Figure 6.1   A General Model of Career Development

and structure of a general model of career development. The figure displays the bias that the similarities and differences between women's and men's careers may be captured by the same model. Actually, whether a single model or separate models are used to describe women's and men's careers does not seem that important an issue. What is more important is that further attempts be made to arrive at and test such models.

FACTORS THAT INFLUENCE
CAREER PATTERNS

Societal Factors

As we have discussed in previous chapters, *societal norms* regarding women's and men's proper roles may influence the decisions women and men make about whether to work and, if so, in what capacity. Traditional norms say that the proper place for men is at work and for women at home. As behavior has changed in recent years, however, belief in these norms has sharply diminished. Nonetheless, traditional norms still have an influence on some individuals. We might expect individuals who profess a greater belief in traditional norms to display more of a sex difference in career patterns than those who profess less belief in the norms.

Legal factors, that is, laws, the extent to which they are enforced, and the nature of judicial decisions concerning them, may also affect career patterns. Discrimination against women was once legislated as necessary to "protect" their childbearing and maternal functions. Federal laws such as the Equal Pay Act, Civil Rights Act, and executive orders, however, now prohibit discrimination in employment under federal contracts and on the part of the federal government itself as an employer. Despite the existence of these laws, presidential administrations have varied in the extent to which they have sought to enforce them. States also have differed in the extent to which they have enacted such laws and enforced them. Through their decisions on particular cases brought before them, federal and state courts have worked at articulating and refining the situations to which the laws may properly be applied. Judicial decisions have been made regarding such matters as sex differences in pay for the same job, the use of hiring and promotion quotas for work organizations or admissions quotas for schools, the permissibility of forcing mothers to take unpaid leaves for pregnancy or allowing them to have paid leaves, and the necessity of offering comparable leaves to fathers. These legal factors affect organizational hiring and promotion practices and employee benefits, thereby affecting the career patterns both of employees and of unhired applicants. We shall discuss legal factors further in the next chapter.[16]

The *sex segregation of occupations*, discussed in detail in Chapter 3, influences individuals' career patterns by sending a message about which occupations are more appropriate for males and which are more appropriate for females. It particularly affects the occupational aspirations and expectations of adolescent girls and boys and their initial decisions to pursue careers in some occupations and not others. It may also affect men and women when they later decide to change occupations.

Government programs may indirectly affect individuals' career actions and organizational practices. For example, money and other resources provided by federal or state governments for child care could affect parents' decisions about careers and the level of organizations' efforts to satisfy the child care needs of their employees.

Organizational Practices

There are four types of organizational practices that may influence individuals' career patterns. One type consists of the programs and techniques that organizations use to meet their own staffing needs, such as human resource forecasting, succession planning, and job posting. A second type consists of the training and development programs that organizations offer to or mandate for employees. A third type consists of the career planning services that organizations provide for individuals, such as personal career counseling and career planning workshops. Other organizational practices such as the availability of alternative work patterns and child care support also affect how individuals manage their careers.

Organizations use several types of *staffing systems* to assist them in making personnel decisions and in managing their employees' careers. These systems include promotion and transfer policies, standard operating procedures, human resource forecasting and planning, succession planning, job matching, job posting, and mentoring programs. Affirmative action programs, to be discussed at length in the next chapter, also influence staffing decisions. Sex discrimination that occurred as a result of the presence or absence of any of these systems in organizations would be likely to contribute to a sex difference in individuals' career patterns. For example, if an organization did not have a job posting or mentoring program and job openings were filled with mostly male employees who were actively promoted by their mentors, then the lack of such programs would give male employees an advantage over female employees in pursuing their careers.[17]

Organizations influence individuals' career patterns through the *training and development programs* that they encourage or require their employees to take. The primary goal of these programs for organizations is to have fully effective employees at all levels. Well-run programs, however, also give individuals the opportunity to acquire the skills necessary for career success.

These programs could contribute to a sex difference in career patterns if men and women were systematically diagnosed to have different developmental needs and tended to go through different programs as a result, or if men and women were deliberately segregated in such programs. Some writers have argued that women and men have different skills and attitudes toward the managerial role and therefore require different management development activities. Our review has suggested the opposite, particularly for men and women who are already in management positions. Others have argued that women need to be separated from men in training activities to learn to be assertive rather than passive and to acquire other necessary management skills. The counterargument is that women ultimately must learn to deal with men effectively and gain little by being separated from them in training and development activities. Both sexes could benefit from training programs that alert them to the dangers of gender stereotyping; with men and women present during such training, the limitations of both traditional sex roles may be more easily discussed. Any training and development programs to which women and men are assigned at different rates, whether because of gender stereotyping or deliberate segregation, or that reinforce stereotypical roles, may contribute to a sex difference in career patterns.[18]

Organizations also affect career patterns through the *career planning services* they offer. Although individuals bear the final responsibility for developing their own career goals and plans, organizations can provide them with necessary information and resources. Four types of career planning activities have been identified: individual activities, counselor-client activities, boss as counselor or coach, and group activities. For example, organizations can provide self-help materials for individuals to use in their personal career planning, or at least suggest materials that would be helpful. They also may refer individuals seeking career advice to outside counselors or provide such counseling themselves. Supervisors may assist subordinates by providing them with feedback, suggestions for improvement, and information on career opportunities. Finally, organizations can provide the opportunity for individuals to generate information about themselves by going through assessment centers and career planning workshops. These services could contribute to a sex difference in career patterns if they were not made equally available to women and men. On the other hand, not offering these services to employees could maintain a sex difference in career patterns that otherwise would be reduced.[19]

Other organizational practices also affect individuals' career patterns by the ways in which they help or hinder employees to meet both their work and their family needs. For example, they may offer *alternative work patterns* such as job sharing, flexitime, flexiplace (or telecommuting), and part-time work. *Parental leaves* at the time of childbirth can help couples to adjust successfully to new responsibilities without one parent having to leave the work force. Counseling services for employees to deal with dual-career issues may assist employees in their resolution of work and family conflicts.[20]

Organizations also may provide *child care support* such as on-site day-care centers, day-care facilities operated by a consortium of organizations in the area, contractual arrangements with community-based day-care centers or individual providers to care for employees' children, referral services, and vouchers to be applied to the costs of day care. In 1985, about 2500 companies were assisting employees with their child care needs. This figure was up from 600 companies in 1982. Most organizations, however, had taken little or no action and were skeptical about the economic benefits. They were more concerned with the potential problems, such as costs, insurance arrangements, and obligations, than with the potential advantages of making themselves more attractive employers and decreasing the absenteeism, tardiness, and turnover that may result from poor child care arrangements. By making options for child care assistance available, organizations can help themselves while helping parents to pursue their desired careers.[21]

These practices give employees more flexibility in planning their careers by removing or alleviating constraints that would otherwise be placed on their careers by organizations. Given that women tend to carry the primary burden of household activities, the lack of such practices maintains a sex difference in career patterns.

Personal Factors

There are two types of individual factors that could affect individuals' actions and organizations' decisions. One type consists of personal factors pertaining to the individual when considered by him- or herself. A second type consists of family factors pertaining to the individual when considered as a member of a family unit. We shall discuss personal factors first.

Family background may affect individuals' career patterns by influencing their career-related attitudes and actions. For example, one study examined the effect that schooling and family economic status had on the attitudes of successful women. Women in this group who came from economically and educationally disadvantaged households were more likely to see themselves as in control of their lives (i.e., have an internal "locus of control"), were less likely to be reward-oriented, and felt a greater separation between themselves and their early support system than those with more middle-class backgrounds. Locus of control is likely to affect the individual's confidence in making career decisions, while being less concerned with rewards is likely to affect the kinds of career choices that are made.[22]

Another effect on career patterns may come from whether an individual's parents played traditional or nontraditional roles. We might expect the influence to be "like father and mother, like son and daughter." Men are expected to work no matter what the family background; however, career patterns could differ between men whose fathers worked in nontraditional versus male-dominated occupations. Women whose mothers did not work or worked in a female-dominated occupation might have different career patterns than woman whose mothers worked in male-dominated occupations.

The potential influence of *socialization experiences* was described in Chapter 2. These experiences are shaped by the family and also by the educational system and mass media. Their influence is most likely to be seen in the occupational aspirations and expectations of adolescents and in early career choices.

Past work experiences often differ according to sex. Women tend to have careers that begin later and are interrupted more often than men, although these differences are diminishing. Past work experiences have a strong influence on individuals' present and future career success. For example, a study distinguished between plateaued and nonplateaued managers (over forty years old with less than seven years in their present positions). The study further divided the plateaued managers into a "deadwood" group (ineffective plateaus) and a "solid citizens" group (effective plateaus) according to their recent salary increases. There were clear-cut differences between the prior work experiences of individuals in the three groups.[23]

What happens to individuals in their first job positions can have a particularly powerful effect on their later career success. If, for example, women were initially placed in less challenging jobs or had less contact with their first supervisors than men as some studies have suggested, they would be expected to achieve lower career success. Larwood and Gattiker, however, concluded that the effect of first job assignments on career success is weaker for women than for men due to changes in the treatment of women by organizations prompted by societal factors.[24]

Demographic factors such as age, education, and race also affect individuals' career patterns. A study of the career patterns of women over age 30 found that those between 30 and 35 years of age who were college graduates were the most likely to have uninterrupted career patterns. Another study found that education had a similar positive effect on the level achieved in the same organization for women and men, but that age had a more positive effect for men than for women. The latter finding agreed with Larwood and Gattiker's observation that age has the weaker effect on women's career patterns. Race also has been shown in various studies to influence career patterns.[25]

Individuals' *needs and abilities* also affect their career patterns. As discussed in Chapter 5, more successful managers tend to differ in motivational needs from less successful managers, and entrepreneurs tend to differ in needs from those of the general population. Individuals' abilities to perform well at their jobs have a considerable influence on their career success. Few general sex differences in needs and abilities have been found, however.

Career attitudes also affect the kinds of actions that individuals take to pursue their careers. We have already mentioned several types of career attitudes. For example, individuals differ in their occupational aspirations and expectations developed prior to working and in their commitment to work, career, and their present organizations once they are working. They also vary in their attitudes about how their careers are progressing. Attitudes such as fear of stagnation (the extent to which individuals are unwilling to accept career plateauing) and career impatience (the extent to which individuals are unwilling to be patient with their career progress) differ according to the career pattern followed. Individuals differ in the extent to which they are satisfied with various aspects of their present jobs, such as achievement, responsibility, recognition, salary, supervisor, and coworkers.[26]

Career attitudes may be influenced by an individual's family situation. They also may be influenced by other personal factors as socialization experiences, family background, education, and past work experiences. Finally, they may be affected by societal factors such as norms about male and female roles and the sex segregation of occupations.

Family Factors

If everyone who worked was single and childless or had a spouse who did not work and assumed all family responsibilities, there would be little reason to include factors such as *marital status* and *children* as influences on career patterns. Employed individuals would be free to pursue their careers without having to worry about homemaking or child-rearing activities. As the opening passage of the chapter suggests, however, this is hardly the case. In 1968, 45% of married couples had two earners and 45% had only the husband as breadwinner. By 1980, over half of all married couples had two earners and less than a third had only the husband bringing home a paycheck. These trends have continued, and the vast majority of married couples now have two earners. Also, even though couples now delay when they have children and have fewer children than in past years, most couples still become parents eventually.

Whether members of dual-career couples or not, men and women theoretically need not differ in their career patterns due to family concerns. (The terms *dual-earner couple* and *dual-career couple* will be used interchangeably for convenience, although the latter term typically implies a greater commitment to career by both members than the former term.) Sex differences, however, exist in the effect of family factors on career patterns. Women typically handle the bulk of family responsibilities, even when both members of the couple have full-time jobs. Although husbands in dual-career couples are more involved in household activities than husbands in the past, wives still bear the primary responsibility for most dual-career households.

As a result, women often are more constrained by family responsibilities in pursuing their careers than men. One effect of this constraint is that women are more likely to interrupt their careers to raise children than men. When there are no children, the career paths of husbands and wives are more likely to stay parallel. On the other hand, except for men in their first marriages who began their careers at the same time as their wives, few men see marriage or family as even potential constraints on their career commitment or productivity. Remarried men are usually older and more established in their careers than their wives and see little impact of their wives' careers on their own.[27]

Of course, not everyone who works is a member of a couple or family. Some women feel they must choose between pursuing a career and having a family, and they choose the career. As mentioned in Chapter 5, female managers are more likely to be single, separated, or divorced and less likely to have children than male managers. This could be because married male managers are more likely to have a stay-at-home spouse than married female managers. When married, female executives still handle more of the household chores and child-rearing activities than their spouses. Thus, in order to apply themselves fully to their careers and compete with male managers on more equal terms, many successful female managers may avoid marriage or get out of it once they are in it.[28]

This discussion points out the potential for *work-family conflict* for married or cohabiting individuals. Three types of conflict can occur. *Time-based conflict,* the first type, results from the limited time that is available to handle both work and family roles. Time spent working generally cannot be devoted to family activities and vice versa. Parents experience more time-based conflict than nonparents, parents of younger children (who are particularly demanding) more than parents of older children, and parents of large families more than parents of small families. Also, men who are married to managerial/professional women experience more of this conflict than those who are married to nonmanagerial/nonprofessional women, probably because they are expected to handle a greater share of the family responsibilities than they would otherwise, even though their wives still bear the primary burden of such responsibilities.[29]

Strain-based conflict, the second type of work-family conflict, results when strain in one role "spills over" into the other role. Family strains could decrease performance at work and thereby negatively affect career success. On the other hand, strain at work could also affect one's behavior as a parent or spouse. This type of conflict occurs in married couples most when the husband and wife disagree about their responsibility for family roles or about the wife's employment status. Working women who have husbands with nontraditional attitudes are less affected by it.

Behavior-based conflict, the third type of work-family conflict, occurs when incompatible behaviors are required for work and family roles, for example, aggressiveness and objectivity at work and warmth and nurturance at home. An individual has to be able to "shift gears" from one role to another to avoid this type of conflict. Managers who are carrying out the masculine stereotype at work, whether female or male, may feel caught between the emotional detachment exhibited at work and the openness expected at home.

Family factors are unlikely to operate to the same extent at all career stages, because the needs of the family and the family-related needs of individuals vary over the life cycle. For example, some writers have concluded that men in midcareer are most likely to turn to their family lives and question their earlier preoccupation with work. Family factors are likely to operate to some extent at all stages of an individual's career, however, when that individual is a member of a family unit.

IMPLICATIONS FOR MANAGEMENT

Sex differences in career patterns are diminishing, but still remain to some extent. The proposed model of career development suggests that career patterns are affected by a combination of societal, organizational, and individual factors. In this section, we shall consider what organizations can do to minimize their contribution to a sex difference in career patterns and what individuals can do to help themselves gain career satisfaction.

What Organizations Can Do

Organizations make several types of *decisions about individuals* during their careers, including hiring decisions, salary increase decisions, disciplinary decisions, promotion decisions, and transfer decisions. The need for such decisions leads organizations to evaluate individuals' recent performance and to estimate their potential performance frequently. Any sex bias that enters into evaluations of individuals could influence organizational decisions about them and contribute to a sex difference in career patterns.

In Chapter 3, we concluded that the less information that organizational representatives have about applicants, the more likely they are to exhibit a sex bias in their evaluations. By the same reasoning, we may also conclude that the greatest potential for sex bias in evaluations occurs at the time of hiring, when the least is known about individuals, and that there is less sex bias in the evaluations of individuals who are already employed by organizations. Recent research on sex bias in performance appraisals supports this reasoning. Although earlier laboratory studies suggested that sex effects in performance appraisals were considerable, the amount of sex bias in the performance appraisals of actual management employees is low when compared to other types of bias. For example, individuals are likely to evaluate more favorably others whom they perceive as similar to themselves. This perception could contribute to sex bias, but not necessarily.[30]

Decisions to fill position vacancies by promoting or transferring insiders rather than by hiring outsiders may be based on several types of information about applicants, including past work experiences, performance appraisals, interviews, and assessment center results. The use of past work experiences could introduce a sex bias if individuals with uninterrupted work careers were favored over those with interrupted careers. Performance appraisals and interviews could be influenced by sex bias, although the more that is known about candidates, the lower the likelihood of sex bias. Assessment centers do not appear to contribute to sex bias in decisions to fill open positions, as assessment center ratings appear similarly to predict the career success of men and women. These decisions could also vary according to sex if organizational factors such as characteristics of the decision maker(s), promotion policies, and techniques for identifying candidates contributed to differential treatment of female and male candidates.[31]

By paying attention to the *organizational practices* specified in the model, organizations contribute to a reduced sex difference in career patterns while meeting their own staffing needs. For example, they should offer training and development programs that are directly connected to individuals' developmental needs. Although men and women in an organization could be diagnosed to have different developmental needs on the average, they should be assigned to training programs according to their needs rather than their sex.

Organizations also may offer a variety of career planning services to individuals, ranging from personal counseling or referrals for outside counseling to career planning workshops. Managers may provide career assistance to their subordinates by giving them accurate appraisals of their performance and future potential and by actively promoting them within the organization. Staffing systems may be designed to facilitate individuals' access to job openings in the organization regardless of their sex. Organizational practices also may help individuals to reduce their levels of work/family conflict. The use of alternative work patterns and addressing of the needs of parents would provide individuals with more freedom to pursue their careers. Organizations would benefit from reduced absenteeism and turnover and more satisfied employees.

In summary, organizations can contribute to the elimination of a sex difference in career patterns by refraining from sex bias in the decisions they make about individuals, by helping employees with setting and achieving career goals, and by providing the opportunity for women and men to pursue careers to equal satisfaction. Programs such as job posting and mentoring programs reduce the advantage that men have had over women in the pursuit of careers. Programs such as career planning services and training and development programs help both male and female employees to set career goals and to achieve them. Programs such as child care support and alternative work patterns lighten the burden placed on the adult female in most families and also contribute to a reduced difference between women's and men's careers.

What Individuals Can Do

Individuals enhance their careers through the *career actions* that they take as well as the ways in which they deal with personal and family factors. Career actions may take several forms, beginning with the establishing of career goals by individuals. *Goal setting* is not required for individuals to progress in their careers, but it can help. Goal setting is consistently linked with effectiveness in occupational choice. In order to set career goals successfully, however, individuals need either external support or strong self-esteem. Due to their different socialization experiences, women have experienced less external support and lower self-esteem and thereby have been reinforced less for goal setting than men.[32]

Goal setting is not effective unless it is accompanied by *career planning*. Career planning may range from the more proactive strategy of acquiring skills seen as necessary for later career progress early in one's career to the more passive strategy of working hard and hoping to be rewarded through later career progress. The proactive strategy is recommended. Gutek and Larwood's model of women's career development suggests strategies taken for granted by most men that may specifically enhance women's careers. When women embark on a work career without delay and do not let marriage or children interrupt it, they are able to compete on more equal terms with men. Unless organizations change their views of what makes for a desirable career pattern, individuals will achieve the greatest career benefits from having an uninterrupted career pattern and from beginning full-time work as soon as possible.[33]

Individuals contribute to their own career success by adopting *career tactics* that are carefully thought out and well timed. We have already discussed the benefits of having a mentor. Men and women also may further their careers by seeking membership in informal networks. By becoming members of key informal groups, individuals enter a world of "ties of loyalties and of dependence, favors granted and owed, mutual benefit, protection, . . . promises that must be kept if you want to be operative in the future, [and] connections with people who already have influence."[34] Such membership is often beneficial to career advancement.

These actions represent a more active stance taken toward one's career than simply relying on one's own competence. They emphasize the development of opportunities through the informal system rather than waiting for them to develop through the formal system. They have relatively little precedent for women. Informal networks traditionally have been called "old boy networks," reflecting the fact that men dominate them, and have accepted few women. Until recently, there haven't been enough women managers to have separate "old girl" networks. As more women enter management ranks, however, mixed-sex and "old girl" networks are becoming more prevalent. For the same reason, women now have more opportunities to have mentors.[35]

The *personal factors* included in the model suggest ways in which individuals can promote their own career success while reducing the sex difference in career patterns. Although most of the personal factors listed are beyond their control, individuals may take some steps during adolescence to prepare themselves for their careers. For example, they can obtain information about the careers available, participate in activities that develop skills and abilities that may be useful in the workplace, and gain the necessary education for the occupations in which they are interested. Gaining a college degree remains a valuable way to enhance one's career. Once in their careers, individuals may take advantage of the training and development programs and career planning services that their organizations offer.

Individuals can address *family factors* by reaching accommodations with other family members that enable them to satisfy both their career and family needs. Four categories of dual-career couples have been identified: superordinate partners, synchronized partners, synthetic partners, and severed partners. *Superordinate partners* value both work and family activities and set the goal of achieving satisfaction in both domains for both partners. They may not achieve spectacular success in their careers, because they do not devote their energies solely to career success, but they feel considerable satisfaction with their family lives and try to build a sense of interdependence among family members. They are typically androgynous people to whom careers are important but not the only interest in life.[36]

Synchronized partners help each other to achieve complementary individual goals. For example, one spouse may be interested primarily in career and less in family affairs while the other spouse is primarily interested in family and less in career pursuits. Couples possessing traditional sex role identities, with the work-oriented man being more masculine and the family-oriented woman being more feminine, fit into this category. The combination of a family-oriented, feminine man and a career-oriented, masculine woman or other combinations, however, are also possible.

Synthetic partners have relationships in which one or both members feel that they have compromised their aspirations. For example, the wife may feel that she has to subordinate her career to her husband's career to carry out family responsibilities, or the husband may feel that he has to suppress his involvement in his career to devote more of himself to the family. Such couples frequently experience frustrations and survive only through makeshift agreements or periodic resolution of tensions. The quality of life in their families, however, is medium at best.

Severed partners possess highly incompatible values, such as a nontraditional woman committed to her career and not her family married to a traditional man with high family and low career involvement who expects his wife also to be strongly committed to family. Such couples are the most contentious and require one member to make a considerable sacrifice in personal goals to preserve the relationship. The majority of dual-career couples may consist of synchronized and synthetic partners, but superordinate partners may achieve the greatest satisfaction in all spheres of life.

There is more to life than work. Ultimately, individuals most help themselves by keeping a balance between career, family, and other interests in their lives. Obsession with getting ahead can lead to type A behavior and its accompanying symptoms of ill health. On the other hand, giving little thought to career issues can lead to lack of achievement and a resulting sense of anger, frustration, or disappointment. When individuals achieve a sense of balance in their lives, they will be able to reject old and new stereotypes and shape their own, more fulfilling life patterns.

NOTES

1. "The Woes of Yuppie Love and Marraige," by Paul Galloway. *Chicago Tribune*, March 26, 1985. © 1985, Chicago Tribune Company, all rights reserved, used by permission.

2. E. H. Schein, Chapter 4, "The Stages and Tasks of the Career Cycle," in *Career Dynamics: Matching Individual and Organizational Needs* (Reading, MA: Addison-Wesley, 1978); D. T. Hall, Chapter 3, "Career Stages," in *Careers in Organizations* (Pacific Palisades, CA: Goodyear, 1976).

3. E. E. Diamond, "Theories of Career Development and the Reality of Women at Work," in *Women's Career Development*, ed. B. A. Gutek and L. Larwood (Newbury Park, CA: Sage, 1987); L. F. Fitzgerald and J. O. Crites, "Toward a Career Psychology of Women: What Do We Know? What Do We Need to Know?" *Journal of Counseling Psychology* 27 (1980): 44-62.

4. D. E. Super, Chapter 1, "Career Patterns and Life Stages," in *The Psychology of Careers* (New York: Harper, 1957); K. H. Meuller, *Educating Women for a Changing World* (Minneapolis: University of Minnesota Press, 1954), quoted in Super, "Career Patterns and Life Stages," p. 76.

5. E. Ginzberg, S. W. Ginzburg, S. Axelrad, and J. L. Herma, Chapter 5, "The Case Materials," and Chapter 12, "Women," in *Occupational Choice: An Approach to a General Theory* (New York: Columbia University Press, 1951), p. 42.

6. Schein, *Career Dynamics*, Chapter 3, "The Stages and Tasks of the Biosocial Life Cycle," and Chapter 5, "The States, Stages, and Tasks of the Family," p. 27.

7. D. J. Levinson, C. N. Darrow, E. B. Klein, M. H. Levinson, and B. McKee, Chapter 1, "The Life Cycle and Its Seasons," in *The Seasons of a Man's Life* (New York: Ballantine, 1978), pp. 8-9.

8. H. S. Astin, "The Meaning of Work in Women's Lives: A Sociopsychological Model of Career Choice and Work Behavior," *The Counseling Psychologist* 12 (1984): 117-26; Comments on this article by L. W. Harmon, L. A. Gilbert, L. F. Fitzgerald and N. E. Betz, and H. S. Farmer, in the same issue.

9. B. A. Gutek and L. Larwood, "Introduction: Women's Careers Are Important and Different,"in *Women's Career Development*, ed. Gutek and Larwood; L. Larwood and B. A. Gutek, "Working Toward a Theory of Women's Career Development," in *Women's Career Development*, ed. Gutek and Larwood, p. 172.

10. L. Stewart and W. B. Gudykunst, "Differential Factors Influencing the Hierarchical Level and Number of Promotions of Males and Females Within an Organization," *Academy of Management Journal* 25 (1982): 586-97; A. S. Tsui and B. A. Gutek, "A Role Set Analysis of Gender Differences in Performance, Affective Relationships, and Career Success of Industrial Middle Managers," *Academy of Management Journal* 27 (1984): 619-35.

11. J. F. Veiga, "Female Career Myopia," *Human Resource Management* 15, no. 4 (Winter 1976): 24-27.

12. L. Larwood, L. M. Radford, and D. Berger, "Do Job Tactics Predict Success? A Comparison of Female with Male Executives in 14 Corporations," *Proceedings of the Annual Meeting of the Academy of Management* (Detroit, 1980), pp. 386-90.

13. K. E. Kram and L. A. Isabella, "Mentoring Alternatives: The Role of Peer Relationships in Career Development," *Academy of Management Journal* 28 (1985): 110-32, p. 111.

14. D. M. Hunt and C. Michael, "Mentorship: A Career Training and Development Tool," *Academy of Management Review* 8 (1983): 475-85; Levinson et al., Chapter 9, "Settling Down: Building a Second Adult Life Structure," and Chapter 16, "Modifying the Life Structure During the Mid-Life Transition," in *The Seasons of a Man's Life*.

15. L. Larwood and U. E. Gattiker, "A Comparison of the Career Paths Used by Successful Women and Men," in *Women's Career Development*, ed. Gutek and Larwood.

16. M. D. Levin-Epstein, *Primer of Equal Employment Opportunity*, 4th ed. (Washington, DC: Bureau of National Affairs, 1987).

17. M. London and S. A. Stumpf, Chapter 8, "Career Management Support Systems," in *Managing Careers* (Reading, MA: Addison-Wesley, 1982).

18. L. Larwood, M. W. Wood, and S. D. Inderlied, "Training Women for Management: New Problems, New Solutions," *Academy of Management Review* 3 (1978): 584-93; M. H. Brenner, "Management Development for Women," *Personnel Journal* 51, no. 3 (March 1972): 165-69; A. G. Sargent, "Training Men and Women for Androgynous Behaviors in Organizations," *Group & Organization Studies* 6 (1981): 302-11.

19. D. D. Bowen and D. T. Hall, "Career Planning for Employee Development: A Primer for Managers," *California Management Review* 20, no. 2 (1977): 23-35; London and Stumpf, *Managing Careers*, Chapter 5, "Organizational Career Planning Programs."

20. U. Sekaran, Chapter 7, "Developing Other Organizational Policies," in *Dual-Career Families* (San Francisco: Jossey-Bass, 1986).

21. D. E. Friedman, "Child Care for Employees' Kids," *Harvard Business Review* 64, no. 2 (March/April 1986): 28-34.

22. S. K. Boardman, C. C. Harrington, and S. V. Horowitz, "Successful Women: A Psychological Investigation of Family Class and Education Origins," in *Women's Career Development*, ed. Gutek and Larwood.

23. J. F. Veiga, "Do Managers on the Move Get Anywhere?" *Harvard Business Review* 59, no. 2 (March/April 1981): 20-38; J. F. Veiga, "Plateaued Versus Nonplateaued Managers: Career Patterns, Attitudes, and Path Potential," *Academy of Management Journal* 24 (1981): 566-78.

24. D. E. Berlew and D. T. Hall, "The Socialization of Managers: Effects of Expectations on Performance," *Administrative Science Quarterly* 11 (1966): 207-24; M. S. Taylor and D. R. Ilgen, "Sex Discrimination Against Women in Initial Placement Decisions: A Laboratory Investigation," *Academy of Management Journal* 24 (1981): 859-65; J. R. Terborg and D. R. Ilgen, "A Theoretical Approach to Sex Discrimination in Traditionally Masculine Occupations," *Organizational Behavior and Human Performance* 13 (1975): 352-76; Larwood and Gattiker, "A Comparison of the Career Paths."

25. Z. K. Gyorky, "Influence of Psychological and Situational Variables on Women's Career Patterns" (Paper delivered at the American Psychological Association Annual Convention, Washington, DC, 1982); Stewart and Gudykunst, "Differential Factors Influencing the Hierarchical Level."

26. Veiga, "Plateaued Versus Nonplateaued Managers"; F. Herzberg, "One More Time: How Do You Motivate Employees?" *Harvard Business Review* 46, no. 1 (January/February 1968): 53-62.

27. Sekaran, *Dual-Career Families*, Chapter 2, "Overlap Between Work, Family, and Personal Needs"; L. A. Gilbert, Chapter 2, "Career Aspirations and Development," in *Men In Dual-Career Families: Current Realities and Future Prospects* (Hillsdale, NJ: Lawrence Erlbaum, 1985).

28. L. Rogan, "Executive Women Find It Difficult to Balance Demands of Job, Home," *Wall Street Journal* 204, no. 85 (30 October 1984): 31.

29. J. H. Greenhaus and N. J. Beutell, "Sources of Conflict Between Work and Family Roles," *Academy of Management Review* 10 (1985): 76-88.

30. L. H. Peters, E. J. O'Connor, J. Weekley, A. Pooyan, B. Frank, and B. Erenkrantz, "Sex Bias and Managerial Evaluations: A Replication and Extension,"

Journal of Applied Psychology 69 (1984): 349-52; V. F. Nieva and B. A. Gutek, "Sex Effects on Evaluation," *Academy of Management Review* 5 (1980): 267-76; E. D. Pulakos and K. N. Wexley, "The Relationship Between Perceptual Similarity, Sex, and Performance Ratings in Manager-Subordinate Dyads," *Academy of Management Journal* 26 (1983): 129-39.

31. London and Stumpf, *Managing Careers*, Chapter 7, "Organizational Staffing: Promotion and Transfer Decisions"; R. J. Ritchie and J. L. Moses, "Assessment Center Correlates of Women's Advancement into Middle Management: A 7-Year Longitudinal Analysis," *Journal of Applied Psychology* 68 (1983): 227-31.

32. S. D. Inderlied, "Goal Setting and the Career Development of Women," *New Directions for Education, Work, and Careers* 8 (1979): 33-41.

33. Larwood and Gutek, "Working Toward a Theory of Women's Career Development."

34. M. Hennig and A. Jardim, *The Managerial Woman* (Garden City, NY: Anchor Press/Doubleday, 1977), pp. 12, 25.

35. G. N. Powell, "Career Development and the Woman Manager: A Social Power Perspective," *Personnel* 57, 3 (May/June 1980): 22-32.

36. Sekaran, Chapter 3, "Quality of Life in Dual-Career Families," in *Dual-Career Families*.

7

Promoting Equal Opportunity

A Dinner Conversation

A high-ranking senior administrator from a west-coast university recently had dinner with two nationally prominent female academics. In the course of a friendly conversation about sex discrimination, the administrator proudly volunteered the information that his institution had decided to search the United States to find a first-rate female physicist to help sexually integrate the ranks of the tenured science faculty. His female companions, who had only minutes before acknowledged concern over the lack of highly qualified female academics in the "hard" sciences, became quite vocal in their disapproval of this strategy. He was astonished. Why were these women resisting an affirmative action effort, the objective of which they strongly supported?

—Gregory B. Northcroft and
Joanne Martin, 1982[1]

Since the 1960s, organizations have been under legal pressure to refrain from sex discrimination and to counteract the effects of past discrimination. Most organizations have been required to take "affirmative action" to promote equal opportunity in employment. Employers who "act affirmatively" make sure that current decisions and practices enhance the employment, development, and retention of members of protected groups such as women workers. This goes beyond merely refraining from discriminatory practices. Although enforcement of equal opportunity laws has varied from one presidential administration to the next, organizations have learned that violation can be quite costly, not only through awards for back pay and other damages but also from the loss of government contracts and the effect of negative public relations.[2]

Organizations may be held at least partly responsible for two major types of inequality according to sex. One is the uneven distribution of men and women across occupations and across jobs within organizations. As we have shown, women and men are concentrated in different types of jobs, with men tending to hold the jobs at higher levels in organizations. Numerical inequalities cannot be attributed solely to discriminatory practices by organizations. Other factors such as education, interests, aspirations, and qualifications also play a role. Nonetheless, the existence of such inequalities creates pressure on organizations to work toward eliminating them.

The other major type of inequality pertains to the difference between men's and women's earnings. As noted in Chapter 3, the ratio of the earnings of full-time female workers to those of full-time male workers was 70% in 1986. Although this figure represented a slight improvement from previous years, it still indicated considerable inequality in wages. The ratio of the earnings of full-time female managers and administrators to those of their male counterparts was only 61%. The greater the proportion of women in an occupation, the lower the average wage level in the occupation. Men earn the higher wages in most occupations, even those that are numerically dominated by women. Moreover, we have yet to achieve equal pay for equal work, with men still tending to receive higher wages than women for the same work. Again, organizations are not solely responsible for this type of inequality. Labor market forces and differences in the preparation and qualifications of men and women may also be responsible. Organizations, however, are under pressure to do something about the earnings gap.[3]

Bringing about changes to prevent future discrimination and to counteract past discrimination is not simple. *Affirmative action* or *equal opportunity programs* (the terms will be used interchangeably) that increase the chances that members of one group will be hired, promoted, paid more, and so on are likely to be objected to as "reverse discrimination" by members of other groups. Moreover, as the opening passage suggests, when individuals feel that they or members of their group are receiving preferential treatment rather than recognition of their competence, they are likely to object to the programs as well.

Are organizations then faced with a "lose-lose" situation, whereby they will be the target of complaints whether they act to reduce statistical discrepancies within their ranks or ignore the discrepancies altogether? Not necessarily. Organizations may take positive steps to eliminate inequalities in treatment of different groups without alienating members of any group, *if* they carefully choose their actions and their implementation strategies.

In this chapter, we shall first review the various laws that restrict sex discrimination and how they have been interpreted and applied in practice. Next, we shall review the different explanations of why sexual inequalities exist in organizations and why affirmative action programs may be resisted by beneficiaries of the programs as well as other employees. Finally, in light of these legal requirements and explanations, we shall reach conclusions about how organizations may best promote equal opportunity for applicants and employees.

SEX DISCRIMINATION:
WHAT THE LAW SAYS

The actions of employers are governed by a vast number of federal, state, and local statutes and executive orders. We shall focus our attention on federal laws and executive orders, because they have had the broadest impact on organizations.[4]

Title VII of the Civil Rights Act of 1964 and the Equal Pay Act of 1963 are the most significant pieces of federal equal employment opportunity (EEO) legislation. Title VII prohibits discrimination on the basis of sex, race, color, religion, or national origin in any employment condition, including hiring, firing, promotion, transfer, compensation, and admission to training programs. It was extended to cover employees of government and educational institutions as well as private employers with more than 15 employees, to ban discrimination because of pregnancy, childbirth, or related conditions, and to ban sexual harassment (see Chapter 4). The Equal Pay Act makes it illegal to pay members of one sex at a lower rate than the other if they are in jobs that require equal skill, effort, and responsibility under similar working conditions in the same establishment.

Executive Order 11246 is the one most relevant to sex discrimination in organizations. As amended, it prohibits organizations with contracts of more than $10,000 per year with the federal government from discriminating against any employee or job applicant because of sex, race, religion, color, or national origin. In addition, all organizations with 50 or more employees and federal contracts exceeding $50,000 per year are required to develop written affirmative action plans and to take positive steps to eliminate discrimination. An acceptable affirmative action program must include an analysis of areas in which the organization is deficient in the use of women and specific goals and timetables to correct the deficiencies. The organization also must commit itself to good faith effort to achieve the goals of the program. This obligation extends to working conditions and facilities, hiring, firing, layoff, recall, promotion, and compensation.

Several agencies are involved in the administration and enforcement of EEO laws. The Equal Employment Opportunity Commission (EEOC) is charged with administering Title VII and the Equal Pay Act. It has the authority to investigate and reconcile charges of discrimination against employers, unions, and employment agencies. The Department of Justice enforces Title VII in cases involving a state or local government agency or political subdivision. The Office of Federal Contract Compliance Programs, part of the Department of Labor, is responsible for administering Executive Order 11246. Individuals also may go to court on their own behalf or on behalf of a class of employees or potential employees to seek compliance with the laws.

Since these laws and executive orders have been passed, the courts and the agencies involved have wrestled with a wide variety of issues involving claims of sex discrimination. The EEOC has had more difficulty in clarifying and applying the Title VII ban on sex discrimination than it has in administering any other provision of the law. Title VII was primarily written to deal with discrimination based on race, national origin, and religion. The ban on sex discrimination was inserted one day before its passage, with little accompanying discussion to clarify the legislative intent. Thus the distinct problems of discrimination according to sex were not taken into account in the drafting of Title VII. Moreover, the EEOC has had to relate the Title VII ban on sex discrimination in compensation to the overlapping provisions of the Equal Pay Act. In the remainder of this section, we shall review the major issues regarding sex discrimination that have been the subject of court rulings and agency guidelines.

Nonpay Issues

Two basic types of organizational practices have been considered discriminatory under Title VII, those that involve disparate treatment and those that result in disparate impact. *Disparate treatment discrimination* refers to the use of sex (as well as race, color, religion, or national origin) as a basis for treating people unequally, such as rejecting women applicants of childbearing age for certain jobs but not men of the same age group. Under the disparate treatment standard of what constitutes discrimination, an organization is allowed to impose any requirements as long as they are imposed on all employees alike.

In contrast, *disparate impact discrimination* refers to any organizational practice that affects women and men unequally, unless it can be justified as job related and essential to the safe and efficient operation of the organization. For example, a company's use of a minimum height requirement for certain jobs was rejected as discriminatory when it was shown to rule out more women than men and was not essential to job performance. Licensing requirements for teachers and apprenticeship training for skilled craft positions, however, are legitimate job-related requirements. Under the disparate impact standard of discrimination, whether or not an employer has discriminated intentionally in a personnel action is irrelevant. All that matters is whether the action has unequal results, unless it can be shown to serve a legitimate need and there is no alternative that would have less of a disparate impact.[5]

Discrimination because of pregnancy-related issues has been prohibited since 1978 by the Pregnancy Discrimination Act amending Title VII. This law was inspired by a 1976 Supreme Court decision that General Electric did not violate Title VII by excluding pregnancy from coverage in its disability plan. The court ruled that the disability plan did not exclude anyone because of sex (even though only women get pregnant) but merely removed one physical condition, pregnancy, from the list of compensable disabilities. The 1978 law was passed to ban unequal treatment of pregnant women for all employment-related purposes. It prohibits firing or refusing to hire or promote a woman solely because she is pregnant, prohibits mandatory leaves for pregnant women arbitrarily set at a certain time in their pregnancy rather than because of an individual inability to work, protects reinstatement rights of women on leave for pregnancy-related reasons, and requires employers to treat pregnancy and childbirth the same way they treat other causes of disability under fringe benefit plans.

The Title VII ban on sex discrimination makes an exception of discrimination that involves a "bona fide occupational qualification." The EEOC has construed this exception narrowly, however. For example, despite the Age Discrimination Act, an elderly person could be rejected as a bus driver on the basis of age due to a concern for public safety. The refusal to hire an individual due to stereotypical assumptions about the characteristics of women and men is more likely to be considered illegal discrimination. This reasoning was invoked in a court ruling against Pan American Airways in 1971 for limiting its flight attendants to women. At the time, the idea of a male flight attendant was unheard of because the airlines felt women were superior at such activities as comforting passengers and serving them food and beverages. Male flight attendants are now commonplace, and air travelers still get their food and beverages.

Another exception to Title VII permits discrimination that is based on a seniority system, as long as the system is not a guise for discrimination. For example, the Supreme Court ruled that an employer cannot be ordered to ignore a seniority system when making layoffs, even if the effect is to reduce the number of women or minorities hired under an affirmative action plan. The courts may award retroactive seniority to individuals who are the victims of past discrimination, but seniority systems themselves are not illegal.

Employee selection procedures such as testing that have a disparate impact on the employment opportunities of men and women are illegal under Title VII and Executive Order 11246 unless they are justified by business necessity. The Uniform Guidelines on Employee Selection Procedures, adopted by several government agencies, recommend an "80 percent" rule of thumb for determining adverse impact. According to this rule, a selection rate for either sex that is less than 80% of the selection rate of the other sex shall be regarded as evidence of disparate impact. This restriction may be applied to promotion and layoff decisions as well as selection decisions.

Employers are not required to meet hiring or promotion quotas for specific groups of workers (e.g., 45% of the area's labor force or population is female, therefore, 45% of hires should be female). The language of Title VII has been interpreted, however, to allow hiring quotas to remedy an imbalance caused by past discrimination. If prior hiring practices promoted sex discrimination, stronger affirmative action may be expected of employers than if prior hiring practices were nondiscriminatory. EEOC guidelines state that employers may give temporary preference to qualified applicants from underrepresented groups to achieve a long-term balance in the representation of those groups among their employees.

Pay Issues

The terms used by the Equal Pay Act have been elaborated by various court decisions. The equal work standard requires only that jobs be substantially equal, not identical. In one case, women received 10% less pay than their male counterparts who did the same, basic job. The men occasionally did heavier work, but this was infrequent and not all men did it. The court, ruling that the employer's lower wage rate for women was based on an artificially created job classification and that the extra duties of some men did not justify paying all of them more, awarded back wages to the women.

Equal work is defined by four factors: skill, effort, responsibility, and working conditions. *Skill* refers to the experience, training, education, and ability needed to perform the job. The skill level of the job, not the job holders, determines whether two jobs are equal in skill. For example, female nursing aides and male orderlies in hospitals have generally been found to perform equal work because similar skills are required. *Effort* refers to the amount or degree of effort, mental or physical, required for a job. *Responsibility* refers to the degree of accountability required in the performance of a job. For example, a wage differential may be justified for employees who are required to become acting supervisor in the absence of a regular supervisor. *Working conditions* refer to the physical surroundings and hazards of a job, such as inside versus outside work, heating, and ventilation. The fact that jobs are merely in different departments is not sufficient to demonstrate a difference in working conditions.

The Equal Pay Act permits pay differences between men and women engaged in equal work if they result from a seniority system, a merit system, a system that measures earnings by quality or quantity of production (e.g., a piecework incentive system), or some factor other than sex such as a shift differential or a difference in experience. For example, a court upheld higher pay for salespeople in the men's department over those in the women's department of Robert Hall Clothes because the company demonstrated that the men's department was more profitable than the women's department.

The Equal Pay Act is based on the principle of "equal pay for equal work." An additional principle that has been proposed for determining whether wage discrimination exists is "equal pay for work of comparable worth or value." According to this principle, jobs that require comparable (not identical) skill, effort, and responsibility warrant equal pay.[6]

Claims of sex discrimination according to the comparable worth principle have been filed under the Title VII prohibition on sex discrimination in compensation, which is not governed by the equal work restriction of the Equal Pay Act. In considering such cases, the courts have typically examined an employer's conduct and not attempted to establish a general standard for illegal wage disparity. The Supreme Court based a 1981 ruling against the County of Washington (in Oregon) on the fact that the county had already established an evaluation system that showed that the wage rates for women were too low. In a different case, a federal Appeals Court held in 1985 that the State of Washington could legally pay employees in predominantly male job classes more than employees in predominantly female job classes, even though a state-commissioned study had concluded that the two types of job classes were comparable in worth. The court's opinion was that Title VII did not obligate the state to eliminate an inequality in wages that it did not create. In other cases, data showing that the differential value of jobs within the organization reflected their differential value in the external labor market, combined with affirmative actions by employers, have led courts to reject charges of wage discrimination.

While comparable worth has not been accepted as a legal doctrine by the federal courts, it has not been rejected either. Its advocates have been more successful in getting new laws mandating pay equity enacted at the state level, particularly for state workers, than in arguing wage discrimination under existing laws at the federal level. Elected officials close to home are perhaps more responsive to the concerns of their constituents than federal regulatory agencies or the court system.[7]

In summary, EEO laws ban sex discrimination by organizations in several forms. Organizations may not discriminate in the ways in which they treat women and men regarding hiring, firing, promotion, layoff, compensation, and other types of employment conditions. They also may be held responsible for the unequal impact of their policies on men and women, unless there is a legitimate need that has been served by the policies in question. Most organizations are expected to take positive steps to eliminate inequalities according to sex in the distribution of individuals across jobs and in wage rates. In addition, they must demonstrate on a regular basis that they are taking such steps by filing compliance reports and keeping their records open for monitoring to assure compliance.

EXPLANATIONS FOR INEQUALITIES ACCORDING TO SEX

Despite the passage of EEO laws, inequalities according to sex remain in the workplace. These inequalities are at least partially due to sex discrimination by organizations. Inequalities according to sex may exist, however, for reasons other than organizational discrimination. In this section of the chapter, we shall consider the inequalities from two perspectives. We shall first review explanations of why they exist, including the explanations offered in previous chapters. We shall then examine the reasons why employees resist attempts by organizations to eliminate them.

Why Do the Inequalities Exist?

So far in this book, we have primarily attributed sex discrimination in organizations to individuals' tendencies to engage in gender stereotyping. Gender stereotyping is a psychological process that results from societal norms about men's and women's roles and early socialization experiences that reinforce these norms. Some individuals have a greater tendency to employ gender stereotypes than others, however, and gender stereotypes are employed more in some situations than in others. Individuals who are more traditional in their attitudes, lower in self-esteem, less educated, and more authoritarian are more likely to rely on gender stereotypes than individuals with the opposite characteristics. Experience in working with opposite-sex individuals tends to reduce individuals' tendencies to apply gender stereotypes in their work relationships. Having more information about individuals also reduces the tendency to base employment-related decisions on gender stereotypes. Token members of a group are more likely to be victims of gender stereotyping than minority members of a group with a more balanced sex ratio.

Thus sex discrimination may be viewed as an inevitable result of gender stereotyping, with individual characteristics and situational factors influencing the extent to which gender stereotypes operate at any moment. This explanation does not allow for the influence of the organization itself, other than through the cumulative effect of employment decisions about individuals on the sex ratio of groups and individuals' work experiences with members of the opposite sex. Organizations, however, also provide the context in which these decisions are made.

Organizations may be divided into three categories according to their basic attitudes toward equal employment opportunity. *Category I* organizations were equal opportunity employers before EEO laws were passed. They have actively recruited female employees for male-dominated jobs and, as a result, have a stable population of female talent for promotion. These organizations use a combination of career planning services, training and development programs, staffing systems, and other developmental activities to keep themselves vital and adaptive. *Category II* organizations merely react to EEO laws. They typically attempt minimal compliance with the laws by adding token women to groups. Because their emphasis is on tokenism, these organizations are vulnerable and they need to strengthen their legal staff to fight sex discrimination cases. They are inclined toward prolonged law suits. *Category III* organizations do nothing to eliminate sex discrimination or to alleviate its effects. They see government activity in this area as a misguided and hopefully passing fad. These organizations are inclined to wait to see if laws really will be enforced before they do anything to promote equal opportunity. Inequalities according to sex are more likely to occur in Category II and III organizations.[8]

Sex discrimination may be exhibited by organizations in several ways. It may result directly from an individual's decision to hire, pay, promote, train, be a mentor for, evaluate favorably or unfavorably, or otherwise reward or punish another individual. It may result indirectly from decisions about the nature and availability of career planning services, training and development programs, and alternative work patterns. Finally, if these programs are available, decisions about who may use them can result in differential treatment of women and men.

Organizations also may institutionalize sex discrimination in their personnel practices. Prior to a 1973 settlement with the federal government, all formal recruiting by the American Telephone and Telegraph Company was sex specific, and applicants could not pursue jobs that the company had decided were inappropriate for their sex.[9] Nepotism rules may exclude spouses with similar backgrounds and training from working in the same department or section, thus favoring the career of one over the other. Rules and procedures about seniority, job posting, promotion eligibility, and so forth also may have unequal impact on men and women. For example, if job posting is not organizationwide, women in female-dominated areas may not learn of openings in male-dominated areas.

Sex discrimination by organizations may be attributed specifically to managers as decision makers. Managers vary in their attention to their own self-interest. At the lowest level of self-interest, managers are unconcerned with pressures on themselves to discriminate, seek only the individuals with the best skills for the organization, and are willing to pay accordingly. Sex discrimination in pay or job opportunities then arises only if men and women are perceived, either correctly or incorrectly, as bringing different characteristics to the labor market.[10]

In contrast, at the highest level of self-interest, managers exhibit a "rational bias" by making decisions that are solely to their advantage rather than the organization's. They are highly sensitive to what will help or hinder their own careers and seek information about what decisions are expected of them and may be personally advantageous. These decisions may coincidentally result in hiring the best employees and helping them to succeed; however, the decisions are made without reference to such concerns. Self-interested managers may find personal advantage in sex discrimination even though they may not care for discrimination personally, may be aware of the laws against it, may understand that the people being discriminated against are as capable as anyone else, or may even themselves be members of the group being discriminated against.

How self-interested managers behave depends on the type of organization in which they work. Managers in Category I organizations are expected to refrain from sex discrimination and actively to promote equal employment opportunity through their decisions. In contrast, managers in Category III organizations are expected to ignore equal opportunity considerations. Self-interested managers have no trouble in deciding how to behave in either type of organization. Category II organizations call for more subtle behavior by managers. Self-interested managers in these organizations are likely to sense that they will be rewarded for operating the way they have always operated without regard for EEO laws, but that they will also be rewarded for a superficial change in behavior. They will pay lip service to equal opportunity considerations, will be appreciated by their organizations for so doing, but will modify their actual decision-making behavior little if at all. Who is to blame for the discriminatory patterns of behavior exhibited by managers in Category II and Category III organizations? If managers are presumed to act only on the basis of their own self-interest and are held blameless for this tendency, then we can only blame their organizations for fostering a climate that encourages sex discrimination in managerial decisions.

Inequalities according to sex also have been attributed to factors beyond the control of organizations, such as the personal characteristics of individuals (other than the tendency to stereotype others), labor markets, and societal institutions. According to the "individual deficit" explanation, the inequalities result from the different qualities that women and men bring to the workplace. Women's relative weaknesses are suggested as the reason why they are paid less than men and work at lower levels in organizations. The implication is that women need to be taught how to remedy these deficiencies in order to eliminate the inequalities. We have already rejected this explanation in previous chapters. The women and men who apply for particular jobs tend to be quite similar in personal qualities. Women may be influenced by different socialization forces, however, and affected differently by situational factors such as family concerns than men, supporting a "sex roles" explanation of the inequalities.[11]

Economic or labor market theories have been used especially to explain wage inequalities. Economists generally see the equilibrium price of labor as determined by the point at which the supply of labor equals the demand for labor by employers. Considering the supply side of this relationship, men and women would occupy different labor markets and therefore receive different wages if they offered employers differences in education, productivity, turnover, absenteeism, or mobility. Gender stereotyping, however, could cause employers to see differences between women and men that are not really there, leading to the existence of dual labor markets despite the facts.

Considering the demand side of the relationship, employers, employees, or customers could exhibit a "taste" for distance from members of one sex or the other that resulted in wage disparities. An employer who discriminates in hiring women pays for that taste by bidding up the wage for men. Such an employer would only hire women if they were willing to work for a wage low enough to compensate the employer for the "distaste." Even if employers are unprejudiced, however, economic considerations could lead them to offer different wages to women and men. If, for example, male employees prefer distance from females, they will work in a sex-integrated job only if they are paid a premium for doing so. Employers would then have to lower the wages of women in order to compensate for the higher rate they must pay men if women are hired. Likewise, if customers prefer not to deal with female employees, prices will have to be lower to prevent the loss of those customers to firms that require them to deal only with male employees. The employer would then have to pay women less than men to compensate for the lower prices.[12]

Other explanations for inequalities according to sex focus on societal forces or institutions other than the labor market. For example, explanations that focus on social class argue that employers segregate workers into different wage groups to prevent the development of a cohesive working class. Because a unified work force would hold more bargaining power, the sex segregation of the work force lowers wages for both men and women, though not by the same amount, thus enhancing an organization's profitability. Unions also have been assigned some of the blame. At one time, many unions maintained sex-segregated bargaining units or pursued practices that excluded women. Collective bargaining agreements between unions and management were often openly discriminatory, specifying male and female jobs and sex-segregated policies regarding promotions, transfers, layoffs, and recalls. The passage of the EEO laws led to the demise of the more blatant forms of sex discrimination by unions.[13]

In summary, many types of explanations have been offered for inequalities according to sex in organizations. Some of these explanations refer to basic organizational attitudes that can be improved if someone in charge has the desire. Other explanations refer to phenomena for which organizations are not responsible but that they can try to control, such as the effects of gender stereotyping and rational bias on employment-related decisions. Still other explanations refer to phenomena that are beyond the responsibility or control of organizations, such as labor market and societal forces and the personal characteristics of individuals. Even when organizations try to change and correct the effects of past discrimination, however, they are often resisted by all parties concerned. Let's now examine why the best intentions of organizations to promote equal opportunity are often unappreciated by the employees affected.

Why Are Attempts to Alleviate the Inequalities Resisted?

Efforts to promote equal opportunity through the design and implementation of affirmative action programs, just as other attempts to introduce change in organizations, often run into some form of resistance by employees. People do not always resist change, and instead may respond positively to or even embrace it. Many organizational efforts to initiate change fail, however, because they do not anticipate or effectively deal with the resistance that materializes.

People may resist change for several reasons. They may have a low tolerance for any change, thus opposing even what they realize is an improvement. General attitudes toward change tend to be less positive for individuals who are older, less educated, less tolerant of ambiguity, less competent, and more senior in service to the organization. People may resist proposed changes when they do not trust the managers who are initiating the changes. They may object to the way in which the changes have been decided and implemented. Or they may simply feel that they will lose more than they will gain.[14]

Resistance to affirmative action programs by employees other than the intended beneficiaries is not difficult to explain. These employees are unlikely to recognize the need for change or to trust the initiators, who may be top management or government officials responsible for EEO laws. They may be unhappy with the process of change. Some individuals are psychologically ready to charge "reverse discrimination," even when it is not applicable, because of their general resistance to change and their expectations that affirmative action changes in particular will invariably be harmful to their personal interest.

On the surface, the resistance of potential beneficiaries seems harder to explain; however, the reasons people oppose any type of organizational change come into play. For example, in the dinner conversation at the beginning of the chapter, the successful female academics may not trust the motives of the administrator. They may see his intention to hire a prominent woman simply as a means of pacifying the demands for equal employment. They also may see themselves as having more to lose than to gain from his strategy, which suggests that their success may be due to preferential treatment rather than their competence. Finally, they may anticipate that the woman who is hired by this strategy also may lose more than she gains because she would be chosen as an outstanding representative of her sex rather than as an outstanding physicist.

Gregory Northcroft and Joanne Martin described the different ways women may react to affirmative action programs intended to benefit them. For example, full-time homemakers with traditional attitudes may oppose the goals of affirmative action programs because they are threatened by societal changes that challenge the legitimacy of their roles. Other women may approve affirmative action goals but disagree with the ways they are pursued. Affirmative action strategies can range from efforts to attract qualified female candidates to imposed hiring quotas that are met with little regard for the competence of applicants. Even women who strongly believe in affirmative action goals may object to strategies that make applicant sex the primary basis for personnel decisions.[15]

Still other women may support goals and implementation strategies but be painfully aware of their negative effects. For example, a study found that women managers who believed that they were hired primarily because of their sex were less committed to their organizations and less satisfied with their jobs than those who believed that they were hired primarily because of their ability. These results indicate a backlash against preferential treatment among women managers. Those who feel that their organizations have ignored their competence and focused on their sex are likely to mistrust the motives of top management and to express their displeasure by displaying less commitment.[16]

The method of leader selection can also affect the perception of female managers and their subordinates. A laboratory study found that female undergraduates who were selected as leaders on the basis of sex devalued their leadership performance, took less credit for successful outcomes, reported less interest in continuing as leaders, and characterized themselves as more deficient in leadership skills than those who were selected on the basis of merit. In contrast, the self-perceptions of male undergraduates were unaffected by how they were selected as leaders. Another laboratory study found that leaders were evaluated more favorably by subordinates when they were perceived to have been chosen because of their competence rather than their sex.[17]

Northcroft and Martin described the difficult situation of the lone woman in a group who is seen to have acquired her position due to an affirmative action decision. They extended Rosabeth Kanter's thinking, described in Chapter 4, by using "solo" instead of Kanter's term "token" to refer to a single minority individual in a group of majority members, such as a woman in an otherwise all-male setting. They used the term "token" to refer to a solo who is somehow identified or associated with an affirmative action effort.

The distinction between solos and tokens helps us to understand why potential beneficiaries would resist equal opportunity programs. One reason is simply that the programs often create solos, who face the many problems Kanter outlines in her description of "tokens." These problems create "single jeopardy" for solos. In contrast, tokens face "double jeopardy" by having all the problems of solo status plus the additional problems of tokenism.

Tokens acquire their status partly because of how they are selected for their jobs and partly because of how other employees assume that they have been selected. Let's assume for the moment that organizations may adopt two opposing philosophies of affirmative action. According to one view, competence is the first candidate screening criterion for hiring or promoting. Members of underrepresented groups, such as female applicants for male-dominated jobs, are given preference if they pass the screen. According to the opposite view, preference for underrepresented groups is the first screen, and competence is then used to choose among the candidates who remain. In the first case, affirmative action yields qualified and competent employees. In the second case, the best of the available affirmative action candidates are chosen, whether qualified or not.

Many people in organizations believe that the second view best captures how affirmative action operates. When they learn that a woman has been hired or promoted, they jump to the conclusion that she has obtained her position as a result of affirmative action and, therefore, is likely to be incompetent. If this line of reasoning is adopted by coworkers, the woman suffers from double jeopardy. She has all the difficulties of solo status, plus the added difficulty of being assumed incompetent. Thus the very existence of an affirmative action program leads some individuals to assume that any female employee was hired or promoted because of the program, not her qualifications. This assumption can make it very difficult for a woman to be recognized and accepted as a competent employee.

IMPLICATIONS FOR MANAGEMENT

So far, we have examined equal opportunity from a legal and theoretical perspective. Now, it's time to look at these issues from a practical perspective—what should organizations try to accomplish, and how?

Unfortunately, research offers little help. Only organizations that are proud of their efforts to promote equal opportunity have been willing to tell the outside world about their success. Organizations less committed to or less successful at achieving equal opportunity have been unwilling to call attention to themselves. As a result, there are no comparative studies that identify the factors that most contribute to organizational success or failure in promoting equal opportunity—we have to reach our own conclusions.

Setting the Proper Goal

We need to begin by considering the organization's goals regarding equal opportunity. Earlier, we placed organizations into three categories based on their commitment to equal opportunity: no commitment (Category III), commitment to meet legal obligations (Category II), or commitment as a guiding principle of conduct (Category I). Whether considered as a moral, legal, or business issue,

Category I commitment is the most appropriate for today's work environment. To see why, let's evaluate the consequences of equal opportunity commitment for each organizational category.

Category III organizations are taking a foolish risk hoping that the EEO laws will fade away or that they will not be caught for ignoring them. Some federal administrations may be lax at enforcing the laws, but, with the large number of women in the workplace, they will not be forgotten. Category III organizations operate at considerable danger to their own livelihood as well as to their relations with employees by disregarding EEO laws.

Category II organizations may achieve the minimal compliance with EEO laws that they desire; however, strategies of tokenism and double standards regarding equal opportunity foster resistance. These organizations are not really ending sex discrimination and they are likely to resort to reverse discrimination to achieve the numerical balance that they think satisfies the law. Thus they leave themselves vulnerable by attempting to follow an intermediate, halfhearted strategy regarding equal opportunity, and they are likely to find themselves in constant trouble over this issue.

Category I organizations promote equal opportunity as a good business practice. They recognize that the composition of the labor pool has changed, with larger proportions of women in the labor market than ever before except at times of national emergency such as World War II. If they were to deny opportunities to women, they would not be taking full advantage of the labor supply and would be limiting themselves to the relatively shrinking supply of male workers. They also would find it difficult to deal with companies who were taking advantage of the increased number of women workers.[18]

Imagine, for example, that Company X has a sales force consisting entirely of white males and that Company Y has a sales force that is diverse. Imagine also that both companies are competing for business from Company Z, whose purchasing department reflects the diversity of Company Y rather than the homogeneity of Company X. All other things being equal, including the quality of the products and services that Companies X and Y offer, which company is likely to win Company Z's business? Company Y, of course. The Company Y sales force will understand and relate to Company Z purchasers and be viewed positively by them. Thus organizations will meet their operating goals better by having a work force that reflects the heterogeneity of the labor force.

While a likely by-product of equal opportunity is a heterogeneous work force, it's not the primary goal. If the goal were to balance men and women in all jobs and at all levels, and managers were evaluated according to their contribution to achieving this balance, then they could further their own self-interest by making *all* employment-related decisions on the basis of sex, assigning women and men to positions according to formula. This would not be desirable, to say the least. Its result would be sex discrimination institutionalized as organizational policy, the opposite of equal opportunity intent.

The proper goal of an organization is to prevent sex discrimination from affecting its employment-related decisions in any way. This is attained by aggressively recruiting, hiring, and promoting the most qualified individuals without regard to their sex, and by not treating employees in any way differently on the basis of their sex. If the organization's goal is to end sex discrimination and managers are evaluated by how well they help achieve this, then *all* decisions must be made in a nondiscriminatory fashion, no matter what their outcome. This is what is really intended by EEO laws. And it is the business practice regarding equal opportunity that makes the most sense for an organization, because it emphasizes making the best use of the human resources available.

Achieving the Goal

Assuming that the goal of an organization is to be nondiscrimin-atory in its employment decisions and practices, we now need to consider what it should do to achieve this goal. The Conference Board asked senior personnel executives of large corporations about the effect of various factors on the success of their EEO efforts on behalf of women. The executives were given a list of 23 factors and asked to rank order the ten that they considered had made the greatest contribution to the overall success of their company's effort. The top ten factors are listed in Table 7.1.

Although the goals and timetables approach required of government contractors by Executive Order 11246 was rated highly, the risk of losing government contracts and the need to undergo rigorous compliance reviews did not make the list of the top ten factors. The risk of a Title VII class-action suit was perceived as very real, however, even though few companies reported that an actual complaint

TABLE 7.1
Factors Contributing to the Overall Success of EEO Efforts

1. Awareness of federal laws and regulations.
2. Commitment on the part of the chief executive officer.
3. Establishment of goals and timetables for action.
4. Development of an EEO policy.
5. Analyses of the company's utilization of women.
6. Awareness of large back pay awards in class-action suits.
7. Monitoring of EEO results against plans.
8. Dissemination of the EEO policy.
9. Identification of special problem areas in utilizing women.
10. Changes in personnel practices or special programs to improve
    opportunities for women.

SOURCE: R.G. Schaeffer and E.F. Lynton, *Corporate Experiences in Improving Women's Job Opportunities* (New York: Conference Board, 1979).
NOTE: Factors are listed in order of endorsement by senior personnel executives.

against them had spurred their efforts to improve job opportunities for women. It was noteworthy that changes in personnel practices and special programming for women barely made the list.[19]

The survey results seem realistic when they suggest that the most important factor contributing to success is awareness of the relevant laws and regulations. Before EEO laws, few organizations thought about improving job opportunities for women. Remember that inclusion of sex in Title VII was an afterthought rather than a primary purpose of the law. It was only after the Supreme Court endorsed the disparate impact definition of illegal discrimination under Title VII in 1971, after government contractors were required to file written affirmative action plans in 1971, and after AT&T signed its multimillion-dollar consent agreement with the government in 1973, that most organizations took note of the EEO laws. Those that are not fully aware of these laws may take ineffectual steps to bring themselves into compliance.

Demonstrating top management commitment. Most writers conclude that top management commitment to an affirmative action program is critical to its success. *In Search of Excellence* authors Tom Peters and Bob Waterman have stressed the importance of the leader in setting an organization's primary values.[20] Writers on organizational change also have stressed the importance of top management commitment; however, how this commitment is demonstrated and implemented is equally important.

One CEO demonstrates his strong commitment to equal opportunity by walking out of any meeting in his organization that consists only of white males. How effective is this action? It certainly catches people's attention; however, it could lead to token representation of lower-level women at meetings with the CEO. Because the only reason for their presence at the meetings would be to respond to the CEO's gesture, both the women and the group would be uncomfortable. Unless this action by the CEO was accompanied by other actions intended to promote equal opportunity throughout the organization, it would be likely to be counterproductive.

Another CEO routinely sends a letter to employees stating that the company is an equal opportunity employer and that sex, race, color, religion, and national origin should not enter into any employment-related decisions by company employees. The letter is the same, word for word, each time it is sent, which is at the same time each year, a common practice in large organizations. It is also company policy not to reveal to any internal or external source, other than to the government in its required affirmative action plan, its goals and timetables for promoting equal opportunity for women employees and its progress to date.

The development of an affirmative action policy and its dissemination to employees are two items on the Conference Board's "top ten" list and they are required of government contractors by Executive Order 11246. When employees are denied knowledge of the company's affirmative action goals and its progress in achieving the goals, however, they find it difficult to know how well they personally are doing and whether they should do anything differently. Employees may then conclude that the real purpose of the letter is to meet government requirements, rather than to promote any particular action on their part, and may be inclined to ignore it.

Top management demonstrates its actual commitment to equal opportunity in its assignment of responsibility and its allocation of resources to the organization's equal opportunity efforts. Executive Order 11246 requires the appointment of a director of Equal Opportunity Programs, who should be given the necessary support to execute the assignment. To demonstrate maximum commitment and also provide maximum leverage, the equal opportunity officer needs either to report to or to be a top executive with line responsibilities. This person should also have a support staff specifically assigned to EEO-related activities. If, for example, the chief operating officer of the organization is also given responsibility for Equal Opportunity Programs, the message is conveyed that equal opportunity is very important to the organization. The EEO officer then has immediate access to and control over the managers who hold the key to program success or failure. To cite the opposite situation, however, if this responsibility is buried in the lower professional ranks of the personnel department, the role of the EEO officer is reduced to the collecting of data and has less impact on the organization. This gives the message that promoting equal opportunity is not really that important to the organization.[21]

Top management may be committed, but how it "sells" equal opportunity to employees plays a large role in determining whether it will be achieved. One company sold equal opportunity first as a moral issue, then as a legal issue, and finally as a business issue. Sold as a moral issue, equal opportunity didn't work, because few people do the "right" thing unless it is personally advantageous. Selling equal opportunity as a legal issue promoted the mentality of a Category II organization. It suggested that numerical compliance with the law was more important than ending sex discrimination, and led to token rather than substantive changes. Sold as a business issue, equal opportunity has worked because it points to the effect on bottom-line profits, which most employees see ultimately affecting their own livelihood.

The EEO management system. A good sales pitch alone does not overcome resistance to equal opportunity efforts. As the Conference Board list suggests, an organization needs a sound management system that analyzes its utilization of women, identifies its problem areas, establishes a plan for action based on specific goals and timetables, and then monitors EEO results against the plan. As one executive in the Conference Board survey said: .

> How do you go about achieving EEO results in a company? The same way you achieve any other results. You analyze the problem carefully, determine what you need to do, and then set up an overall management planning and control system to make very sure that it happens—and on schedule.[22]

Such a system begins with an analysis of whether women are equitably represented throughout the organization. Required by Executive Order 11246 for government contractors, this analysis should compare the utilization of women in each job category with the availability of women in the relevant labor force who are qualified to fill jobs in that category. The relevant labor force could be defined as that located in the immediate city or town, the metropolitan area, or the nation, depending on the job category. Areas that underutilize women then become the appropriate targets of equal opportunity programs. Although not required by law, this analysis also could identify areas of underutilization of men, which the organization may wish to address.

Next comes the specification of equal opportunity objectives. Managers will put more effort into promoting equal opportunity if they are expected to meet numerical objectives. For example, a marketing research manager's objectives might be to hire at least five female market analysts within two years and to have at least 40% of all market analysts be female within five years, with the stipulation that all analysts hired be fully qualified. Such an objective, however, focuses on affirmative action results but ignores the issue of discrimination. If the real goal is nondiscriminatory personnel decisions, objectives should focus on the way decisions are made rather than their outcomes.

The PQ Corporation, a specialty chemicals manufacturer in Valley Forge, Pennsylvania, has implemented a unique procedure to meet the objective of discrimination-free employment decisions. The procedure measures the nature and frequency of discriminatory incidents. By fully documenting each hire or promotion—including job descriptions, a contrast of required skills to candidate skills, and a checklist of actions—it forces managers to confront and acknowledge discriminatory behavior in the hiring and promotion process.[23]

The key to the procedure is the "selection checklist," a two-part document that the manager completes for each internal or external candidate interviewed for a position. The first part contains questions that address how free each step in the selection process was from possible discrimination. The following are examples of questions: Did you perform or do you have a current job analysis for this position? Was the position posted internally? Were reasons for rejection based on job-related deficiencies and not related to non-job-related factors such as a handicap or religious beliefs? Each question must be answered "yes," "no," or "not applicable." The questions answered "no" reflect possible incidents of discrimination. The second part of the selection checklist documents the correlation between the job criteria and the attributes of the candidate. It compares the skills and knowledge required to perform major job functions with the attributes of the candidate interviewed.

Both parts of the document are intended to make managers aware of the process they use to make their decisions. If a manager reports a potential incident of discrimination, upper management is able to take corrective action if necessary. If a manager does not complete the form accurately and attempts to cover up discrimination, it is a conscious decision made with awareness that he or she is exposing the company to the possibility of an EEO lawsuit. Each manager's checklists are passed on to his or her superior, who is expected to investigate if the percentage of incident-free decisions is low. EEO objectives for managers are then stated in terms of percentages of discriminatory incidents. The focus of this procedure is clearly on discriminatory behavior rather than numbers of nontraditional hires and promotions.

Once an organization develops specific objectives and assigns them, they should become part of the manager's overall performance appraisal. The appropriate measure of performance is the degree to which each manager achieves the objectives. Managers should feel that their supervisors will evaluate their EEO results as they do any others.

Finally, good performance should be reinforced with tangible (preferably financial) rewards, and poor performance should be punished. Deliberate failure to comply with EEO objectives should result in decreased salary or promotion opportunities, whereas exceeding EEO objectives should lead to increased salary, promotion opportunities, or bonuses. These actions speak much louder than words of approval or disapproval. Note that the emphasis is on the reinforcement of behaviors rather than attitudes. Unlike attitudes, behaviors can be readily observed, allowing progress or lack of progress to be directly monitored. Moreover, if people are motivated to support equal opportunity despite their other beliefs, they often come to believe in what they are doing.[24]

Designing and implementing EEO programs. An EEO management system gives managers tangible incentives for achieving equal opportunity objectives and helps to overcome any resistance they might feel toward equal opportunity. Their resistance will be further reduced, however, if they are encouraged to participate in the design and implementation of the organization's equal opportunity programs. Furthermore, nonmanagerial personnel who are the intended beneficiaries of the programs, as well as other nonmanagerial employees, should also be encouraged to participate. Participation in goal setting and decision making leads to acceptance and commitment; therefore, it is useful to have individuals from all levels involved in setting equal opportunity goals and timetables and in solving the problems that hinder their achievement. With this involvement, we could expect greater understanding of the reasons for equal opportunity and a greater sense of shared responsibility for the attainment of equal opportunity objectives.[25]

The participation of first-line supervisors, the people most responsible for getting work done in organizations, is especially critical to the success of equal opportunity programs. If these programs are designed by staffing experts at the corporate level without consulting lower-level managers, there may be problems with implementation. Supervisors may feel that preferential hiring is taking place without regard to competence and may resent individuals whom they see as affirmative action hires in their units. The biggest problem most supervisors have with affirmative action programs is that they are perceived to result in the use of differential criteria for hiring and promotion and in differential treatment of employees with respect to discipline and discharge. Whether these perceptions are accurate, they may seriously affect morale in the supervisor's unit. Such perceptions are prevented by including the supervisors in the development of equal opportunity programs and by assuring them that qualifications and competence, not sex, will be the primary basis for employment decisions.[26]

The participation of nonsupervisory personnel in the design and implementation of affirmative action programs, while not absolutely necessary, is helpful. They need to be assured that the programs are based primarily on qualifications and competence and that affirmative action is secondary. The best way to instill these beliefs is to have such employees participate in the equal opportunity process. Unless these beliefs are instilled, no one will gain from affirmative action. The intended beneficiaries will lose because others will assume that they are incompetent and resent them. Other employees will lose because they will feel resentful about perceived reverse discrimination, even if it did not actually take place.

Thus reverse discrimination hurts everyone. Conceivably, individuals who could not gain a job otherwise may have a chance to show how well they can do. Resentful coworkers, however, could make working conditions very difficult and success virtually impossible. Perceptions of reverse discrimination are in some ways are more important than the reverse discrimination itself, because they trigger the negative attitudes that cause all parties to resist equal opportunity programs. The best way to keep such perceptions from forming is to have women and men from all levels of the organization participate in the design and implementation of equal opportunity programs.

Areas that EEO programs should address. There are many kinds of discriminatory practices that equal opportunity programs should address. Sex discrimination may be reflected in nonpay areas such as recruitment and selection procedures, promotions and factors that determine upward mobility, demotions, terminations, layoffs, employee benefits, training opportunities, subsidization of educational expenses, use of facilities, antinepotism policies, part-time and flexible employment policies, and union contracts. Sex discrimination also may appear in the form of unwarranted disparities between the wages paid to women and men. Pay disparities deserve our special attention, because it is not immediately obvious how they arise.

Pay disparities are often linked to job evaluation, a measurement procedure that helps organizations to set pay differentials. Job evaluation typically focuses on *key jobs*, characterized by a standard and stable content across organizations, within *job clusters*, or groups of jobs that have emerged as a function of technology, administrative practices (e.g., lines of promotion), location, and common job content. For example, computer programming may be defined as a key job, because it exists in many types of organizations. Wages are assigned to the key jobs within a job cluster according to the wages typically paid in the labor market for that geographical location. Wages are then assigned to non-key jobs according to how they compare in rated worth with the key jobs in the same job cluster. Thus a computer programming job that requires familiarity with advanced programming languages or has more senior responsibilities may be rated as worth more, and thereby deserving of more pay, than one that only requires familiarity with simple programming languages or has fewer responsibilities. The starting point for the setting of wages, however, is what the marketplace currently pays for key jobs. The result is a pay structure that is based on concern for both internal equity—the relationship between pay and job content within the organization—and external equity—the relationship between the pay for key jobs inside and outside the organization.[27]

Employers need to make sure that sex discrimination does not enter into job evaluation or any other element of the compensation system. Wage discrimination does not legally exist if factors other than sex, such as skill, effort, responsibility, and working conditions, account for pay disparities. If the difference between the wages paid for male-dominated and female-dominated jobs is reflected in the marketplace, most courts also have concluded that wage discrimination does not legally exist. If an organization has identified pay disparities that cannot be accounted for by job-related or market factors, however, then wage discrimination does legally exist and should be the target of corrective action. This does not necessarily mean immediately rectifying all differences or lowering anyone's pay, but rather a commitment over the long run to eliminate unjustifiable disparities. Such a commitment is an important part of an organization's equal opportunity efforts.[28]

In conclusion, equal opportunity programs are necessary and desirable for all organizations. Even organizations that have demonstrated enlightened attitudes toward equal opportunity throughout their existence need to make special efforts to ensure that they have a pool of qualified male and female applicants for all jobs, because forces beyond their control have a large impact on who actually applies for job openings. When used to end sex discrimination, and with sensitivity for employees, equal opportunity programs benefit all members of an organization as well as the society at large.

NOTES

1. G. B. Northcroft and J. Martin, "Double Jeopardy: Resistance to Affirmative Action from Potential Beneficiaries," in *Sex Role Stereotyping and Affirmative Action Policy.*, ed. B. A. Gutek (Los Angeles: University of California, Institute of Industrial Relations, 1982), p. 82.

2. M. Eastwood, "Legal Protection Against Sex Discrimination," in *Women Working: Theories and Facts in Perspective*, ed. A. H. Stromberg and S. Harkess (Palo Alto, CA: Mayfield, 1978).

3. U.S. Department of Commerce, Bureau of the Census, "Male-Female Differences in Work Experience, Occupation, and Earnings: 1984," *Current Population Reports*, series P-70, no. 10 (Washington, DC: Government Printing Office, 1987); A. A. Kemp and E. M. Beck, "Equal Work, Unequal Pay: Gender Discrimination Within Work-Similar Occupations," *Work and Occupations* 13 (1986): 324-47; J. O'Neill, "Role Differentiation and the Gender Gap in Wage Rates," in *Women and Work: An Annual Review*, vol. 1, ed. L. Larwood, A. H. Stromberg, and B. A. Gutek (Beverly Hills, CA: Sage, 1985).

4. This section of the chapter is primarily based on M. D. Levin-Epstein, *Primer of Equal Employment Opportunity*, 4th ed. (Washington, DC: Bureau of National Affairs, 1987).

5. J. Ledvinka, Chapter 2, "Basic Principles of EEO," in *Federal Regulation of Personnel and Human Resource Management* (New York: Van Nostrand Reinhold, 1982).

6. D. J. Treiman and H. I. Hartmann, eds., *Women, Work, and Wages: Equal Pay for Jobs of Equal Value* (Washington, DC: National Academy Press, 1981).

7. T. A. Mahoney, "Understanding Comparable Worth: A Societal and Political Perspective," in *Research in Organizational Behavior*, vol. 9, ed. L. L. Cummings and B. M. Staw (Greenwich, CT: JAI, 1987).

8. G. C. Pati, "Reverse Discrimination: What Can Managers Do?" *Personnel Journal* 56 (1977): 334-38, 360-62.

9. P. A. Wallace, ed., *Equal Employment Opportunity and the AT&T Case* (Cambridge: MIT Press, 1976).

10. L. Larwood, E. Szwajkowski, and S. Rose, "When Discrimination Makes 'Sense': The Rational Bias Theory of Discrimination," in *Women and Work: An Annual Review*, vol. 3, ed. B. A. Gutek, A. H. Stromberg, and L. Larwood (Newbury Park, CA: Sage, in press); L. Larwood, B. Gutek, and U. E. Gattiker, "Perspectives on Institutional Discrimination and Resistance to Change," *Group and Organization Studies* 9 (1984): 333-52.

11. V. F. Nieva, "Equity for Women at Work: Models of Change," in *Sex Role Stereotyping*, ed. Gutek.

12. G. S. Becker, *The Economics of Discrimination*, 2nd ed. (Chicago: University of Chicago Press, 1971).

13. B. F. Reskin and H. I. Hartmann, Chapter 3, "Explaining Sex Segregation in the Workplace," in *Women's Work, Men's Work: Sex Segregation on the Job* (Washington, DC: National Academy Press, 1986).

14. G. N. Powell and B. Z. Posner, "Resistance to Change Reconsidered: Implications for Managers," *Human Resource Management* 17, no. 1 (Spring 1978): 55-60.

15. Northcroft and Martin, "Double Jeopardy."

16. T. I. Chacko, "Women and Equal Employment Opportunity: Some Unintended Effects," *Journal of Applied Psychology* 67 (1982): 119-23.

17. M. E. Heilman, M. C. Simon, and D. P. Repper, "Intentionally Favored, Unintentionally Harmed? Impact of Sex-Based Preferential Selection on Self-Perceptions and Self-Evaluations," *Journal of Applied Psychology* 72 (1987): 62-68; M. B. Jacobson and W. Koch, "Women as Leaders: Performance Evaluation as a Function of Method of Leader Selection," *Organizational Behavior and Human Performance* 20 (1977): 149-57.

18. F. C. Shipper and F. M. Shipper, "Beyond EEO: Toward Pluralism," *Business Horizons* 30, no. 3 (May/June 1987): 53-61.

19. R. G. Schaeffer and E. F. Lynton, *Corporate Experiences in Improving Women's Job Opportunities* (New York: Conference Board, 1979).

20. T. J. Peters and R. H. Waterman, Jr., *In Search of Excellence: Lessons from America's Best-Run Companies* (New York: Harper & Row, 1982).

21. J. Cunningham, "Avoiding Common Pitfalls in Affirmative Action Programs," *Personnel Journal* 55 (1976): 125-27, 136.

22. Schaeffer and Lynton, *Corporate Experiences in Improving Women's Job Opportunities*, p. 21.

23. J. C. Poole and E. T. Kautz, "An EEO/AA Program That Exceeds Quotas—It Targets Biases," *Personnel Journal* 66, no. 1 (January 1987): 103-5.

24. F. E. Gordon, "Bringing Women into Management: The Role of the Senior Executive," in *Bringing Women into Management*, ed. F. E. Gordon and M. H. Strober (New York: McGraw-Hill, 1975).

25. D. A. Brookmire, "Designing and Implementing Your Company's Affirmative Action Program," *Personnel Journal* 58 (1979): 232-37; F. S. Hall and M. Albrecht, Chapter 7, "Developing Systemwide Commitment," in *The Management of Affirmative Action* (Palisades, CA: Goodyear, 1979).

26. T. H. Hammer, "Affirmative Action Programs: Have We Forgotten the First-Line Supervisor?" *Personnel Journal* 58 (1979): 384-89.

27. D. P. Schwab, "Job Evaluation and Pay Setting: Concepts and Practices," in *Comparable Worth: Issues and Alternatives*, ed. E. R. Livernash (Washington, DC: Equal Employment Advisory Council, 1984).

28. G. P. Sape, "Coping with Comparable Worth," *Harvard Business Review* 63, no. 3 (May/June 1985): 145-52.

8

Looking Ahead

A Brave New System?

There will be two large categories of changes between the working world of the present and that of the future (when equal opportunity is achieved). First, in the future there will be a greater accommodation of family life. In other words, there will be recognition by the working organization of the personal maintenance work of house and family care and a less rigid separation of these two aspects of their employees' lives. No one will be able to be treated as though he or she had no personal life or children. Second, the business and industrial organization will be less of a male-oriented, male-image culture. This will come about both through the greater participation of women in the actual processes of management and decision-making and through greater emphasis upon personal and emotional sides of men's personalities.

—Jane W. Torrey, 1978[1]

This book has portrayed a combination of new dynamics and old dynamics in the current work relationships between women and men. For example, we have seen the following:

(1) Traditional norms about women's proper role (i.e., at home) have been rejected in practice by the majority of women. Traditional norms about men's proper role (i.e., at work), however, are still accepted in practice by the vast majority of men. As a result, women and men have experienced considerable conflict and confusion over what their new roles relative to each other should be.

(2) There are new conceptions of what it means to be male or female. A blend of masculine and feminine characteristics called androgyny has been touted as the new ideal for both sexes. Endorsement of gender stereotypes as accurately depicting the typical member of each sex, however, remains strong. The socialization experiences of

young females and males and the effects of these experiences on occupational aspirations continue to differ greatly.

(3) Barriers to the entry of women in many male-dominated occupations, including management, have been breaking down, and a greater proportion of women have been preparing themselves for and entering these occupations than ever before. Men still remain in the majority, however, in almost all occupations that historically have been male-dominated.

(4) As male-dominated occupations have increased their proportions of women, the sex ratios of work groups within them have shifted from uniform (all males) to skewed (greater than 85% males) or tilted (65% to 85% males). Balanced sex ratios have seldom been achieved, however, and majority/minority dynamics remain between men and women in most work groups.

(5) EEOC guidelines banning sexual harassment in the workplace have been implemented and successfully enforced in many organizations. Sexual harassment still occurs at an alarming rate, however. In addition, men and women have sharply different views over what constitutes sexual harassment and what should be done about it, making it difficult for organizations to police themselves.

(6) Myths about women's allegedly inferior abilities to manage have been shown to be just that. Women and men managers generally do not differ in essential aptitudes, abilities, and behaviors, and there are excellent, average, and poor performers within each sex. Women remain in the minority in the management profession, however, especially in its upper echelons.

(7) There is evidence that better managers are androgynous in their behavior. Support for the belief that better managers are masculine remains strong, however, among women and men, even though masculine managers seem to be only average performers.

(8) The difference between women's and men's general career patterns appears to be diminishing; however, important differences remain. Women with families are less likely to pursue careers in management than men with families. Also, married male managers are more likely than married female managers to have a stay-at-home spouse who handles family responsibilities. No matter what her occupation, the woman continues to perform most household activities in dual-career families. Thus having a family typically imposes a greater constraint on a woman's career than on a man's.

(9) Almost all work organizations have acted to provide more equal

opportunity to their employees and applicants. These actions are often token attempts to achieve minimal compliance with EEO laws, however, rather than a true commitment to end sex discrimination. When they consist of or are perceived as reverse discrimination, such actions encourage attitudes of resistance to equal opportunity among employees, even the intended beneficiaries. As a result, two decades of affirmative action have not made a significant dent in the sex segregation of occupations or in the difference between men's and women's wages.

We have evidence of both persistence and change in the dynamics of male/ female work relationships. "How much persistence versus how much change?" is difficult to answer objectively. It's the same type of question as, "Is a glass that contains 50% liquid half-full or half-empty?" While most people agree there has been change, some see mostly progress and others mostly delay in achieving equal opportunity. For example, a reader suggested that a 1987 *Business Week* cover story, "Corporate Women: They're About to Break Through to the Top," would have been titled more appropriately "Corporate Women: The Barriers to the Top Still Persist."[2]

In this chapter, we shall consider potential changes, addressing questions about the future rather than trying to predict it. We may not be able to offer definitive conclusions about the future, but we should be able to identify the key issues that are most likely to shape it.

TRENDS IN MANAGEMENT

How Large Will the Proportion of Women Managers Become?

Table 1.2 shows that this proportion has risen consistently by decade, although there have been fluctuations within decades, throughout the twentieth century. The increase in this proportion has been particularly large in recent years. The proportion more than doubled between 1970 and 1987, increasing from 16% in 1970 to 38% in 1987.

Will the proportion of managers who are women continue to rise? If so, to what level—40%? 50%? 60%? 70%? 80%? Higher? Fewer women than men managers currently are married or have children. If family constraints on women's careers do not change, the proportion of women managers may remain below 50%. On the other hand, if family life becomes less constraining or if women forgo family lives to pursue managerial careers, this proportion could rise above 50%. Changes in the managerial aspirations of women relative to men, the amount of organizational support for employees' pursuit of their family lives, and the nature of hiring decisions for management positions could also influence the future proportion of women managers.

How Will the Proportions of Women at Various Managerial Levels Differ?

The proportion of women managers is greatest at the lower levels of management, smaller at the middle management levels, and smallest at the top management levels. This imbalance is not surprising, given that new managers start at the bottom of the management ranks, which most women have entered in recent years. If there were no barriers to upward mobility for women managers, the proportions of women at middle and top managerial levels should increase simply as a function of time.

An alternative view is that the present imbalance may continue for any of the following reasons: sex discrimination in hiring and promotion for middle and top management positions; sex discrimination in the development of lower-level women managers, which leaves them unprepared to rise within management ranks; or less interest among women to succeed in management careers. There is some evidence to support the first two reasons, but little evidence to support the last reason.

Organizational efforts to promote equal opportunity and end sex discrimination within the ranks of management will play a big part in answering this question. Individual commitment and decisions about management careers will also be a factor. It seems likely that the proportions of women in middle and top management levels will rise to some extent because they are in the lower management levels now. Because few women are presently at the very top of organizations and because most organizations do not fully commit to equal opportunity, it also seems likely that imbalanced distribution of women across managerial levels will remain.

What Will the Predominant Management Style Be?

The increase in women managers in recent years has not affected beliefs about what makes a manager more effective. Support for a stereotype of the "good manager" as masculine has remained steady among women and men, who as managers see themselves as masculine on the whole. As long as women managers remain similar in style to men, we may have little reason to expect a change in the predominant management style.

On the other hand, women managers may have adopted a masculine style because men have been the majority group in management. In the opening passage, Torrey suggests an androgynous organizational culture; she predicts that equal opportunity will lead to less of a male orientation as women are involved in essential management activities and men are freer to express their feminine qualities. If women ever became the majority sex in power, perhaps a female-oriented culture would emerge and men would feel compelled to conform to a new standard of behavior set by women. What that standard of behavior would be—androgynous, feminine, masculine, or something else—is unpredictable.

An androgynous management style actually may lead to greater success as a manager. If this is indeed the case (and more research is needed to determine whether it is), astute managers may eventually realize it and shift their behavior accordingly. Predominant management styles are very difficult to change, however, even for the right reasons.

Future trends in management will depend on a host of factors pertaining to trends in society, organizational practices, and how individuals make decisions about work and family issues. Therefore, we need to pose additional questions about the factors that seem likely to affect male/female work relationships and sex differences in the workplace.

SOCIETAL TRENDS

Will Traditional Norms About Women's and Men's Roles Disappear?

The proportion of individuals who believe that the proper place for women is at home and for men at work has decreased considerably in the latter half of this century. If these prescriptions for behavior become even more out of touch with the reality of how women and men live their lives, we can expect the size of this group to shrink even further.

Will EEO Laws Become Modified in Practice, and, If So, in What Direction?

Although concern for women played a small role in the initial passage of Title VII legislation, support for EEO laws has increased as the proportion of women in the workplace has risen. Unless a sudden and sharp reversal in this proportion occurs, it seems highly unlikely that the laws will be curtailed. If anything, the laws are more likely to be strengthened, especially at the state and local levels, where organized groups of voters have greater influence than at the federal level. Interpretation and enforcement of the laws at the federal, state, and local levels have varied, however, between strictness and leniency according to the political and social philosophy of elected officials and ruling judges. It seems more likely that this kind of variation will continue than that the laws themselves will change.

Will the Sex Difference in Socialization Experiences Disappear?

These experiences are primarily influenced by parents, school systems, and the mass media. We might expect the latter two influences to reflect general changes in society concerning women's and men's roles, although on a delayed basis. Children also learn a great deal from how their parents live. Given the considerable change in the economic roles of parents, which has led to the proportion of dual-earner families being greater than that of single-earner families, it would seem that young boys and girls are receiving more similar messages about who should work. If the mother's work continues to contribute less to the family's total income than the father's work, however, as is true in most families at present, the message will also be given that women's work is less important and essential than men's work.

The nature of their parents' occupations also influences children. For example, we have already noted that, compared to men, relatively few women in management have children. The influence of parents on socialization experiences will not change very much if couples with more traditional occupations remain the individuals most likely to have children.

TRENDS IN ORGANIZATIONS

Will Gender Stereotyping of Coworkers End?

Gender stereotyping most often occurs when people know little about individuals except their sex. Thus the degree of gender stereotyping in the workplace depends on the extent to which women and men actually work with each other in their jobs. After working with women, men have more positive attitudes toward them as coworkers and are less apt to see them in stereotypical terms. A similar shift in attitudes and perceptions about men occurs for women who have men as coworkers for the first time. If the experiences that women and men have at work become more similar and the sex ratios of work groups become more balanced, gender stereotyping will be less frequent. If work groups remain imbalanced, however, or if any increase in minority group members is seen as due to preferential treatment rather than competence, gender stereotypes will remain in force.

Will Organizations Make It Easier for Employees to Satisfy Family Needs?

The opening passage suggests that this will happen if or when equal opportunity is achieved. There is a trend in this direction at the present time. Some organizations have provided alternative work patterns, parental leaves, assistance with day care, and counseling services, which help employees to satisfy their family needs better. Most organizations, however, still have a long way to go in responding to work/family conflicts.

For the proportion of women in the work force to increase further while women still handle most household responsibilities, organizations either will have to make it easier for their employees to satisfy family needs or will have to offer higher wages to attract and retain qualified female employees. If dual-career couples reallocate their household responsibilities to free women and constrain men, organizations will not need to change their policies as much. If, however, dual-career couples do not change their present allocation of household responsibilities, and organizations do not make it easier for employees to satisfy their family needs, the proportion of women in the work force and seeking to enter it may level off or decrease soon. The result could be a reduction in the overall skill level of the work force.

Will More Organizations Try to Achieve Equal Opportunity?

The behavior of organizations in this area is affected by EEO laws, top management attitudes, and the composition of the labor market. If the enforcement and interpretation of EEO laws moved toward greater leniency, top management would feel less compelled legally to promote equal opportunity in employment-related decisions and policies. More enlightened top executives may still decide, however, that promoting equal opportunity is a good organizational practice. If the individuals seeking entry to the work force continue to be primarily female, then organizations that emphasize equal opportunity will have an advantage in attracting new talent. This would encourage even top managers who do not see equal opportunity as a moral imperative to promote it for their own good. The answer to this question may depend on whether more top executives are able to overcome their prejudices to make good strategic decisions for their organizations that also happen to promote equal opportunity.

Will More Organizations Succeed in
Achieving Equal Opportunity?

Sex discrimination is most difficult to eliminate when there is little information about the individuals being judged, typically when hiring decisions are made. Because an organization's recruiters are critical to the achievement of equal opportunity, they should be experienced employees who understand the organization's equal opportunity goals. Periodic training that cautions recruiters against the possibility of unconscious gender stereotyping entering their decisions also could help to prevent sex discrimination in hiring decisions.

Sex discrimination in other employment-related decisions is less likely to occur unconsciously because more is known about the individuals who are the subject of decisions. Managers could be influenced by rational bias, however, if the organization does not reward the achievement of affirmative action goals. Discrimination also could occur if the equal opportunity program promotes—or is perceived to promote—preferential treatment rather than decisions based on the qualifications and competence of individuals. Thus how organizations design and implement equal opportunity programs plays a large role in determining whether they ever achieve equal opportunity in practice.

INDIVIDUAL AND FAMILY TRENDS

Will the Sex Difference in
Occupational Choices Disappear?

Individuals' decisions about whether, where, and when they work are influenced primarily by their socialization experiences and by the distribution of men and women across occupations. Sex differences in socialization experiences contribute to a sex difference in occupational choices; occupations sharply segregated according to sex also contribute to a sex difference in occupational choices. These differences will be reduced in the long run only if the occupational choices of males and females become more alike and men and women are admitted to occupations in more similar proportions. Given this vicious cycle, any change in the nature of women's and men's occupational choices is amazing.

Once the sex ratio of an occupation changes, it spurs further change by affecting the occupational choices of individuals who are entering the labor market. Occupational choices are influenced by individuals' aspirations and expectations. Past studies have shown that the difference between aspirations and expectations is greater for females than for males. The proportion of adolescent girls who say they would like to work in male-dominated occupations is larger than the proportion who expect to work in these occupations. When the opportunities for women in a given male-dominated occupation seem to be greater, these girls revise their expectations about working in it. They become more likely to make it their occupational choice and to prepare themselves by gaining the necessary education or training. Adolescent boys, on the other hand, see fewer constraints on the achievement of their occupational aspirations and show little interest in female-dominated occupations.

The sex difference in occupational choices seems likely to be reduced if women continue to desire greater entry to male-dominated occupations and if the success of female "pioneers" in these occupations leads other women to believe that their aspirations also can be achieved. Unless there is a corresponding change in men's aspirations to enter female-dominated occupations, however, the sex difference in occupational choices will remain to some extent.

Will Women's and Men's Careers Become Equally Affected by Family Concerns?

Working individuals always have to decide how much time and energy to put into their careers versus their home life or other interests. They also vary widely in the potential demands placed on them by their family situations, ranging from the minimal demands of the single person with no children to the slightly higher demands of "dinks" (double income, no kids) to the heavier demands of dual-career parents to the heaviest demands of the single parent. Aside from having children, they also may have to care for their own parents or elderly relatives. Men's and women's careers presently tend to be affected differently by their family situations. Women perform more of the household activities than men, leaving them less time and energy to pursue work careers. When one member of a couple takes time off from the work force or leaves it altogether to care for children or elderly relatives, it is invariably the woman.

Two changes could occur that would reduce the sex difference in the effect of family situation on work career. One is that couples could choose to allocate their household responsibilities more equally, shifting more of the burden from the female to the male. This would require even further change in societal norms about women's and men's roles.

Organizations also could reduce the impact of family if they revise their policies and practices in an accommodating manner, by providing flexible schedules, on-site child care, or subsidization of child care or elder care expenses. Any such change would remove some of the burden from women and enable them to have careers that are more like men's careers, that is, uninterrupted and free of concerns about family arrangements during working hours. It also could be welcomed by men, because it would require less renegotiation of their own household roles. Unless something changes, men's and women's careers probably will continue to be affected differently by family considerations.

THE ULTIMATE EFFECT OF THESE TRENDS: TWO SCENARIOS

A number of trends have been raised as likely to have a significant effect on the future of women and men in management. Most of these trends have been stated in positive versus negative terms. That is, it has been suggested that (a) if the trend goes one way, its effect will be to promote equal opportunity in organizations, to reduce sex differences, and to improve female/male work relationships; and (b) if the trend goes the other way, its effect will be to discourage equal opportunity in organizations, to maintain or increase sex differences, and to fail to improve or worsen female/male work relationships. Thus we can project two opposite scenarios, one that would be achieved sometime in the future if all of these trends turned out to be positive and the other if all of the trends turned out to be negative. Let's elaborate on these scenarios.

The Positive Scenario

Virtually all organizations have been striving to achieve the goal of complete equal opportunity for some time, and they have achieved it to the extent that it can ever be achieved. Sex discrimination is a taboo behavior in the workplace, thought to be both offensive and dumb. Managers who commit sex discrimination in their decisions are subject to immediate dismissal or other punitive action. At the same time, EEO laws are being rigorously enforced, leaving organizations that do not adhere to both the letter and the spirit of the laws at considerable risk to their livelihood.

Organizations have made great strides in helping their employees to satisfy both their work and family needs. Couples have also been making their own internal adjustments to enable both members to pursue their careers with equal satisfaction. As a result, family concerns are having less of a negative effect on the career of either member of the couple. These changes have affected the socialization experiences of children. Because their parents lead more similar work lives, young girls and boys have come to acquire similar perceptions of the workplace, develop similar aspirations, and see few barriers to their working in any career they would like to pursue.

With the resulting reduction in the sex segregation of occupations, most work groups now have balanced sex ratios. Male and female coworkers treat each other essentially as individuals, without regard to sex. Gender stereotyping in the workplace is a subject that arises only in books or articles discussing what it was like to work in the United States up to the late twentieth century.

Within the ranks of management, the proportion of women managers has reached the proportion of women in the workplace overall, which itself primarily reflects the wishes of individuals rather than family or organizational constraints. The proportion of women at different levels of management is about the same, with neither sex having a monopoly on the positions of greatest power. Androgynous individuals now are preferred as managers, because they have the capability of varying both their task orientation and their people orientation according to the demands of the situation.

Organizations are run better than ever, because they finally are making the best possible use of all the talent available to them. They have also developed systems to distribute monetary and other rewards in the most equitable fashion. At the same time, their employees are more satisfied than ever, because they are achieving personal job satisfaction by holding jobs that are best suited for their skills and interests.

The Negative Scenario

EEO laws are largely unenforced, being seen as more relevant to a distant past (if they were ever relevant then) than to the present. Organizations pay lip service to these laws at most. Affirmative action plans, which have no connection with reality and are not intended to be the basis for any action, are submitted to the government. Top executives occasionally make speeches about how important equal opportunity is to them and send out form letters to employees to that effect, but everyone knows that this is simply a mock effort. Organizations do not really worry about whether they are engaging in sex discrimination. Managers are free to take sex into account in employment-related decisions if they believe that it is an important consideration.

Through lack of action to the contrary, organizations let their employees fend for themselves in satisfying their family needs. Work is assumed to be a good employee's primary concern, with family issues dealt with and left at home. As for working couples, decisions about how to handle household responsibilities are slanted to favor the male's career, because it is implicitly seen as more important than the female's career. This message is reinforced in the socialization experiences of children. Young girls and boys learn that, if there is a future choice to be made, the female should expect to place her own career interests second to those of her male partner.

The sex ratios of groups are heavily skewed in favor of either males or females depending on the occupation or job. Anyone who pursues an occupation that is atypical for his or her sex has a high likelihood of becoming a solo member of a work group, an unenviable position.

Gender stereotypes are the primary basis for predicting the behavior of others and evaluating how others actually behave.

Within the ranks of management, the proportion of women managers has stabilized at a level below 50%. The higher you look in the ranks of management, the fewer women managers you see, with very few women in the ranks of top management. A masculine management style, which places an emphasis on attention to task rather than the needs of people, remains the norm.

Organizations are achieving about the same productivity levels as before, because they essentially have not made any changes in their utilization of people. Men continue to receive a higher share of monetary and other rewards than women. Not surprisingly, men also report generally high levels of satisfaction with their jobs and careers. Women, however, report either active frustration with or reluctant acceptance of the constraints placed by their families and by organizations on what they are able to achieve in their careers.

Which Shall It Be?

Are these extreme scenarios? Very much so. They are presented to illustrate the dramatic difference in the potential effects of the trends that have been discussed.

Which one more reflects today's realities? That's an "is the glass half-full or half-empty?" type of question. I believe the negative scenario. What do *you* believe?

Which one would be better to achieve? I have made my preference known through the choice of labels for the scenarios. I vote for the positive scenario. Because you picked up this book and have read this far, I suspect that you do too.

Toward which scenario have we been heading in recent years? I believe the positive scenario, primarily because women have made substantial progress in entering male-dominated professions such as management and the difference in women's and men's typical career patterns in management has been reduced. The sustained sex segregation of occupations and sex difference in earnings argue in favor of lack of progress, however, and suggest the negative scenario.

Toward which scenario are we more likely to proceed as a society? It's hard to tell. All of us, women and men, have a large stake in how this question is answered. Further research is needed that will give us more guidance on how to eliminate sex discrimination and minimize the relevance of sex as an individual characteristic in the workplace.[3] In the meantime, if we encourage the promotion of equal opportunity in our organizations as best we know how, encourage each other in the pursuit of satisfying careers, share the family responsibilities that are there to be shared, and personally strive to do in life what we are best at and most enjoy, we can contribute to making the positive scenario happen in our lifetimes.

NOTES

1. J. W. Torrey, "The Consequences of Equal Opportunity for Women," in *Women in Management*, ed. B. A. Stead, 1st ed. (Englewood Cliffs, NJ: Prentice-Hall, 1978), pp. 304-5.

2. "Corporate Women: They're About to Break Through to the Top," *Business Week*, no. 3004 (22 June 1987): 72-78; "Readers Report," *Business Week*, no. 3007 (13 July 1987): 10-13.

3. L. Larwood and G. N. Powell, "Isn't It Time We Were Moving on? Necessary Future Research on Women in Management," *Group and Organization Studies* 6 (1981): 65-72.

Appendix
Additional Resources

If you are teaching a course on women and men in management or women in management, or offering a training program on either of these topics, there are several sources of additional materials that may be of assistance. *Women and Men in Organizations: Teaching Strategies*, edited by Dorothy M. Hai and published by the Organizational Behavior Teaching Society (OBTS) in 1984, is an invaluable reference. It contains articles on teaching issues (including one by me on "Issues for the Male Teacher"), classroom exercises, sample course syllabi, and a bibliography on the topic of women and men in management. It costs $9.95 and can be ordered from the OBTS, Center for Economic and Management Research, University of Oklahoma, Norman, OK 73019. Another excellent book for teachers and trainers, which contains articles, exercises, and a bibliography of books, films, and videotapes, is *Preparing Professional Women for the Future: Resources for Teachers and Trainers*, edited by V. Jean Ramsey and published in 1985 by the Division of Research, Graduate School of Business Administration, University of Michigan, Ann Arbor, MI 48109.

A 1984 article that Dorothy Hai and I wrote for the OBTS's quarterly journal, *Organizational Behavior Teaching Review*, describes further resources. It is titled "Integrating Knowledge Regarding Women and Men in Management into the Organizational Behavior Curriculum" and appeared in Volume 9, Number 4, pp. 86-103. Write me at Box U-41, 368 Fairfield Road, University of Connecticut, Storrs, CT 06268 for a copy.

If you wish to use a supplementary book of readings in addition to this book, I recommend any of the following three:

1. Lynda L. Moore, ed., *Not as Far as You Think: The Realities of Working Women* (Lexington, MA: Lexington/Heath, 1986).

2. Bette Ann Stead, *Women in Management*, 2d ed. (Englewood Cliffs, NJ: Prentice-Hall, 1985).

3. Alice G. Sargent, *Beyond Sex Roles*, 2d ed. (St. Paul: West, 1985), also contains classroom exercises.

Finally, for teachers and trainers, two series published by University Associates, the *Annual* series and the *Handbook of Structured Experiences for Human Relations Training* series, contain numerous exercises that you may find useful. University Associates, located at 8517 Production Avenue, San Diego, CA 92121, also publishes a reference guide to its previously published exercises, which is updated yearly.

If you are *not* a teacher or trainer but are interested in further reading on the topics in this book, I recommend any of the following books:

1. Anne F. Scott, ed., *The American Woman: Who Was She?* (Englewood Cliffs, NJ: Prentice-Hall, 1971).

2. Joe L. Dubbert, *A Man's Place: Masculinity in Transition* (Englewood Cliffs, NJ: Prentice-Hall, 1979).

3. Carol Gilligan, *In a Different Voice: Psychological Theory and Women's Development* (Cambridge, MA: Harvard University Press, 1982).

4. Joseph H. Pleck, *The Myth of Masculinity* (Cambridge: MIT Press, 1981).

5. Rhoda K. Unger, *Female and Male: Psychological Perspectives* (New York: Harper & Row, 1979).

6. Robert D. and Candida G. Brush, *The Woman Entrepreneur: Starting, Financing, and Managing a Successful New Business* (Lexington, MA: Lexington/Heath, 1986).

7. Laurie Larwood, Ann H. Stromberg, and Barbara A. Gutek, eds., *Women and Work: An Annual Review*, vols. 1 and 2 (Newbury Park, CA: Sage, 1985, 1987).

8. Barbara F. Reskin and Heidi I. Hartmann, eds., *Women's Work, Men's Work: Sex Segregation on the Job* (Washington, DC: National Academy Press, 1986).

9. Barbara F. Reskin, ed., *Sex Segregation in the Workplace: Trends, Explanations, Remedies* (Washington, DC: National Academy Press, 1984).

10. Rosabeth M. Kanter, *Men and Women of the Corporation* (New York: Basic Books, 1977).

11. Constance Backhouse and Leah Cohen, *Sexual Harassment on the Job: How to Avoid the Working Woman's Nightmare* (Englewood Cliffs, NJ: Prentice-Hall, 1981).

12. Dail A. Neugarten and Jay M. Shafritz, *Sexuality in Organizations: Romantic and Coercive Behaviors at Work* (Oak Park, IL: Moore, 1980).

13. Natasha Josefowitz, *Is This Where I Was Going?* (New York: Warner, 1983).

14. Natasha Josefowitz, *Paths to Power: A Woman's Guide from First Job to Top Executive* (Reading, MA: Addison-Wesley, 1980).

15. Alice G. Sargent, *The Androgynous Manager* (New York: AMACOM, 1981).

16. Ann M. Morrison, Randall P. White, Ellen Van Velsor, and the Center for Creative Leadership, *Breaking the Glass Ceiling: Can Women Reach the Top of America's Largest Corporations?* (Reading, MA: Addison-Wesley, 1987).

17. Barbara A. Gutek and Laurie Larwood, eds., *Women's Career Development* (Newbury Park, CA: Sage, 1987).

18. Uma Sekaran, *Dual-Career Families* (San Francisco, Jossey-Bass, 1986).

19. Lucia A. Gilbert, *Men in Dual-Career Families* (Hillsdale, NJ: Erlbaum, 1985).

20. Francine S. and Douglas T. Hall, *The Two-Career Couple* (Reading, MA: Addison-Wesley, 1979).

21. Heidi I. Hartmann, ed., *Comparable Worth: New Directions for Research* (Washington, DC: National Academy Press, 1985).

22. Michael D. Levin-Epstein, *Primer of Equal Employment Opportunity*, 4th ed. (Washington, DC: Bureau of National Affairs, 1987).

Index

About the Author

Gary N. Powell, Ph.D., is Professor of Management and Organization in the School of Business Administration at the University of Connecticut. He is a nationally recognized scholar and educator on women and men in management. He has published over 40 articles and made over 40 presentations at professional conferences. He has served as Chairperson, Program Chair, Newsletter Editor, and on the Executive Committee of the Women in Management Division of the Academy of Management. He is currently a member of the Editorial Board for Sage Publications' *Women and Work* series and for the *Academy of Management Review*. His graduate course on women and men in management won a $10,000 award for innovation in education from the Committee on Equal Opportunity for Women of the American Assembly of Collegiate Schools of Business.

He is a former project engineer with General Electric, having graduated from that company's Manufacturing Management Program. At GE, he designed and implemented automated project scheduling systems as well as systems for inventory control, production control, materials procurement, facilities management, and so on. He also assisted in training technical personnel for supervisory positions and in developing leadership. He has worked on management training and development with several companies, including Apple Computer, Monroe Auto Equipment, All-State, and CIGNA, and has conducted numerous other workshops.

He received his Ph.D. and a master's degree in business administration from the University of Massachusetts and a bachelor's degree from MIT. He has also held office in the Eastern Academy of Management, having served as President, Program Chair, Secretary, Treasurer, and now as Director. He is also a member of the American Society for Training and Development and Beta Gamma Sigma, a business honorary association.

NOTES

NOTES

NOTES

NOTES